I0605522

NO PLACE FOR PILGRIMS

NO PLACE FOR PILGRIMS

SOLVING THE MURDER OF WILLIAM MOORE, THE LAST COLD CIVIL RIGHTS CASE

MIKE MARSHALL

NewSouth Books
An imprint of
The University of Georgia Press
Athens

NSB

Published by NewSouth Books,
an imprint of the University of Georgia Press
Athens, Georgia 30602
www.ugapress.org

Designed by Mary McKeon
Set in Bembo Book by Mary McKeon
Printed and bound by Sheridan Books, Inc.
The paper in this book meets the guidelines for
permanence and durability of the Committee on
Production Guidelines for Book Longevity of the
Council on Library Resources.

Most NewSouth / University of Georgia Press titles are
available from popular e-book vendors.

Printed in the United States of America
25 26 27 28 29 C 5 4 3 2 1

EU Authorized Representative
Easy Access System Europe—Mustamäe tee 50, 10621 Tallinn, Estonia,
gpsr.requests@easproject.com

Library of Congress Control Number: 2025939830
ISBN 9781588385598 (hardback)
ISBN 9781588385604 (epub)
ISBN 9781588385611 (PDF)

By St. Peter's standards, I may well deserve to go to hell, but of one thing I am thoroughly convinced—If I had had the great privilege of knowing Jesus personally and being one of His followers, I would gladly have gone to the cross also rather than desert Him. And not one of Jesus' disciples can make that statement.

And if I had St. Peter's present job, there is no doubt the way I would judge others. I would open the Gates wide open and shout, "Everyone is welcome. Blessed are you all. Blessed are the saintly. Blessed also are the damned!"

And if any hypocrite[e] who led a "saintly" life should complain that he is too good for the company of the others; let him beware, for I might send him down below until he learns a little tolerance and understanding.

Life is hell. It is a terrible lottery, an awful game whereby no one really wins and none ever survive. As reward for having to struggle through life on earth, heaven is but a fitting payment.

—William Moore, *The Petal Paper*, 1961

CONTENTS

NO PLACE FOR PILGRIMS

INTRODUCTION

A Walnut Tree Dies in Keener

A black walnut tree stood on the edge of Keener, between the Alabama Great Southern railroad tracks and the highway from Chattanooga to Birmingham. It was an old tree, tall and thick, with yellow and green leaves that bloomed in the late spring. The branches dangled over a roadside park at the foot of Lookout Mountain, and they held husks that fell in the fall, after the farmers had gathered their corn and hay. Tourists on their drives to the Gulf Coast beaches stopped to eat picnic meals in the shade, and men proposed marriage at the concrete table under the tree. A locomotive thundered past the park now and then, the boxcars loaded with hobos who roamed the narrow valley between Sand and Lookout Mountains in search of meals. The more charitable women of Keener left meals for them on the steps of their back porches.

A gas station attendant and his pregnant wife passed the walnut tree each night around eight thirty, after the evening shift at Doc Cleveland's Gulf in Attalla, and the park was usually empty. On the night of April 23, 1963, they saw a black car pull under the tree. They thought the car belonged to an Alabama highway patrolman who was setting a speed trap or to a motorist who had run out of gas. They were confused as they passed the park and looked to see who was in the black car. They saw no one. Up ahead, about forty yards away, they spotted a tall, husky man pushing a cart and wearing a sign over his windbreaker. The headlights of their car, a 1956 Ford, flashed off his cart, piercing the night, cool and windy as a cold front passed through Little Wills Valley. They didn't understand what they had seen until the next morning, when they heard the news on a radio station from Gadsden. They had seen a civil rights protester only seconds before he was murdered, and they decided not to talk about it. They could get into trouble if they talked. They talked, though, because some federal and local lawmen found them, and the gas station attendant returned to the black walnut tree to tell what he had seen.

Soon, just as the tree had bloomed, some men from the state destroyed it. The picnic table was hauled away, and the state cut down the tree. The road crew finished the job in a day or two, but the protester's blood stayed on the highway, a pool clustered among the potholes and streaks of tar. The blood spilled across the warning stripe and into the chipped concrete, staining the road for days, until the rains came hard, then harder, and washed away the remains. Only the stump of the walnut tree survived, and people drove long distances to preach on it and put flowers near the edge of the highway, until the state dynamited the stump and roots.

The removal of the tree and picnic table were among the changes that soon came to U.S. Highway 11. Most of the traffic went away after the interstate highway opened, and many of the businesses in Keener closed. The last of the tree roots crumbled from decay, and the sympathizers found new tragedies to mourn. With the final reminders of the murder gone, the county prosecutor agreed it was best to forget about what happened at the park. No one in Little Wills Valley or Gadsden, the county seat, wanted a jury trial after all the troubles they had endured since the textile plant had closed four years earlier and more than two thousand people lost their jobs. They had already suffered enough with industry continuing to struggle and unemployment still so high that the federal government had declared the county a depressed area a year before the murder. The prospect of putting the killer or his accomplices on trial and telling how the black car arrived at the park might jeopardize the area's chances of luring another major manufacturer for years.

I knew the importance of new industry to Gadsden, even as a child. I rode that highway over and over on trips from my maternal grandparents' home on Sand Mountain to my paternal grandparents' home south of Gadsden. The local economy was among my paternal grandparents' favorite subjects, discussing Gadsden's business troubles as if they were mourning a terminally ill relative. Gadsden had once been among the leading manufacturing cities in the South, with fifty plants that employed 13,701 workers who had salaries and wages of $36.34 million in 1947. By 1962, after the closing of pipe foundries and textile mills, the local newspapers reported that the area was "hampered by a resource base which is too weak to attract the resource-oriented growth industries of the present era."

My maternal grandparents, though, seemed oblivious to such worldly matters. They were more interested in farming, family, and long hours at the nearest gas station and general merchandise store. Until I was five, my favorite place on earth was a gas station near their home on the eastern rim of Sand Mountain. The owner was Zenas Zadok Richey, a retired farmer who was known as "Z. Z." to the steel plant workers and sock mill hands who gathered at his store on Alabama 35, the chert and tar-slick highway that stretched past the kudzu-covered hills and the fields of thin, sandy soil. Z. Z. was a legendary figure in my family, mainly to my cousins and me, the beneficiaries of his generosity. He allowed us to eat all the candy we wanted and invited us to reach into his soft drink cooler whenever we needed refreshment on hot summer afternoons, neglecting to tell us that my grandfather was paying the bill. We spent long hours on the church pews in front of his store, talking with his regular customers as eighteen-wheelers loaded with chickens barreled down the mountain toward the new poultry plant in Collinsville in the southern part of the valley.

In the late spring of 1966, my maternal grandparents moved to a larger town on the mountain, a development that saddened many in my family because it meant the end of our friendship with Z. Z. For the rest of his life, my grandfather spent his afternoons at another Shell service station, where the owners were almost as charitable as Z. Z., but things were never the same. From then on, I spent many of my weekends at my paternal grandparents' farm near the banks of the Coosa River, listening to my grandmother's analysis of local affairs. Occasionally, I heard her curse the Black residents of Gadsden, unaware of why she spoke so contemptuously of people she never knew. There were no African Americans near her—at least for ten miles, as far as I could tell, until downtown Gadsden.

I was fourteen when I discovered an explanation for her anger. As I researched a term paper on civil rights for my ninth-grade civics class, I found an article in *Time* magazine about William Moore, a thirty-five-year-old postman from Binghamton, New York. On the afternoon of April 20, 1963, Moore arrived at the Chattanooga bus station from Washington, D.C., and strapped on his protest signs. He planned to walk to the governor's mansion in Jackson, Mississippi, and give a letter to Governor Ross Barnett, considered perhaps the nation's leading segregationist after his resistance the previous fall to the enrollment of James Meredith, the first African American student to enter the University of Mississippi.

On the third day of his walk, Moore pushed his cart through Keener, about fifteen miles north of Gadsden and twenty miles from my paternal grandparents' home. He stopped at a general merchandise store, ate a can of corn and a pecan pie, and read the *Gadsden Times*, the area's afternoon newspaper. About an hour later, he rounded the curve that led to the park and saw a black car parked under the walnut tree, its headlights and motor off. In the distance, he saw the headlights of the 1956 Ford stabbing the night and listened to the Ford's glasspack muffler echo through the valley. After the Ford passed, he heard a familiar voice, a high-pitched twang, summoning him to the black car. He had been introduced to that voice earlier that morning when he had been invited to walk across the highway for a discussion with some of the regular customers of Floyd Simpson's general merchandise store in Collbran. He heard that voice off and on for the remainder of the afternoon as a black car followed him down U.S. 11, pursuing him until he reached the picnic area in Keener. The driver instructed him to head to the car, and he shot him in the head and neck. The murder led to four months of protests in Gadsden, culminating in one of the largest mass arrests in American history on August 3, 1963, when about one thousand marchers, including women holding babies, filed through downtown. The police used electric cattle prods, among their favorite enforcement tactics during the long summer of protests, as the arrests swelled to more than 680.

A photo of Floyd Simpson accompanied the story in *Time*. I thought he looked like some of the men at Z.Z. Richey's store—short, patches of gray hair at his temples, piercing eyes that flashed defiance at the newsmen who had gathered after his release on bond from the Etowah County jail.

"The Sand Mountain area between Chattanooga, Tenn., and Gadsden, Ala., is no place for pilgrims," read the opening paragraph. "It is a land of mountaineers who tote rifles in their cars, glare in suspicion at strangers, and believe unshakably in racial segregation. Last month William Moore . . . thought he might change things by walking through the area displaying civil rights signs. It cost him his life; he was found shot dead on U.S. Highway 11."

I had never seen residents of Sand Mountain carry rifles in their cars or watched them glare in suspicion at strangers. I knew segregation was part of life on the mountain, but I thought it was because only white people lived there. I made a promise after reading the article: I would solve the murder when I was old enough to handle a murder investigation. I was sure I could quickly unravel the murder, relying on my relatives and their neighbors for guidance. My father's family was from Etowah County, the site of the murder, and my mother was from DeKalb County, where the suspect lived. I was from Huntsville, about seventy miles from Keener, but I thought those long hours at Z. Z. Richey's store had taught me how to talk to people from the mountain and the valley.

More than twenty years later, I still remembered the promise. As my mother was dying of cancer, she asked me about my plans for the rest of my life, and I told her about my pledge to solve the murder. I thought she would approve. The murder was unique in the history of civil disobedience in America. Moore was the first civil rights activist who was killed during a protest, and his murder was still unsolved. His murder had confirmed to white supremacists that authorities in the Deep South were unwilling to pursue civil rights killers, and Ku Klux Klansmen soon committed more murders.

"First fighter to die in the Revolutionary War in 1776 was Crispus Attucks," the *Baltimore Afro-American* wrote. "First fighter to die on the side of freedom in the new revolution against racial tyranny is this white Mississippian, Bill Moore. Thus does this man tell his brothers, 'I have atoned, when will you?'"

Six weeks after Moore's death, Medgar Evers, the National Association for the Advancement of Colored People's (NAACP's) first field secretary in Mississippi, was murdered outside his home in Jackson. Early on the morning of September 15, 1963, just more than a day after a grand jury in Gadsden announced it had freed the only man arrested for Moore's murder, Ku Klux Klansmen planted almost twenty sticks of dynamite attached to a timing device outside the Sixteenth Street Baptist Church in Birmingham. About eight hours later, the bomb exploded as the church filled for Youth Day services, killing four African American girls who were in the women's lounge in the northeast corner of the basement.

William Moore's death was mourned around the world. Four songs were written about him, including "Ballad of the Letter Carrier William L. Moore" by Wolf Biermann, a German singer, songwriter, and poet. A British Broadcasting Company show, *That Was the Week That Was*, produced a song and a skit about his death. Six men in Rhodesia started a memorial fund in his honor.

My mother, though, was unimpressed with my plan to solve his murder. At first, I thought she was worried about my safety, but that seemed preposterous. By then, the murder was almost forty years old, and the only man arrested had died earlier that year.

"Don't go stirring up trouble," she told me.

Looking back on it, I wondered if my mother knew what I was about to find. She, of all people, would have likely known.

PART I

THE WALK

CHAPTER 1

William Moore was New York born and Mississippi bred, a medley of cultures and convictions. With a father who misunderstood him and a mother who died when he was two, he was a drifter and an outcast almost from the start, an oddity to almost everyone who knew him. He pursued life as he saw fit, usually alone, never letting go of his childhood ambition to save the world from conflict and suffering. He believed he was bound for heroic achievements, a national and perhaps international leader in the making, a budding champion of the oppressed. He traveled great distances in pursuit of his destiny, first to Guam for the final months of World War II, then to England, France, and Spain after the fighting in the Pacific ended. He returned to New York, sailed to Europe, and hopscotched across America—Maryland, New York, Florida, Georgia, and back to New York. Finally, he settled in his native Binghamton after marrying a divorcée with three children, but he was too restless for family life. Crusaders did not settle for typing letter after letter in their basement, watching the kids play in the backyard, as William Moore had done at his trailer home high on a hill. They joined the fray, and the fray was far from Binghamton, where he had spent much of his life. He returned to Baltimore, the city that had once tortured him, and found a row house apartment on East Twenty-Fifth Street, a three-room dwelling that he rented for $65 a month. From there, he plotted his greatest adventure, a four hundred–mile walk to Mississippi.

It started on the afternoon of April 20, 1963, a rainy Saturday in Baltimore. He hurried through his living room, dressed in a short-sleeved shirt and slacks, a car waiting downstairs. His long arms were latched on to the cart that contained his books, clothes, and letters, his possessions for the next two weeks. He was a formidable man—six feet two and about 190 pounds—with brown hair and blue eyes. He spoke slowly and softly, sometimes stuttering when he tried to emphasize a point about human rights and world peace, his favorite topics of discussion. He was eight days away from his thirty-sixth birthday, an occasion he planned to celebrate alone, fitting for a loner. Using two weeks of vacation from his job at the Hamilton post office, he intended to walk from Chattanooga, Tennessee, to Governor Ross Barnett's mansion in Jackson, Mississippi, with two homemade signs.

"EAT AT JOE's, Both Black and White," read the sign he planned to wear across his chest.

"EQUAL RIGHTS FOR ALL, Mississippi or Bust," said the sign that he was to place across his back.

At the end of his walk, he planned to deliver his letter to Barnett, his plea for civil rights.

> Dear Governor Barnett:
>
> I have always had a warm place in my heart for Mississippi, the land of my childhood and ancestors. I dislike the reputation this state has acquired as being the most bigoted in the land. Those who truly love Mississippi must work to change this image.
>
> Frankly, I do not know which is worse—to be raised to believe that one should be happy to live in poverty and die twice as fast as the white man and to be told to reject the ideas of those who tell you democracy means the right to vote whatever the color of one's skin; or is it worse to be raised as members of sort of a "master race" which fights a losing battle to preserve injustice with barbaric laws and police state methods.
>
> The British were wise in that they dissolved their empire before they were force to do so. Consequently, the government of countries such as India and Nigeria are stable and friendly and democratic. The French, on the other hand, held onto their empire as long as they could. Thus the bitter strife in Laos, Vietnam, Algeria.
>
> The end of Mississippi colonialism is fast approaching. The only question is whether you will help it to end in friendship like the British, or try to hold onto what is already lost, creating bitterness and hatred, as did the French. For our sake, as well as the Negro's, I hope you will decide to try the British way.
>
> The white man cannot be truly free himself until all men have their rights. Each is dependent upon the other. Do not go down in infamy as one who fought the democracy for all which you have not the power to prevent.
>
> Be gracious. Give more than is immediately demanded of you. Make certain that when the Negro gets his and his vote that he does not in the process learn to treat

> the white man with the contempt and disdain that, unfortunately, some of us now treat him.

To prove that he was different than other Northern activists, he carried a key ring with a Confederate battle flag emblem. It was more than protection or a sign of his attachment to the area where he was raised. It was an example of his approach to his activism, a philosophy he described as "love your enemy." Less than a month earlier, he told an interviewer that he was already preparing for the day when all men had their rights. The white man, he said, owed it to himself to have such foresight so he did not experience the same injustices as Black men when stronger civil rights legislation was passed.

William Moore's fierce attachment to the oppressed—African Americans in search of equal rights, mental health patients in need of help after they left the hospital, students and professors seeking freedom of speech—had bewildered many in Binghamton. Only his relatives and closest friends knew the reason for his devotion to the downtrodden: a troubled and lonely childhood. He was born on April 28, 1927, in Binghamton, in the bowl-shaped valley near the Pennsylvania border. He lived there until he was two, when his twenty-two-year-old mother, Ruth, died of cancer early on the morning of November 14, 1929, at her home near the Susquehanna River. With an Atlantic & Pacific grocery store to manage and no wife at home, William's father, Robert, was faced with the prospect of raising two young children alone. His solution was to send William and his older sister, Louise, to his childhood home in Russell, Mississippi, in the timber country near the Alabama state line. William and his sister were raised by their grandparents, William and Lella, and their teenage aunt, Helen. Three more aunts lived near the Moores' farm, and another aunt, Grace, was in Birmingham, Alabama. About 150 miles to the north, an uncle lived in Tutwiler, Mississippi, in the section of the Delta where the mutilated body of Emmett Till, a fourteen-year-old African American from Chicago, was found in the Tallahatchie River in the summer of 1955.

With the Deep South crippled by the Great Depression, William yearned to return to Binghamton, envisioning the North as a utopia, where his father's customers were awash in wealth and the streets were paved with gold. He returned when he was nine, but Binghamton was no utopia. It was so turbulent, in fact, that William Moore offered a precursor to his walk to Mississippi in the winter of 1938, when he was eleven. He left home on his bicycle, bound for the Holy Land, ready to go to Jerusalem to fight for Jesus. Later that night, he returned home, cold and wet, his clothes torn by a barbed wire fence. He still had the rebel spirit of many Mississippians, but he no longer shared their views on race as he had when he lived in Russell. The public schools in Binghamton were integrated long before *Brown v. Board of Education*, the U.S. Supreme Court's ruling in 1954 that outlawed segregation. Two African Americans were among the members of his high school graduation class, the Central High School Class of 1945.

The violent images of the Freedom Rides of 1961—the burning Greyhound bus in Anniston, Alabama, the charred-out remains of the bus parked outside Forsyth and Son Grocery Store, the beatings at the Trailways terminal in Birmingham—had stirred his interest in civil rights. More disturbing photographs—streets littered with tear gas canisters and burning cars, local lawmen wielding nightsticks as they prepared for battle, troops aiming their bayonets at student protesters—were published after James Meredith had integrated the University of Mississippi in the fall of 1962. Almost thirty thousand U.S. troops were needed to repel the first armed conflict between the U.S. government and Southerners since the Civil War, a battle so deadly that a French journalist and a Mississippi jukebox repairman were killed during a night of rioting on September 30, hours before Meredith's enrollment. Now, the brutality had struck in William Moore's adopted homeland, and the reports from Mississippi were more than he could stand.

Six weeks later, William Moore was transferred to the post office in Baltimore, a move he requested so he could be closer to the civil rights movement. He spent his mornings working at the Hamilton post office and his afternoons and evenings at the Congress of Racial Equality (CORE) office on North Avenue. After only three months in Baltimore, he became a celebrity in the local movement, a white man who had gone to jail for the cause of Blacks. The largest newspapers in Baltimore and Washington, D.C., chronicled his role in the Northwood Theater protests on the night of February 18, 1963, when he was the only white man among 151 who were arrested. He had now achieved what he was unable to attain in Binghamton: a public acknowledgment that he was someone to be taken seriously, a legitimate advocate for the cause he was promoting. He had become "quite respectable of late," as he wrote a close friend, Bill Griffen, a professor in the State University of New York system. Sensing the moment he had waited on since childhood—the chance to "pursue the impossible," as he once wrote—he planned his walk to Mississippi.

One of Moore's closest friends in the civil rights movement, James Peck, had written a book about his experiences during the Freedom Rides. The opening paragraphs described the violence he had encountered on Mother's Day 1961, when he received fifty-three stitches in his face and head because of beatings by Ku Klux Klansmen. The first lines of Peck's book, *Freedom Ride,* were questions from reporters as he lay on the operating table at Hillman Clinic in Birmingham.

"Was the Freedom Ride worth it?" he was asked. "Would you do it again?"

Yes, he told the reporters.

But Peck refused William Moore's offer to go to Mississippi with him. He considered the trip too dangerous, even more risky than the Freedom Rides. At least Klansmen were forced to consider policemen, reporters, and photographers when making plans to beat activists in Birmingham. Most of the communities along U.S. 11, especially those in northwest Georgia and northeast Alabama, had no newspaper, radio station, or policemen.

"Get a group to go with you," Peck told him.

No one wanted to go, though.

Moore, like Peck, planned to write a book about his civil rights journey. His book, however, would be about a one-man walk through some of the poorest and loneliest sections of the South.

He wrote his notes on a dime store notepad.

"Walk to Mississippi," he scribbled across the top in his small, slanted handwriting.

Being a career substitute postman, William Moore chose the most logical method to deliver a letter. He intended to walk to the Mississippi governor's mansion and put his letter to Ross Barnett in a mailbox. Examining the maps that he kept on his nightstand, Moore devised a route that took him through the industrial centers of Alabama and into the familiar timber country of Mississippi. Walking forty miles a day, Moore planned to arrive in Jackson on April 30. He chose U.S. Highway 11 as his primary route, a road he had ridden most of his life. It was one of the longest roads in America, beginning in northern New York near the Canadian border and ending in eastern New Orleans. The Moores knew it as the road that connected Binghamton to their family in Russell, Mississippi.

U.S. 11 passed through or near some of the South's toughest cities for civil rights activists. Gadsden policemen scuffled with the Reverend Fred Shuttlesworth's children in 1960 because they had refused to move to the back of a Greyhound bus. Birmingham was the site of the Freedom Riders' attack at the Trailways bus station in 1961 and seventeen bombings by segregationists since 1957. Tuscaloosa, Alabama, was the headquarters of the National Knights of the Ku Klux Klan, the most powerful white supremacist organization in America. Robert Shelton, the imperial wizard of the National Knights of the Ku Klux Klan, occupied a corner office on the fourth floor of the Alston Building in downtown Tuscaloosa, less than five miles from U.S. Highway 11.

Undaunted, Moore reached for the Confederate key chain in his pants pocket, locked his apartment door, and headed down the stairs, where Lloyd Taylor, the public relations director for the Baltimore chapter of CORE, waited to drive him to the bus station on the afternoon of April 20. In his last phone call to his wife, Mary, the night before, he had been brave, doing his best to ease her worries.

"Where are you going to sleep?" she asked him. "Where are you going to eat?"

"I'm a Marine," he told her. "Remember?"

All his life, he had put himself in unfamiliar and uncomfortable situations, traveling the world by ship and motorcycle, pursuing the most daring adventures. This trip, though, was more grueling and audacious than anything he had attempted, but he was sure that his previous journeys had prepared him. In a letter to Mary, he called the trip "something for which my whole life has been sort of a preparation."

His preparations included every form of communication—signs, letters to the editor, speeches, and protests—to express his views and create debate about the world's biggest problems.

"The important thing to bear in mind is that if people will not keep their gripes to themselves, but air them openly in a friendly manner to those in a position to do something about them, what a wonderful thing free society is!" he had written a year earlier. "And because so comparatively few take an active interest in such things as community improvement, the efforts of those who do something count for that much more."

Riding through downtown Baltimore, he reviewed his itinerary with Taylor on the short drive to the bus station. After his arrival in Washington, D.C., he planned to walk to the White House and ask an honor guard to see President Kennedy. He had made a similar request almost a month earlier, after he had walked from Baltimore to Washington as a warm-up for the walk to Mississippi. On the afternoon of March 22, he approached the White House gate and asked the guard if he could give his letter to the president.

"You can't come in here," the guard said.

Moore asked him how he could deliver the letter.

"Drop it in the mailbox," he said.

He headed to the State Department and left the letter at the office of Chester Bowles, Kennedy's special representative and adviser on African, Asian, and Latin America affairs.

> Dr. Mr. President:
>
> I have just finished walking from Baltimore, Maryland to the White House. I am a mailman, and this is the farthest I have ever walked to deliver a letter. Recently, I walked from Baltimore to the State Capitol at Annapolis with an appeal for more effective Civil Rights legislation.
>
> It is not so much that I need the exercise as that I must do what I can toward achieving human brotherhood. Walking and letter delivering are my so-called "professional skills," as legislation and administration are yours—and we must do the best we can with the abilities that we have.
>
> Two of my great-grandfathers from Mississippi fought for the South in the Civil War. I was raised for seven years in that state: relatives of mine live there and in Alabama, Georgia, Florida, Tennessee, Arkansas, and Texas. The South is like my second home. I used to think as they now think. But I have had the advantage of living most of my life in states with greater racial tolerance; I am now employed in your totally

integrated Post Office Department. I can see the harm to the white man as well as to the Negro, whose racial prejudice and denial of civil rights is the custom.

So within the next month or two, I will start walking from the White House here, destined for Mississippi on my back saying END SEGREGATION IN AMERICA and EQUAL RIGHTS FOR ALL MEN. If I may deliver any letters from you to those on my line of travel, I would be most happy to do so.

At this moment, I have neither sufficient accumulated vacation time nor adequate funds to complete this proposed thousand mile journey. It is my hope that if I get started and walk for a week or two, that somehow the means to finish my walk will be made available. I don't believe that any similar walk has ever been undertaken before, and I have the legs to do the job.

Sincerely,

William L. Moore

Bowles was unavailable, but the receptionist told Moore to leave the letter with her, promising him that the president would receive it. Before handing it to her, he added a postscript: He would begin his walk to Mississippi from Chattanooga instead of the White House. Money was too tight. The major civil rights organizations refused to sponsor his trip, believing it was too dangerous. His family, neighbors, and fellow activists warned him, too, but he didn't listen.

"I'll bet $1,000 to one you'll never make it," a neighbor told him. "I agree with you, but the odds are that high."

The walk was too important to call off now that the Southern Christian Leadership Conference (SCLC), Dr. Martin Luther King's organization, was about to begin Project C in Birmingham—C for confrontation.

On his way out of the State Department, he met a reporter for the *Washington Evening Star* who wanted to know more about his walk from Baltimore to the White House.

"I thought it might dramatize the issue more if I walked than if I mailed the letter," Moore said.

He told the reporter about his recent civil rights activities in Baltimore, including the Northwood Theater protests in February. After his release from jail, he walked from Baltimore to Annapolis on a nine-degree morning to deliver a letter to Governor Millard Tawes and the Maryland General Assembly, asking the state to revise the Trespass Act, the charge officers used to arrest the Northwood demonstrators.

As the interview was about to end, Moore had another change of plans. Tired of all the walking, he decided to take the bus back to Baltimore instead of walking the Baltimore-Washington Parkway. He needed the rest, with his shift at the post office scheduled to begin at six the next morning.

A story appeared in the *Evening Star* the next afternoon:

> A mailman inaugurated a private deliver route between Baltimore and the White House, but it won't catch on. William Moore, 35, walked from his home in Baltimore with a letter he wrote to President Kennedy on civil rights. At the swift completion of the unappointed round, Mr. Moore was told by a White House policeman to drop the letter in a mailbox. Rather than let another mailman complete his route, however, Mr. Moore trekked over to the State Department and left the letter at the office of Chester Bowles to be delivered to the President.

The newspapers in Baltimore had already written stories about his walks. The *Baltimore Afro-American* had published a front-page feature that included a photograph of him before his walk to Washington. The headline announced his plans to walk from the White House to Jackson.

> 1,000 Miles to Miss.,
> Walking all the Way

Now he was known in Washington, too. Trying to capitalize on the publicity, he wrote a letter to the editor of a local newspaper to announce he had returned to Baltimore safely.

"I'm the mailman who walked from Baltimore to the White House," he wrote. "People are all worrying about how I got back home. I took the bus. Think I'm stupid or something?"

He was "probably the most educated mailman in the history of the postal service," as Griffen put it. Moore graduated from Harpur College in Binghamton in 1952, enrolled in graduate school at Johns Hopkins, and studied at universities in England, Spain, and France after World War II. He spent his lunch hours reading books and magazines. For his trip to Mississippi, he packed several books, including *This Is What We Found*, the story of how a white father, Ralph Creger, and his son, Carl, became civil rights advocates after the Arkansas National Guard and the 101st Airborne Division of the U.S. Army were needed to integrate Central High School in Little Rock, Arkansas, in the fall of 1957.

William Moore was a writer, too. He had written a book while he was in the service and another in his late 20s—one unpublished and the other he published for $3,500. He was known in Binghamton for writing letter after letter to the morning and afternoon newspapers. He had even considered a career as a journalist, applying for a job at the *Sun-Bulletin*, Binghamton's morning newspaper. On his job application, he said his goal was "to accomplish as much as possible within my lifetime of use to others."

On the ride from Baltimore to Washington, D.C., he planned to do some writing, documenting the opening moments of his trip on his new notepad. Ralph and Carl Creger's book was available for reading.

"As a father and son directly affected by the integration turmoil surrounding Central High School in Little Rock, Arkansas, in September 1957, we were disturbed by what seemed to us a lack of Christian principles in many of our fellow citizens," read the first page. "We were shocked by the willingness of some men in high political office to exploit an emotional crisis for political gain. We felt that causing such tension, ill will and bitterness as we had witnessed justified as much study and research as we could find time for. We saw that we had no right to blindly accept the theories advanced by so many in our community—particularly of the older generation."

If William Moore needed a summary of what he was about to face, he found it in those opening passages of the Cregers' book.

Alabama was tense on the afternoon of April 20, 1963. King and the Reverend Ralph Abernathy, his top aide, were released after eight days in the Southside jail in Birmingham at 12:30 p.m. Just before his release, eighteen demonstrators were arrested downtown for picketing and parading without a permit. In Montgomery, Alabama, Governor George Wallace announced that gunmen had shot at the governor's mansion three times in recent days, the shots coming from the front and back entrances. Always the fighter, Wallace, still the Golden Gloves boxer of youth and now the chief antagonist of the federal government, wondered why his assailants lacked the courage to confront him.

"I can't understand it," Wallace said. "If they want to shoot me, why don't they come up and do it?"

Wallace's aides said Attorney General Robert Kennedy was scheduled to arrive at the capitol late next week to discuss the racial situation in Alabama. To prepare for his visit, Wallace's staff made plans to place the Confederate battle flag on the capitol dome. Wallace pledged "segregation today, segregation tomorrow, segregation forever" in his inauguration speech in January, and his defiance of the federal government was even stronger after his opening months in office. He had been emboldened by a flood of letters, many supporting his views.

"I will never permit integration in this state unless I am compelled to by force," he told an interviewer in March. "They must use force—physical force—directly on me. Let them put their hands on the governor of this sovereign state and see what happens. We're going to show the people of this country what we stand for, and they'll be glad we did. . . . They talk about law and order. Hell, I'm for law and order; law is more important than order."

More than four hundred protesters had already been arrested in Birmingham. King and Abernathy were arrested on April 12 for violating a circuit court order that prevented them from participating in or encouraging racial demonstrations. On his fourth day in jail, King wrote his "Letter from Birmingham Jail," his response to white clergymen who said his campaign was "unwise and untimely." One passage of King's letter was an appeal to activists such as Moore.

"We must use time creatively, in the knowledge that the time is always ripe to do what is right," King wrote. "Now is the time to make real the promise of democracy and transform our pending national elegy into a creative psalm of brotherhood."

Use time creatively to produce a creative psalm of brotherhood? Martin Luther King Jr. had his man in William Lewis Moore. Who else would consider a four hundred–mile walk to Mississippi with integration signs across his chest and back? He had also mimeographed several copies of his letters to Kennedy and Barnett in hopes of passing them out during his walk. His letters included another letter to Kennedy that summarized his plans and motives:

Dear Mr. President:

After I attempt to leave this letter for you at the White House, I will start for my native Mississippi. I will take the bus to Chattanooga, then walk from there wearing signs on my front and back opposed to segregation. I will also bear an open letter for Governor Ross Barnett, which I will attempt to deliver personally.

If you, Mr. President, wish to write to Governor Barnett, I would be delighted to have the opportunity to deliver your letter, also. I expect that the Southern hospitality which I have cherished so much in the past will manifest itself in less desirable forms this time. I may well feel like I am living in the Perils of Pauline, with no hero around to come to my rescue.

I will be engaged in interstate travel, and, theoretically, under the protection of the 14th Amendment to the Constitution, guaranteeing—on paper—equal rights and privileges to all citizens. I am not making this walk to demonstrate either federal rights or state rights, but individual rights. I am doing it, among other things, I feel, for the South, and, hopefully, to illustrate that the most basic of freedoms of peaceful protest is not altogether extinguished down there. I do not believe that such a walk has ever been undertaken before. I want to show that it can be done.

In hopes that I will not leave to eat these words, I leave with you the message, "This time, federal employee notwithstanding, let this be among us rebels."

The cartoon of Jesus on the front of Moore's cart was perhaps his boldest attempt at creativity. The drawing and caption were from a 1917 cartoon by Art Young in *The Masses*, a socialist bohemian publication. Moore attached it to his cart to show Southerners, known as much for their religious faith as their loyalty to segregation, that he also identified with Christ.

Reward

For the Information leading to the apprehension of—JESUS CHRIST

Wanted for sedition, criminal anarchy—vagrancy and conspiracy to overthrow the established government

Dresses poorly, said to be a carpenter by trade, ill-nourished, has visionary ideas, associates with common working people, the unemployed, and bums. Alien—believed to be a Jew. Alias: Prince of Peace, Son of Man, Light of the World. Professional agitator, red beard. Marks on Hands and Feet the result of injuries inflicted by an angry mob led by respectable citizens and legal authorities.

To make sure he was prepared for emergencies, he wired himself money to post offices in Alabama and Mississippi. The American Civil Liberties Union in Baltimore gave him a list of lawyers who would defend him if trouble arose, and he was sure that a few days in jail or a beating was likely. But he wasn't willing to be killed.

"I don't want to be a test case," he said.*

He knew, however, that death was a possibility. In his final letter to Mary, he sent his insurance policy.

"All of this sounds like a lot of unnecessary last detail, and it probably is," he wrote. "But whatever happens and maybe nothing will I'm prepared as best I can be for it."

He paid $1.15 for his bus ticket to Washington, collected his cart and signs, and said goodbye to Taylor. Taylor wished him luck.

"See you when you get back," he said. "Be sure and look me up."

The bus left Baltimore at 6:35 p.m., and Moore recorded the time in his notebook. When Taylor arrived home, he phoned Maurice Sorrell, a photographer for *Jet* magazine in Washington, with a tip: A mailman from Baltimore was about to arrive at the Greyhound bus station, and he was headed to the South to walk for civil rights. Sorrell had the day off, but he drove to the bus station on New York Avenue, less than a mile from the White House. He figured he could sacrifice a few hours of his off day if a white man was willing to march to Mississippi for civil rights.

Moore's bus arrived in Washington at 7:30 p.m., two hours before he was to leave for Chattanooga. He walked through Franklin Park, past McPherson Square, and toward the White House gate. Approaching a guard, he asked if he could deliver the letter to Kennedy. Again, the guard told him to drop it in the mailbox near the gate. Heading back to the bus station, he met Sorrell, the first Black member of the White House Photographers Association. To Sorrell, about five feet four, Moore looked enormous—at least six feet five and 235 pounds.

"He was unafraid," Sorrell was to recall. "He was so big few dared even to tarry long if they disagreed. He was a huge man, but he was sincere. He seemed unaware of any hostile feelings toward him. He was dedicated. He didn't particularly care for any publicity. This was no headline stunt. He seemed like he wanted to do this because he thought it was right to do."

---

* *Civil Liberties* (Monthly Publication of the American Civil Liberties Union), May 1963, 1.

Standing on a sidewalk, Sorrell positioned Moore near a No Parking sign and took his photograph. Waiting for the bus to leave at 9:30, Moore received a final warning from a pedestrian who overheard his conversation with Sorrell.

"You going to Mississippi?" he said. "They'll kill you down there."

The bus barreled through Virginia all night and into the morning, following U.S. 11 through Roanoke and Bristol before entering the Deep South after dawn. During a stop in Tennessee, Moore phoned a reporter in Chattanooga, trying to create some publicity for his walk. Publicity meant protection, but most Deep South news organizations were unsympathetic to the civil rights movement.

The reporter asked if he was worried about his safety.

"I don't think people are going to hurt me," he said. "I'll just have to take that chance."

At 2:30 p.m., he arrived at the Chattanooga bus station with no reporters in the terminal or waiting room. He called the local newspapers—the morning *Times* and the afternoon *News-Free Press*. No one answered. At 2:45 p.m., he grabbed his signs and slipped them over his shoulders, adjusting them across his chest and back. He reached for his cart, and he was off.

The day was warm and sunny, the temperature climbing to eighty-eight as he began his walk in the heat of the day. Because it was Sunday in the South, the downtown streets had little traffic, and the stores were closed. To his left were five-and-dime stores where Black high school students held the second sit-ins in the Deep South, causing two days of violence. Mayor P. R. Olgiati came downtown and ordered firemen to use water cannons to break up the demonstrations on February 25, 1960. The lunch counters were integrated months after the sit-ins, and the integration of elementary schools came in 1962. By 1963, all of Chattanooga's public facilities and its hotels, motels, and theaters were integrated. A Bi-Racial Commission was also formed. Leaders of the local Ku Klux Klan, responsible for seven bombings in 1960, ordered an ending to the bombings and beatings as the Federal Bureau of Investigation (FBI) began an investigation into the group's activities.

With the local Klan in hiding, Moore walked freely through downtown. He turned from Market Street onto Broad Street and headed toward the base of Lookout Mountain, its western rim rising almost two thousand feet above the city. Only a few minutes into his walk, he encountered a Black man who ripped the side of his sign across his chest, tearing "black" off "EAT AT JOE's—Both Black and White."

"Should be colored," the man said.

At the foot of the mountain, Moore veered onto the Cummings Highway, known as the "Dixie Highway," and looked for a restaurant. Among the tourist and motor courts, he found a drive-in and ordered a milkshake. A waitress saw his signs and asked him about his walk. When he told her what he was doing, he saw her concern.

"I hope you make it," she said.

"I hope so, too, if the [Blacks] don't get me," he replied.

Then he told her about the man who had torn the bottom of his sign. He expected trouble from the whites, he said. But Blacks, too?

"No," she said, "I think the whites will get you."

She told him that he would never finish his walk, certain that he would be killed. He agreed, telling her that he thought his walk would end near Birmingham. But he did not stop. He had always believed his stubbornness had been salvation—his "saving grace," as he put it—and he was sure that it would sustain him now. The waitress gave him the milkshake, and he walked through the parking lot, where a Black child asked if he could borrow some money. Moore handed him a dime.

About eight miles into his walk, he left behind the city, turning off the Cummings Highway and finding the hills of Lookout Valley, thick with wood and shade. To his right was the eastern rim of Raccoon Mountain, the start of the plateau known as Sand Mountain in northeast Alabama. At 6:20 p.m., he entered northwest Georgia, with only railroad tracks, a railroad bridge, and more woods in front of him. Over his right shoulder, the sun dipped below the barren rim of the mountain. One hour later, it was dark. In the night, he continued walking on the narrow shoulder of the highway. He reached the community of Wildwood and found a pay phone. Maybe someone at the *Chattanooga Times* would be available now that the early deadlines had passed. This time, a reporter answered, and Moore gave an account of his opening day. He told the reporter about the man who had ripped his sign and his conversation with the waitress on Cummings Highway.

"I told her I doubted I would make it since I was going straight through Birmingham, but I didn't know which ones would get me, the colored or the whites," he said. "I told her most of my trouble had been from the colored people thus far."

He found new trouble now that he was in the seclusion of northwest Georgia. With no motel in sight, he did what came naturally: He slept on the side of the road, as he had done while traveling through Europe after the war and when he had ridden his motorcycle across America after returning home. Finding an abandoned school bus between Wildwood and Trenton around 9:30 p.m., he climbed in and fell asleep, unaware that news of his walk had already traveled down the highway, through Trenton and Rising Fawn and into Alabama.

CHAPTER 2

The sunlight sliced through the bus windows after dawn, awakening Moore around six on the morning of April 22. Since he entered the Marines almost twenty years earlier, he had started many of his days alone or away from home. He was estranged from his father and stepmother, Madeline. He was closer to his sister and brother-in-law, Garth Miller, but they were in Hawai'i, almost five thousand miles away. His aunts and uncles, all residents of the Deep South, rejected him because of his civil rights activism. He considered Mary and his stepchildren the only family he had.

In Binghamton, he was an outcast, called "an oddball" or worse. He was ridiculed for his one-man protests at the Broome County courthouse on frosty winter mornings and his letters to the editor to the *Evening Press* and *Sun-Bulletin*. Unwilling to conform, he withdrew to his basement, where he wrote letters on his typewriter. He wrote about birth control, the elimination of smoking and liquor advertisements, the fluoridation of city drinking water, the display of nativity scenes on the courthouse lawns at Christmas, and tolerance of people with different cultural standards.

He even wrote a letter to the editor about why he wrote so many letters.

"This is a Letter-to-the-Reader who sees my words in this column so much that he either (1) thinks they shouldn't be, (2) wants to know my secret, or (3) wishes I would write about his pet peeve," he wrote. "By way of reply: (1) you can keep me out of this column by writing letters yourself. Don't think the editor doesn't get sick of always printing my name, but if others are too lazy to write, he prints what he can get. (2) My secret is that when my stuff isn't printed, I don't take it personally, but keep on writing.

It's fun, anyway. (3) You write about your own peeves. Your chances of getting printed are better than mine.

"Free speech is only as good as we exercise it. In other parts of the world men may give their lives to speak to a smaller audience than The Sun-Bulletin reaches every day. We should not erode by apathy this freedom so precious to those who do not have it."

After five months in Baltimore, his work at the CORE office on North Avenue had bolstered his reputation. He was usually the only white volunteer, often listening to the other CORE volunteers express their frustrations with white society. He kept stuffing and licking envelopes as they talked, saying nothing. They wondered how he managed to remain quiet when the discussions became so emotional, but they ultimately figured it was because he had been mistreated by many in white society, too.

At the Hamilton post office, he joined the National Postal Alliance, a group composed of 893 Blacks and 7 whites. He was so quiet that he was unknown to many of his coworkers. Herbert Gardner was one of Moore's few friends at the post office. They became acquainted after the integration protests at the Northwood Theater, in a white, middle-class neighborhood four blocks from Morgan State College. For eight years, Morgan State students had tried to integrate the theater, but they had been turned away by the manager, Aaron B. Seidler, who read the Maryland Trespass Act before denying them tickets. The protests resumed on February 15, 1963, and for the first time, the students were arrested. Three nights later, Moore went to the theater to see *Gigot*, starring Jackie Gleason, but he was more interested in the twenty-five demonstrators near the entrance.

"Is this the line for your ticket?" he asked one of the protesters.

"Yes," the protester said. "You can go around if you like."

"No, that wouldn't be polite."

"You don't have to be arrested."

"And you do?"

"Yes, for my dignity."

Police arrested 151 protesters that night—150 black students and 1 white man, William Moore. The next morning, he appeared before Judge Joseph G. Finnerty on charges of disorderly conduct and violation of the state trespassing act. The Black students' bail was $600 apiece; Moore's was $200.

Anne Gardner was among the students who were arrested. When Moore returned to work, he heard Herbert Gardner's name announced over the post office intercom. Moore wondered if he was related to Anne Gardner.

"She's my daughter," he told Moore.

On the afternoon of April 19, Moore shook Gardner's hand and informed him of his plans for his two-week vacation to Mississippi. He told Gardner that he wanted to awaken the "whole world, not only the South, to its racial obligations." Doing it alone would be difficult, he said, but he considered it his job to educate the world.

Gardner gave him $2 and suggested he use the money to buy a sandwich on the trip.

"The time is coming where [people of color] will be in power," Moore told him, "and I only hope that they will be more kind to my people than mine have been to them."

William Moore had been a drifter and a dreamer since the winter of 1938, when he was eleven. He came home from school to an empty house and decided to leave for the Holy Land. The newspapers had been filled with recent reports about Arab extremists occupying Bethlehem and the Old City of Jerusalem, forcing the British army to overtake both cities.

"Suddenly, I told myself, 'I must go to the land of Jesus and fight for him,'" Moore wrote in later years. "Once my mind was made up, I gave no more thought to the wisdom of my plan. Foolish or not, I had made my decision."

He gathered his belongings—his Bible, a toothbrush, a comb, and his savings of $1.15—and left a note for his family.

> I am sorry to have to leave. It is not because I don't like it here, but it is the story of an American who said, "Where you feel you are needed, then go." She was right. I must go, too.

The afternoon was cold and snowy, and the trip lasted only a few miles. He tore his clothes on a barbed wire fence, waded through an icy stream, and found shelter in a barn. Too scared to continue, he headed home to find his father, stepmother, and sister listening to police radio for reports of his whereabouts. From then on, his father and stepmother became his antagonists, trying to suppress his ambitions.

"You think you can go out into the world and do big things," Robert Moore told his son. "You think you can become a hero. But you can't. The world is too large. So just try to be average, to be ordinary. Find your place, stay there, and be satisfied."

But William Moore wanted to travel the world, meet new people. He wanted to be extraordinary, a hero to mankind, a world leader. He believed his purpose was to create a world government and form an organization so powerful that it could prevent wars. His father and stepmother wanted him to pursue a career in business. They wanted him to be like everyone else, another nine-to-five sucker pulling a paycheck. He was more interested in world peace than a daily routine.

Who understood him? Did anyone? Maybe someone at school—a teacher, an administrator, a guidance counselor. He found Gustave Youngstrom, his economics and history teacher at Central High School in Binghamton. Youngstrom had been a professor at Syracuse University and Baker University before joining the Central High faculty in 1936. He was a speaker at the local International Relations Study Group, sharing his knowledge of international affairs. Gustave Youngstrom understood the world and the war in Europe. He also understood William Moore. During his free periods, he counseled Moore on his career choices and which branch of military to choose, encouraging him to find the strength to pursue his goal of changing the world.

As Moore approached his high school graduation on the night of January 30, 1945, his father and stepmother wanted him to enlist in the navy, believing the navy was the safest choice. Youngstrom favored the Marines because the Marines would make him tougher. Youngstrom had been a marine in World War I, and he thought the Marines would make Moore more aggressive. At Central, Moore was so passive that he was named "Most Bashful Boy."

"You have the intelligence," Youngstrom told him. "What you need now is the courage."

Moore continued to fight with his family about his enlistment and Youngstrom's counseling, so much so that his father and stepmother ordered him to stop meeting with his teacher. But the sessions continued.

Then came the breakthrough, his first victory over his father and stepmother, as he later called it. Just before graduation, his father agreed to let him join the Marines.

"It's probably the best thing that ever happened to you," Youngstrom told him.

He joined the Marines on March 16, 1945, six weeks before his eighteenth birthday. He went to Guam and became a member of Casual Company, a unit usually used as a holding place for troops who were awaiting a permanent assignment. The war in the Pacific ended less than six months later with eighteen-year-old William Moore seeing no combat duty.

On March 15, 1949, he received an honorable discharge, the end of his four-year enlistment. Youngstrom was now a resident of Fredonia, Kansas, dying of cancer. On March 14, 1950, Moore met a former high school classmate as he walked through Binghamton.

"Have you heard the news?" the classmate asked him. "Mr. Youngstrom died."

There it was on page 22 of the *Binghamton Press*, a one-paragraph obituary that sent William Moore tumbling into despair. Who could he turn to? Where could he go? Out of the country, for one thing, as far away from Binghamton as possible.

He boarded an ocean liner, the *Mauretania*, from New York City to Southampton, England. He would honor Mr. Youngstrom and do the very thing that his father and stepmother had always opposed. He would get more education. He enrolled in classes at the University of Southampton, the University of Barcelona, and the Sorbonne in Paris, traveling on a British motorcycle and living out of hotels. He returned home a year later, on September 21, 1951, when he walked off a Swedish ship, the *Anna Salem*, with three packages, a suitcase, and his motorcycle.

He was better educated and more sophisticated, as much of a maverick as he ever was.

But Mr. Youngstrom was still with him.

Mr. Youngstrom was with him so strongly that William Moore refused to believe that he was dead. Mr. Youngstrom had faked his death. He was sure of it. Mr. Youngstrom, in fact, had concocted a most clever plan: He had made arrangements with Dwight Eisenhower, the new president, to hire him as a special adviser on foreign policy. To make it easier on Ike, William Moore moved to Baltimore for graduate school at Johns Hopkins University, less than fifty miles from the White House.

Overwhelmed with joy, he returned to Binghamton to inform his family of his new job. News of his appointment, he told them, would come any day. On January 28, 1953, his family had him committed to the state mental hospital in Binghamton, where he stayed for the next year and a half, until August 1954. The diagnosis was paranoid schizophrenia. Moore's doctors said his delusions were created by his belief that he was blessed by a higher power—Youngstrom, in this instance. During his hospitalization, he kept a diary, the basis for his autobiography, *The Mind in Chains*.

"I was made to wish for more—more than the mere possible or even the probable," he wrote. "I must pursue the impossible. . . . Whether I go forward as Don Quixote chasing his windmill or as the pilgrim progressing must be left for you to decide. Indeed in this democratic half of the world, my future is in your hands, at your mercy. I can only give my life."

His life changed in 1955, after he began reading to Bart, a blind graduate student at Harpur College. His work with Bart led to his first full-time job—a social worker with the Binghamton Welfare Department. As Moore went from client to client, he realized the welfare money wasn't enough to feed and clothe the poor, especially during the harsh Binghamton winters. He gave donations to many of his clients, keeping a record of his contributions on a piece of paper that he folded into his shirt pocket. He referred to it as his "sucker list." Before he left the department in 1956, he had given $3,000 to his clients.

Bart also told him about one of his neighbors, Mary Weyant. Mary was a nice woman who was in an unhappy marriage, Bart told him. She also had three young children. Bart believed Mary deserved better, and he suggested Moore meet her. A year later, Bill and Mary moved to Jacksonville, Florida, where she received her divorce. On November 1, 1956, they were married in a small town in south Georgia. Mary had two daughters, Marilyn and

Shirley, and a son, Danny. When the children joined them after their marriage, they were met by their new stepfather, who ran out of their Florida home and scooped them into his arms.

By the summer of 1957, the Moores were back in Binghamton. William shuttled from job to job, first at the Federal Fabrication Company, then at Grand Union Company as a grocery clerk, then at the post office. But he was restless again. In 1960, he told his bosses at the post office that he wanted to consider a transfer to Washington, D.C., where he planned to enroll in graduate classes at American University. America was changing rapidly. The sit-in movement started that year at a Woolworth's lunch counter in Greensboro, North Carolina. More sit-ins were held by college students at department stores and restaurants in Baltimore. He sensed the need to go south, but the transfer to the post office in Washington never came.

A move, though, was inevitable after he saw the photographs of the Freedom Rides on the front pages of the *Evening Press* and *Sun-Bulletin*. A photograph of a bloody and beaten Jim Peck was on the front page of the *Evening Press* on May 16, two days after the attacks in Birmingham. Peck, like Moore, was a pacifist and a member of the War Resisters League, one of the nation's antiwar organizations. In the late summer of 1961, Moore and his fellow members of the Committee of Concern invited Peck to Binghamton to speak at the Arlington Hotel. On the night of September 27, Moore introduced him to a crowd of about one hundred, most of them Harpur College students and members of the Committee of Concern. After the speech, Moore invited Peck to his home for a late-night discussion on world peace and civil rights. Peck's scars were still visible, and Moore's stepson, Danny, asked him how he received so many stitches.

"You mean you got all this because of that?" Danny asked Peck. "Because you wanted [Blacks] to sit in front of a bus? Give me a break."

Moore's life began to shift. He still waged his peace protests, but civil rights became more of a priority. How could he ignore the suffering of African Americans when he had spent his whole life trying to ease the pain of others, especially the oppressed? Binghamton, though, was no place for an activist. The schools and public accommodations had been integrated since he was in high school. Almost 80 percent of Binghamton's residents were white, and many of them ridiculed his protests. There was perhaps no better example of how his hometown viewed him than his peace protest on the courthouse square on the morning of January 31, 1962. No one accepted his invitation to join him. Motorists and passersby gawked at him, trying to decipher the words on his sign.

"TURN TOWARD PEACE," read the front.

"GOOD WILL TOWARD ALL MEN AND WOMEN," said the handwritten words on the back.

Some thought his peace march was an indication that he was sympathetic toward the Communists and against Christianity. He answered his critics in a letter to the newspapers.

"Paradoxically, one reaction of a small minority to my peace placard vigil in front of the Courthouse was to imply that it is somehow un-Christian to suggest friendship to all, including Communists," he wrote. "However, 'good will toward men' was not an expression original with me.

"The following words also come from the same well-known source. 'Love your enemies, bless them that hate you. . . . For if ye love [only] them which love you, what reward have ye?'"

Realizing Binghamton was unresponsive to his attempts to change the world, he went to the post office and made another transfer request. To do the great things that his father considered impossible, he knew he needed to be in a city where he could find people who wanted to protest.

Then came the riots at Ole Miss on September 30 and October 1, and he was sure that he must go to Mississippi. To understand civil rights activism better, he joined Jim Peck and Bayard Rustin in a "peace sail" on October 12, 1962, Columbus Day. They boarded a boat in New Jersey and sailed into the Atlantic, a move designed to support William Worthy, a civil rights activist who faced a five-year prison sentence and a $5,000 fine for violating the Immigration and Nationality Act. Worthy, a foreign correspondent for the *Washington Afro-American*, was charged with violating the act after reentering America from Cuba, the first American charged with defying the act, intended to keep current and former members of the Communist Party out of America.

Moore, Peck, and Rustin sailed beyond the three-mile territorial boundaries of international sea laws and returned to New York Harbor to meet Worthy. They went to the U.S. Immigration and Naturalization Office and surrendered, but there were no arrests. Their protests received a five-paragraph story on page 14 of the *New York Times*. The *Times* said Moore, Peck, and Rustin described themselves as "Freedom Riders," an indication of his commitment to the movement.

Before leaving Binghamton, he wrote his final letter to the editor. The riots and Ole Miss and the Cuban Missile Crisis, the Soviet Union's deployment of nuclear weapons ninety miles off the coast of Florida, had inspired him to write a long letter to the *Sun-Bulletin*.

"In this world of contradictions, it is the super patriots who call for U.S. troops to bring 'democracy' with the sword to countries like Cuba, then find themselves advocating treason and condemning our armed forces in Mississippi. How strange that Senator [James] Eastland of Mississippi, in his diligent search for subversives, did not see himself as being anti-American!

"Segregation and the whole concept of second-class citizenship is a vicious tyranny which does harm to my white Mississippi relatives as much to the Negro. But there is another issue mixed in, which the Civil War has not yet fully resolved for this rebel—that is the right to defy one's country's orders.

"Resistance, brick tossing and shotgun firing at Oxford was senseless and futile. But for a more noble cause, and in a more self-disciplined and responsible manner, may we sometime say that treason is the higher patriotism?

"Do we not consider it right and proper that some revolutionaries defied the established British government to give us these United States? Do we not agree with Jefferson that government is instituted among men and derives its just powers from the consent of the governed? He also said that the tree of liberty must be repeatedly nourished by the blood of martyrs. We have indeed been fortunate in that we have preserved the free ballot so that the will of the people can be expressed with little martyrdom."

Moore was a contradiction, too. Some of his closest friends were Unitarian and nondenominational ministers, but many considered him an atheist because of his opposition to religious zealotry. He was, however, a spiritual man by any measure. He gave Mary a Bible on their third wedding anniversary.

"To dearest Mary on our third memorable anniversary—Bill," he wrote inside the Bible.

He studied religion as intensely as he examined world peace and civil rights. When he read about a tragedy in the newspaper, he often expressed his dismay over bad things happening to good people, unable to understand why there was "a God of love and a God of wrath," as Mary put it. He also disliked the division of religion into different faiths, each believing that their way was the path to salvation. He was baptized twice, though, once when he was a teenager and then in his early thirties. On a Sunday in the summer of 1960, the Reverend Harold Roys delivered a sermon that inspired Moore.

"God loves all faiths and has just one plan for salvation—through Jesus Christ—for all people of all religious beliefs," the Reverend Roys said.

Then the Reverend Roys issued an invitation to the congregation.

"Step out and accept the Lord Jesus Christ as your savior," he said.

Moore walked to the front of the church and approached the Reverend Roys.

"I want this free gift," he told him.

He took baptismal training classes at Park Terrace Heights Gospel Church in preparation for the full-river baptism in the pond behind the Reverend Roys's home. In Baltimore, he attended the First Unitarian Church, where the Reverend Irving R. Murray preached sermons such as "An Affirmative but Not Dogmatic Faith." His closest acquaintances included the Reverend Murray, active in local American Civil Liberties Union affairs, and Madelyn E. Murray, whose court cases to ban religious practices in public schools had made her a controversial national figure.

William Moore was also a contradiction in his home life. He was a strong family man, encouraging his stepson to overcome his fears of the dark and giving one of his stepdaughters the confidence to play the piano, even though she struggled to read music. But he left his family to be closer to the civil rights movement, ignoring his wife's concerns for his safety.

When he left in November, he held her close and tried to comfort her.

"Be strong," he told her.

But he was worried, too.

❖

He settled in the north-central section of Baltimore known as Harwood, living in an apartment on the second floor of a three-story row house. He had a kitchen, a bedroom, and a living room. Among his furnishings were a bust of Abraham Lincoln, his typewriter, and his books. Most days, he came home from the post office, put his cap on the stack of books by his bed, and hopped on his blue Vespa motor scooter, bound for the CORE office on North Avenue.

It took three months for him to announce himself to the rest of Baltimore; the Northwood Theater arrest was his introduction. Baltimore Mayor Phillip Goodman intervened the day after the arrests, saying he was willing to hold discussions with each side "in the interest of having this community problem solved without any further embarrassment to anyone." The theater owner said he was willing to negotiate. On February 21, three days after Moore's arrest, the theater was integrated.

The next day, with postal workers off for George Washington's birthday, Moore headed down the Baltimore-Annapolis Boulevard, bundled in a topcoat and wearing two protest signs.

"END SEGREGATION IN AMERICA," read the sign across the front of his topcoat. "Black or White, Eat at Joe's."

"EQUAL RIGHTS FOR ALL MEN," said the sign on his back.

The winds gusted to 20 mph and the temperature fell to 9°F, the coldest George Washington birthday on record in Baltimore, but he carried his letter to Maryland Governor J. Millard Tawes. At the capitol, he was told Tawes was ill and out of the office, but he spoke with leaders of the Maryland General Assembly and an assistant to Tawes. Before leaving the capitol, he gave a letter to the Maryland Secretary of State, requesting that Maryland "place human rights above property rights and abolish segregation in all forms." On his way home, Joe McConnell, a member of the general assembly from Moore's district in Baltimore, bought him dinner and gave him a ride home.

The walk to Annapolis was so successful that he made plans for a walk to the Deep South. To get more accustomed to longer walks, he decided to walk to the White House in late March and give a letter to President Kennedy.

"A letter carrier at the Hamilton Station, Mr. Moore feels that since he works for President Kennedy he should take the problem right to his boss," the Baltimore *News-Post* reported on March 7.

Two weeks later, a reporter for the *Baltimore Afro-American* came to his apartment as he was about to leave for Washington, D.C. For the first time, he disclosed his plans to walk to Mississippi.

"Aren't you scared?" the reporter asked him.

Moore reached into his overcoat, found a note, and showed it to the reporter.

"Walking for brotherhood," it read, the theme of his walk to Annapolis.

No one had threatened him on his walk. They had been so friendly, in fact, that he immediately made plans for his next walk.

"Yes, but what about Mississippi?" the reporter asked.

"You must not worry about what other people might think but go on and do what you are going to do," William said.

He did not worry when some fellow CORE activists came to his apartment to convince him to cancel his walk.

"Where do you want us to send the body?" one joked.

He told them that he had already sent his insurance papers to his wife.

"At least don't go by yourself," someone else said. "Take someone with you."

"I would," he said. "Only I can't find anyone who wants to go. Why don't you go?"

But she did not want to go either.

"You're white, and they'd get you," she said. "I'm colored, and they'd get me twice as fast. And if they saw us walking together, well . . ."

Aunt Helen, the relative who helped raise him after his mother's death, was more blunt than any of them. Now she was Helen Moore Sims, the fifty-one-year-old wife of the Russell postmaster, Jamie Sims. Moore's grandparents had died, but several relatives were still around Russell—Aunt Ruby, Aunt Dillon, Aunt Fredna, and Uncle Ezra, among others. He wondered if they could get together when he passed through town.

He wrote a letter to inform Aunt Helen of his plans to come to Mississippi on a civil rights walk. Don't bother coming, she replied. She had just had surgery and her nerves couldn't take the stress of seeing her nephew shaming the family this way.

"I sure can't see how you can expect us to welcome you down here, with the motive you have in mind," she wrote. "It's not that we don't love you, cause we do, but we certainly don't love what you stand for. You outsiders walk into an area and cause trouble and unrest, and you're on your way again.

"This is our home, and we have to stay here, and live in peace. And we don't intend to uphold any such thing by welcoming you into our home, and having the public think we are a part of any such thing. So do not send any money in care of us—or we'll probably send it on to Mary and the children, as that's where it should be going, as well as yourself. If you have vacation you better be going to see your family—you did take them to be your obligation, did you not?

"This is very hard for me to take this attitude toward my own flesh and blood. But you don't seem to have any respect for Mama and Daddy's memory. So for their sakes and ours, I'm saying please do not come. Our home will be closed to you on a trip of this nature. And I don't want your name or your picture to appear in a paper in Miss. Mama and Daddy would turn over in their graves if they knew you acted like this.

"You'll probably find out when you hit this section of the South what you are doing is NOT a joke after all."

Aunt Helen was not usually a prophet. Most days, she stayed at home while her husband earned a living at the Russell post office. She tended to the family's vegetable garden, taught Sunday school at the Russell Baptist Church, and participated in Order of the Eastern Lodge activities at the Masonic Lodge. Aunt Helen had only a high school education, but she was a scholar when it came to racial attitudes in the Deep South. Her nephew was about to discover just how prophetic she was.

CHAPTER 3

With the morning sun slanting through the bus windows, William Moore reached for some postcards and scribbled some updates to Mary and the Reverend Murray, who was also the head of the Maryland American Civil Liberties Union, the only organization that had sponsored his walk.

> Everybody quite hospitable, and I am having a pleasant walk. Feeling quite secure by now. But if anything ever happened, I wonder if anybody would ever know. The road is a lonely place.
> Bill

Next, he wrote a letter to the Associated Press in Birmingham, his final attempt to create publicity for his walk. He had been walking since two thirty on Sunday afternoon, he said, and the local reception had been "very courteous." He had walked about twelve miles on Sunday, but with the early start on Monday, he expected to be in Birmingham on Thursday or Friday. Needing to walk at least thirty-five miles a day to make it to Birmingham by Thursday, he was out of the bus and on the highway after six, the traffic to the factories and mills in Chattanooga rushing north on U.S. 11.

Dade County, Georgia, was known as the "State of Dade" and the "Free State of Dade," both references to the county's Confederate allegiances. On July 4, 1945, eighty years after the Civil War ended, the county officially left the Confederacy and rejoined the Union during a ceremony at the county courthouse in Trenton, where a crowd of more than four thousand heard the reading of a congratulatory telegram from President Truman over a national radio broadcast. Even in the spring of 1963, many of the county's 8,600 residents held on to the area's reputation for rebellion.

"You know, this is the 'Free State of Dade,'" a white man said. "We do things out in the open."

Entering Trenton around eight, William Moore passed the American Legion hall where Ku Klux Klan leaders, most of them from Sand Mountain, had changed into their Klan robes on the night of April 2, 1949,* when the "Free State of Dade" did some of its most violent business out in the open. After leaving the American Legion hall, Klan leaders went downtown and met a mob gathered on the square. Among those in the crowd was a Dade County deputy sheriff, Stokes McCauley, who led the procession up Highway 11 and into the community of Hooker, just near the Tennessee line. The Klan burned a cross after the mob arrived. A missionary Baptist preacher supplied the burlap and the wire for the crosses. Dade County Sheriff John Lynch and three of his deputies turned seven African American men over to the mob of fifty to seventy-five men, most of them Klansmen. The African American men were taken in the sheriff's car to a Methodist church and beaten by the mob. Federal authorities arrested Lynch and his three deputies on federal flogging charges—the first time the federal government used civil rights statutes and the Constitution to prosecute law enforcement. In the trials that followed, Klansmen, most of them Sand Mountain farmers, testified that Lynch and his deputies attended Klan meetings in Trenton.

No mobs were waiting on Moore as he approached Trenton. He did, however, create enough of a disturbance that Allison Blevins, the current Dade County sheriff, noticed that his usually peaceful town of 1,300 was disrupted by someone who was walking toward the courthouse.

"Are you a Christian?" asked a man who saw Moore's signs and the poster on his cart.

Confused by the cartoon, the man assumed Moore was an atheist. Moore reached into his cart and handed the man his letters to President Kennedy and Governor Barnett.

"Maybe we can convert each other," he said.

"I've already been converted," the man said.

---

* *Dade County Times*, May 12, 1949, 1.

Blevins rushed out of the jail, wearing his trademark snap brim hat. Seeing the integration signs, Blevins ordered Moore into his patrol car, shoving his signs and cart into the back seat. There would be no chance of a repeat of the Klan violence from the spring of 1949. The "Free State of Dade" would hold no business in the openness of the Dade County courthouse square, as one of Blevins's predecessors had done, especially in the early morning.

Blevins drove for eight miles until he reached Rising Fawn, just north of the Alabama line. Rising Fawn was a cluster of tourist traps that were disguised as gas stations and souvenir shops. The most famous was the Georgia Game Park, which attracted customers with fireworks, chenille bedspreads, and freak animals—Trixie the five-legged dog, Sambo the talking bird, a six-legged cow, alligators, and a dancing bear.

"EVERYONE WELCOME," read the signs on the fence that guarded the animals at the Georgia Game Park. "COME IN AND BROWSE AROUND."

But Moore discovered that he was not welcome at the Georgia Game Park or any other business in Rising Fawn.

"Toilet plugged up," he was told. "I don't think I want your business."

He walked farther south to Deer Park, another gas station with freak animals, and found two men sitting in front of the entrance. Were the bathrooms available, as the sign in front of the store indicated? No response. When he asked again, he was told, "You'll have to use the ladies."

An older woman saw his signs and stopped to ask him what he was selling.

"Integration," he said.

The Alabama state line was up ahead, around the curve. The road was narrow, with no shoulder to walk on, only the edge of the highway. The area was so isolated that he wondered if the state highway officers or local deputies ever patrolled the roads. He had seen only two police cars in two days—one near Chattanooga and Allison Blevins's sedan in Trenton.

Crossing the Alabama state line, he reached for a fallen road sign and stuck it in the ground, wiggling it until it straightened. Up ahead, an elderly woman was stranded on the side of the road with a flat tire, and he changed it for a quarter. The traffic thickened in the late afternoon as the mill workers finished their shifts in Chattanooga. Two men offered him a ride, but he didn't accept. Allison Blevins had already driven him to Rising Fawn. The rides were over.

Another carload of men—five mill workers from Lookout Mountain and Little Wills Valley—stopped him as he was adjusting his integration signs. They were third-shift workers at the DuPont plant in Chattanooga, producing nylon for textiles and tires. Moore gave them copies of his letters to Kennedy and Barnett—"my circulars," he called them.

"You'll never make it through Birmingham without being arrested," one of them said.

The news of Moore's walk had already spread through the northern part of DeKalb County and into the all-white communities of Sulphur Springs and Hammondville, near the base of Sand Mountain. The county was anxious about recent national and international developments, including the integration of Central High School in Little Rock, Arkansas, the Freedom Rides, the integration of the University of Mississippi, and the Cuban Missile Crisis. But its mood appeared to reach a hysteria in the weeks before Moore's walk.

"Troubled People Face 1963," read the headline on the lead editorial of the *Fort Payne Times-Journal* on January 3, 1963.

Communism was the *Times-Journal*'s main concern.

"The year 1963 dawns on a deeply troubled world. Communism jeopardizes world peace and posterity of mankind. Communists continue to push forward aggressively in many areas seeking new land to rule and additional people to regiment. Man—the fallible being that he is—now holds in his hands a destructive force of such great potential that its very existence poses the question of whether or not mankind is to have a future. It is no wonder that people everywhere fear the worst, knowing as they do that a militant force dedicated to world rule possesses such destructive power. In this country Americans are justifiably alarmed at the ever present threat of Communism to the priceless heritage of our great land."

And into their troubled world came a man whom many regarded as a Communist, and their alarm climbed even higher.

About eight thousand cars a day traveled up and down U.S. 11 in the northern part of DeKalb County. Traffic was much heavier there than in the southern part of the county because the traffic came barreling off Sand and Lookout Mountains, filled with men who headed to their factory jobs in Chattanooga. Only 821 of the 40,596 in the county were Black, according to the 1960 census. Whites comprised almost 98 percent of the population, the third heaviest concentration of whites among Alabama's sixty-seven counties. Most were Scots-Irish descendants, known for their independence and suspicion of strangers—the "last gut of the white race," as one local politician called them.

With its thin, sandy soil on Sand Mountain, undesirable for farming, DeKalb County was also poor. Only 4.1 percent of families in the county exceeded the average family income of $6,691 for Americans in 1960, and barely more than 25 percent of the families in DeKalb had incomes in the $4,000–$7,000 range, accounting for more than half of the county's earnings.

The Klan had been influential since the 1920s. A young Albert Rains, now the area's most powerful politician as a longtime member of the House of Representatives, was a speaker at a July 4, 1925, picnic on Sand Mountain that featured a Klan parade, a Klan address, and speeches by the Masonic Order.* Large Klan motorcades said to be as many as one thousand cars wound through the valley and on to rallies on Sand Mountain, where Klansmen and their supporters gathered at a thousand-foot overlook known as Buck's Pocket.

The Collinsville Courier published a banner headline across its front page:

A Klansman's Creed

I believe in God and in the tenets of the Christian religion and that a Godless nation cannot prosper.

I believe that a church that is not grounded on the principles of morality and justice is a mockery to God and to man.

I believe that a church that does not have the welfare of the common people at heart is unworthy.

I believe in the eternal separation of church and state.

---

* *Fort Payne Journal*, June 24, 1925, 8.

> I hold no allegiance to any government, emperor, king, pope or any other foreign, political or religious power.
>
> I hold my allegiance to the Stars and Stripes, next to my allegiance to God alone.
>
> I believe in just laws and liberty.
>
> I believe in the upholding of the Constitution of these United States.
>
> I believe that free public school is the cornerstone of good government and that those who are seeking to destroy it are enemies of our Republic and unworthy of citizenship.
>
> I believe in freedom of speech.
>
> I believe in a free press uncontrolled by political parties or by religious sects.
>
> I believe in the protection of womanhood.
>
> I am a native-born American and I believe my rights in this country are superior to those of foreigners.

The Collinsville Klan grew to 500 members, almost three-quarters of the town's population of 793. Preachers promoted the Klan in their sermons. Politicians embraced them. A crowd estimated at 7,500 came to Collinsville High School for a Klan parade and a naturalization ceremony on the night of June 5, 1925. An estimated 1,500 Klansmen were in attendance and another 200 were naturalized that night.

Collinsville Mayor John Anderson was so impressed with the event that he expressed his appreciation in a letter to the *Courier*.

"Allow me to extend my thanks to those members of the Ku Klux Klan who so ably cared for the traffic situation here at the monster meeting of the Klan on June 5th," he wrote. "Few towns our size have ever had a traffic problem as confronted on the school campus where hundreds of cars were parked, [but] not even a minor accident occurred. I also thank the thousands of visitors for their presence, the perfect order and general spirit and good fellowship shown. Come again."

The Klan remained influential in Fort Payne as its popularity declined in the rest of America. On April 10, 1929, the *Fort Payne Journal*, in a front-page obituary, wrote of a Lookout Mountain farmer, "We are also delighted to be able to state that this grand old citizen was a loyal member of the old Original Knights of the Ku Klux Klan, and that he was a devoted member of Fort Payne No. 121, at the time of his death and had been very active until his illness prevented him from his activities of the Klan."

The Klan was revived in DeKalb County in the fall of 1962, after the

Cuban Missile Crisis and the riots at Ole Miss. The new leader lived in a community in the southern part of the county, near Collinsville. He was a twenty-seven-year-old truck driver who hung out at a general merchandise store operated by Floyd Simpson, an officer in the Fort Payne Ku Klux Klan. Near the front door of Simpson's store, a .22-caliber rifle hung over the fireplace mantel.

In this climate of growing agitation and fear, William Moore encountered the first attempt at violence around 5:15 p.m. on April 22.

"Hey, n—— lover, go back up north where you belong," someone yelled at him as he walked down a hill between Sulphur Springs and Hammondville.

Rocks came flying from behind him, but the man stayed behind the hill, never showing himself.

The crossroads at Hammondville was Moore's first major stop in Little Wills Valley. Across U.S. 11 was the Rock Castle Café, a diner and service station made of stones from the mountains. He bought copies of the Birmingham and Chattanooga morning newspapers, sat on one of the stools near the front counter, and read them. Leafing through the *Birmingham Post-Herald*, he read this article from the Associated Press on page 15:

Equality Is 10 Years Off, RFK Thinks

Says Disturbances Will Continue Over Nation

Washington, April 21—Atty. Gen. Robert F. Kennedy predicted today that racial disturbances will continue in the United States for ten more years before Negroes obtain full equality with whites.

"You are going to have them in Alabama and Mississippi and you are going to have them in Chicago . . . in all parts of the United States," he said.

"This is not a problem that is confined to one section. . . ."

Kennedy, in a taped radio and television interview, said that the interracial difficulties and disturbances that have marked the Negro's rise are a sign of progress—"that the people will not accept the status quo."

He said he realizes this presents problems for the United States both domestically and abroad and then added:

"I think we have to go through that kind of thing [disturbances] for the next maybe ten years before we are going to have full equality."

On the next page was a story about Governor George Wallace's meeting with Robert Kennedy, scheduled for Thursday morning at Wallace's office in Montgomery. In preparation for Kennedy's visit, Wallace had ordered the Confederate battle flag atop the capitol dome, another sign of Alabama's resistance. Wallace said the meeting was an opportunity to "let [Kennedy] know how strongly we resent in Alabama the concerted efforts on the part of the central government in Washington to take over local government and destroy our cherished traditions."

An article near the bottom of page 2 of the *Post-Herald* gave Moore a better example of the city's racial climate. Four white churches allowed fifteen African Americans to attend services on Sunday, while five other churches refused to integrate.

"The church-going came on the 19th day of anti-segregation demonstrations here," the *Post-Herald* reported.

> The demonstrations have resulted in some 400 arrests, mostly for marching without permits and seeking service at white eating places.
>
> Leaders of the demonstration are scheduled to answer contempt of court charges for violating a no-demonstration injunction at the courthouse this morning.
>
> The Revs. Martin Luther King Jr. and Ralph Abernathy, Atlanta Negro ministers who have been here for the demonstrations, were released from City Jail under $300 bond over the week-end. They had not previously sought release. King and more than 100 other Negroes are scheduled to face Judge W. A. Jenkins in the contempt case.

Moore opened his notebook and summarized the news. Robert Kennedy's prediction was encouraging, but the demonstrations in Birmingham were bigger news. Heading out of Hammondville, watching the sun fall beneath the rim of Sand Mountain, he was now 105 miles from Birmingham. At his current pace of twenty miles a day, he would arrive in Birmingham on Friday, putting him in the middle of the nation's most explosive civil rights story as Project C was completing its third week.

As evening arrived, Moore's gait quickened, spurred by the cooler temperatures and the absence of distractions on the road. It was still hot, much hotter than he was accustomed to in the evening, with the high humidity and temperatures in the sixties. The ice cream and soft drinks he had purchased at the Rock Castle, though, had rejuvenated him, and he covered almost four miles an hour—double his pace for much of his walk.

Approaching Fort Payne at around ten o'clock, he checked into Black's Motel, the city's newest and most stylish place for lodging. The large neon sign glowed in the night:

> **BLACK'S MOTEL**
> Air Conditioned
> Electric Heat

John O. Gilbreath, the owner of Black's Motel, was at the front counter. Entering the lobby without his signs, Moore checked in, and Gilbreath walked him to his room. Gilbreath thought his new guest was a salesman on vacation, with his sports shirt, slacks, and well-spoken ways. Approaching the room, he saw Moore's cart.

"You better get a license plate for that," Gilbreath said.

They laughed, then Gilbreath saw Moore's integration signs and Jesus poster.

"But I didn't say anything of course, because they were his privilege," Gilbreath said later.

At ten thirty, he reached for his notepad and made the final entry in his diary for the day.

"Black's Motel, Fort Payne, blisters on both feet and in crotch. A little sunburn, saw one police car, almost without exception, every person along the road was white."

CHAPTER 4

William Moore checked out of Black's Motel around 7:00 a.m. as Fort Payne awakened on an already-warm Tuesday morning. The school traffic and commuters to Chattanooga and Gadsden were passing along Gault Avenue, the main thoroughfare through the city's downtown business district. In the distance, Moore could see the dogwood and cherry trees beginning in bloom on the western rim of Lookout Mountain, a vivid blanket of green against the cloudless sky.

Arriving at the front desk of the motel, John Gilbreath looked out of the office window and saw Moore walking toward Cooper's Restaurant, the city's most popular café. Wearing his signs and pulling his cart as he approached the restaurant, he was the biggest news in Fort Payne since Hank Williams stopped for a haircut at a downtown barbershop and a bottle of whiskey from a bootlegger on Lookout Mountain on December 31, 1952, the day before he died in the back seat of a baby-blue Cadillac.

After breakfast, a downtown crossing guard waved at Moore. Moore was more surprised by the reaction of a man walking downtown. Seeing only the sign across Moore's chest, the man asked him if Joe's was the new restaurant opening down the street.

"No," Moore said, "it's [an] integration sign."

Students and teachers on their way to school knew what the signs meant. So did one of the town's toughest policemen, Bill King, known for once beating a prisoner with a blackjack. On the north end of Fort Payne, Moore passed Tutor Hardware Store, owned by Guyton Tutor, a local Ku Klux Klan and National States Rights Party leader. Tutor, like William Moore, was a prolific letter writer. "Payday is to come sometime, and soon will be here," he wrote in a recent letter to the *Birmingham News*, the largest newspaper in Alabama. "Many are changing [political parties] because they believe it is necessary to save this country."

On the south end of town, Moore walked through the intersection of Alabama 35 and U.S. 11, an area known among the locals as the "South Y." Only a few years earlier, Klansmen from Sand Mountain had seen a Black member of the Naval Air Station in Millington, Tennessee, and forced him to remove his shoes and walk barefooted up the eastern slope of the mountain, shooting at the sailor's feet when he strayed into the grass.

Now that Moore was almost out of Fort Payne, he had a better look at Lookout Mountain, with the midmorning sunlight glinting through the trees. The highway was now closer to the base of the mountain, and he admired the view.

"10 a.m., lovely road, courteous receptions, walking a real chore and feet sore," he wrote in his notebook.

He headed down a hill and past a branch of Little Wills Creek on the edge of Collbran, a farming community that was founded more than a century earlier by three families—the Brandons, Burts, and Killians. Members of each family waited on him at Floyd Simpson's general merchandise store, the center of social life in Collbran.

The road straightened as Moore crossed the creek. Herds of cattle owned by Jack Killian, the master of the Killian farm, roamed the valley. Down the road, a man dressed in a sports shirt and slacks stood on the side of the highway, waiting to invite Moore to the general merchandise store for a conversation with the store's regular customers. Floyd Simpson was a quiet and slender man—about five feet nine and 145 pounds—with brown hair and piercing green eyes. He was the father of five and was about to celebrate the birth of his first grandchild. In four days, he would turn forty-one. He and his wife, Lucille, had lived at the side of the store with their children, ages one to eighteen, since November 1962, when he began renting the building from Gaddis Killian, the rural mail carrier and former proprietor of the store.

Life had been difficult for Floyd Simpson and many of the others at the store. Raised on rental property in Collbran, the eldest of six children, Simpson was the son of a carpenter and a block mason with a fourth-grade education. His full name was Floyd L. Simpson. His parents hadn't seen fit to give him a middle name, only the initial. By seventeen, he was working half the year, an existence that allowed him to complete only the seventh grade. In 1942, when he was twenty, he joined the army and went to Georgia and Tennessee for training. He was sent to California, where he destroyed huts in Japanese concentration camps, and then to France as a member of the 984th Engineer Company. In October 1945, he left the army and came home to marry Lucille Brandon.

Lucille was a member of Collbran's pioneer family. The town was known as Brandon until 1903, when the community was renamed because railroad freight was often mistakenly dropped off in Brandon, Mississippi. A combination of Brandon and Collinsville, the largest town in the southern part of the county, accounted for the community's current name. In the early years of their marriage, Floyd and Lucille Simpson had their struggles, typical of most young couples in Little Wills Valley, where life after school usually meant farming or shifts at the sock mills. But Floyd and Lucille had also experienced tragedy. On November 15, 1947, Lucille Simpson delivered twins—a son, Floyd Ray, and a daughter, Flora Fay. Floyd Ray died that day, and Flora Fay died the next.

Floyd returned to school and earned his diploma from DeKalb County High School, but opportunities remained limited. He and Lucille worked in the sock mills in Fort Payne, and Floyd joined the 151st Combat Engineers of the Alabama National Guard during the Korean War. When the unit was activated, Floyd was promoted to sergeant. His family had grown to two sons and two daughters by the end of the war. He shuttled from one job to another—a fixer in the sock mills, pumping gas at a garage, a carpenter's helper. The family moved from Collbran to Adamsburg, on the rim of Lookout Mountain, then back to Collbran when Floyd began renting Gaddis Killian's store.

When he invited William Moore to his store on the morning of April 23, 1963, he had added a new title—investigator in the Fort Payne chapter of the Ku Klux Klan.

The store sat below a cemetery and a bank of pines, a white frame building with a tin roof and wooden floors. It had been the center of life in Collbran since Highway 11 was finished more than twenty-five years earlier, a place so popular that the fields across the highway had paths leading to the store. An ice-cream freezer was by one of the front windows, a makeshift desk for Floyd Simpson when he tallied the day's business before closing. Beyond the front door, a .22-caliber rifle hung over the fireplace. Out front, under a cluster of pines, his 1950 black Buick was parked next to the store, its usual spot. Some chairs and a spare tire were under the awning, near gas pumps where Gulftane gasoline sold for $0.32 a gallon.

Many of Floyd Simpson's regular customers were at the store when he invited William Moore to head over for a discussion. Most were relatives of Gaddis Killian's, including his brothers, Jack and Gene. Claude Burt, a bridge builder for Southern Railroad, was another lifelong resident of Collbran. Hoyt Kelly* was the most ambitious. He was twenty-seven and the new exalted cyclops of the Fort Payne Ku Klux Klan, a position he had held since the previous fall. He was a short, thin man, married to a woman from Lookout Mountain, and the father of two young sons.

Jack Killian was in his early sixties, a staunch believer in the military and a long day of work. When his father, Demoville, was killed in a horse and buggy accident in 1917, he and an uncle, a local business owner, were responsible for providing for the Killian children, including Gene, now a housepainter, and Gaddis, the youngest of his seven siblings. Many of the area's largest newspapers published accounts of the horse and buggy incident. A runaway horse that belonged to a Fort Payne doctor, R. J. Guest, crashed into the horse and buggy that contained Demoville Killian and his daughter. A Black youth, Ebuckles Chambless, was riding the doctor's horse through an alley near a drugstore when the horse became frightened by a "hand car on the Main street," the *Chattanooga News* reported on September 14, 1917. Chambless was unable to control the horse, and the horse crashed into the Killians' buggy, throwing Demoville Killian onto a pile of brick and crushing his skull. Life had toughened Jack Killian, so much so that he prepared for confrontation when the state highway crew informed him in 1935 that it was coming through the next day to bulldoze his land so it could finish the final leg of Highway 11 from Birmingham to the state

* Pseudonym. To be known from here as Hoyt Kelly or the former exalted cyclops.

line. He built a fence across his land, shielding his prized barn from the bulldozers, and loaded his shotgun. He was waiting when the state road crew arrived the next day, shotgun in hand. The state's compromise was to move Jack Killian's barn to a hill that overlooked the new home he was about to build.

The Killians were "the pillars of Fort Payne, having given money and time to the development of the town," as the *Fort Payne Journal* once put it. They were also established in the southern part of the county, where family members owned a grocery wholesale business and much of the farmland along Highway 11.

The meeting at the store was the sort of moment William Moore had been waiting for, one of the main reasons for his walk. He wondered how the men knew about his trip.

"We heard about it on the first news break," one of them said.

William Moore interpreted the comment to mean that he had made the local television news, but either he had misunderstood the remark or the man had lied to him. The first news break was one of the local radio reports.

The discussion started with some questions about Moore's opinions on social issues. Did he believe in integration?

Yes, he told them.

Did he believe in a Black man marrying a white woman?

Yes, he believed in interracial marriage, he said.

That was when the men at the store were convinced someone was paying William Moore to make his walk. They believed only a Communist had those views.

"Why don't you walk for the Indians?" Hoyt Kelly asked. "They're the most oppressed people ever."

"They're not as bad off as Black people are," Moore said.

The conversation lasted about fifteen minutes, maybe twenty. The store regulars warned him before he returned to the highway: He'd never make it past Birmingham.

As they watched him turn and head for the road, they agreed that William Moore was part of something much bigger than a one-man walk. He was part of something sinister, perhaps something subversive.

CHAPTER 5

A black car began following him. A black Buick or Pontiac had been trailing him since the first day of his walk, but he had not noticed it because of the traffic that hurried toward Chattanooga for the first and second factory shifts. The traffic was lighter in southern DeKalb County, especially around noon, so it was easier for him to spot the black Buick that pursued him after he left the store. It followed him through Portersville and toward Collinsville, and the driver had nothing to fear. He knew many of the county deputies and the local state patrolmen. Some of them were relatives.

Most days, the car was parked in front of the store, under a grove of pines. A hubcap was missing on the driver's side and a taillight was out on the passenger side. It was an old car, and the engine screeched when it was pushed to high speeds. The motor was silent now. The driver pursued him slowly.

"11:15, a touch of diarrhea," Moore wrote in his diary.

He entered Portersville, the only community between Collbran and Collinsville, a village that consisted of a church, a post office, a train depot, and two gas stations. Spotting Moore's signs as he did some chores, a farmer walked across his field.

"What do those signs mean?" he asked.

Moore laughed and said, "I'm one of those n——lovers you hear about."

Around noon, the state of Alabama decided to intervene. Ralph Holmes, a lieutenant with the Alabama Department of Public Safety's Investigative and Interrogation Division, had been monitoring Moore's walk since he entered the state. After the meeting at Floyd Simpson's store, Holmes told his boss, Captain Ben Allen, that Moore might be in trouble. Allen radioed the DeKalb County Sheriff's Department with instructions to find Moore and try to bring him in for mental observation.

George Noles, the chief investigator with the DeKalb County Sheriff's Department, drove south on U.S. 11. He was a former DeKalb County sheriff who had been appointed special investigator by Harold Richards, the recently elected sheriff. Most people in DeKalb County called him "Doodle."

"Are you tired?" Noles asked Moore.

"No, no," Moore replied. "Not too bad."

Noles watched Moore's expression, seeking signs of mental instability. He saw only a gentle face and soft eyes, nothing threatening.

"If you'll allow me, things could get rough for you south of here," Noles said. "I think you should catch the first bus and go back north."

He looked at the sign across Moore's chest and saw the tear in the left corner.

"You could get something more ripped than a sign," Noles said.

Moore ignored Noles's warning, responding with an uneasy laugh. On his way back to Fort Payne, Noles radioed the Investigative and Interrogation Division that Moore was still walking. He said he was unable to find any laws that would allow him to arrest Moore, either unaware or unwilling to use the same law that allowed officers in Birmingham to arrest hundreds of demonstrators.

Now that the state and county were on the case, McKinley Freeman, the sixty-six-year-old police chief of Collinsville, drove from his office and parked near the northern city limits, waiting for Moore to enter his town. He watched a well-dressed man in a black Cadillac stop as Moore entered Collinsville. People in Collinsville weren't known to drive Cadillacs and wear fine clothes on a weekday. Someone from out of town was apparently interested in William Moore.

Moore crossed Highway 11 and entered Byron's Café, a block building on the edge of town. Margaret Osborn, known to her customers as "Mertie," operated Byron's Café, named for her father. Byron's was almost empty when William Moore walked in around 2:00 p.m. for lunch and to use the bathroom. He sat on one of the stools near the front counter and ordered a plate lunch of meat and vegetables. He ate his lunch in silence, an outcast here, too. Mertie was unimpressed with him. She thought he should be back home, trying to earn a living for his family.

Up ahead, the townspeople of Collinsville were waiting for him. Lavonne Williams, the owner of Collinsville Dry Cleaners, met him on the side of the highway for a discussion. Farther south, at the intersection of U.S. 11 and Alabama 68, the heart of town, a group of Black men sat on the bridge over Little Wills Creek and waited for their first look at a civil rights activist. They muttered among themselves after he passed them, wondering what would happen to him after dark. The black car was still following him.

At 3:00 p.m., Gaddis Killian returned to Collbran, his mail route on Lookout Mountain finished for the day. He was the community's most respected citizen, the closest thing Collbran had to a leader. Former Governor John Patterson, George Wallace's predecessor, had named him an honorary member of his staff, sending him a small license plate that he kept at the store. He had also served on the DeKalb General Hospital board. But his business, civic, and political activities had been more than he could stand. In the fall of 1962, he was hospitalized for nervous exhaustion. He was out by the late fall but returned to the hospital in the spring of 1963. On the afternoon of April 23, he had been out of the hospital for about a month when he encountered more anxieties. Walking up the block steps to his store, he heard the regulars still discussing William Moore's visit. What should they do about him, a man who they were now convinced was subversive? Gad Killian decided to have his own conversation with William Moore. He and Simpson headed south on U.S. 11 in Killian's car.

Moore was almost through Collinsville when Killian and Simpson stopped him near the Collinsville Trade Day, the outdoor flea market where people from the mountain and the valley gathered on Saturdays to buy goats, dogs, and mules. There were the usual questions about integration and religion, then one of them, apparently Killian, inquired about the Jesus poster on the front of his cart. In the excitement, Killian and Simpson focused only on the passages that appeared to be minimizing Christ: "criminal anarchy," "dresses poorly," "said to be a carpenter."

They asked many of the questions that he faced at the store, just to make sure they had identified him correctly.

Did he believe in integration?

Yes.

Did he believe in interracial marriage?

Yes.

Was he a Christian?

The answer, of course, was complicated, like most things with William Moore. Perhaps he seemed evasive about religion to Gaddis Killian and Floyd Simpson, lacking the conviction of most Deep Southerners. The mystery, if there was any to Gaddis Killian and Floyd Simpson, had been unraveled.

"Now I know what you are," Killian said.

An atheist. A Communist. An integrationist. The embodiment of all the trouble people of DeKalb County feared as they faced 1963.

"And one was sure I'd be killed for [his political and religious beliefs], such as my Jesus poster on my buggy," he wrote in his diary.

The plot to kill him had become more urgent. In four hours, it would be dark.

But who would kill him?

The Alabama Department of Public Safety moved swiftly, as it had after the meeting at the store. Bill Stone, a state trooper from Fort Payne, was dispatched to the county line. On his way out of town, he stopped to pick up Cecil Reed, a twenty-three-year-old sheriff's deputy; both were charged with making sure Moore left DeKalb County alive.

The road began to twist, and the land was steeper in the southern part of the county. Moore lumbered up a hill, his pace more labored because of the reappearance of the blisters.

"4:10—feet sore all over," Moore wrote on his way out of Collinsville.

Stone parked near the woods at the county line, along a curve on the side of the highway. Stone and Reed watched Moore enter Etowah County, and they returned to Fort Payne, assured of his safety. The road was mostly straight for the next mile or so, running parallel to the railroad tracks where locomotives shuttled hobos and cargo through the valley. Moore was tired and sweaty, and blood seeped through his socks. He stopped near the woods, removed his shoes, and reached for his diary.

"5 p.m.—shoes too painful, walking without them, adopted by hungry, thirsty, road-foolish dog," he wrote.

The dog darted through the fields until Moore reached the hill at the edge of Keener. At the top of the hill was a large building made of stone—the Keener bus stop, as it was known in the valley because of its beginnings in 1937 as a rest area for Greyhound travelers who shuttled between Chattanooga and Birmingham. In its early years, the Keener bus stop had a café, a grocery, and a deck overlooking U.S. 11, but its heyday had long since passed. The café closed first, then the bus station.

The store's new owners, Garvin and Conola Robinson, occupied one of the two upstairs bedrooms. Their son, Bill, and his new wife, Louise, were in the other. Louise ran the beauty shop upstairs. Groceries and gasoline were sold downstairs, where Garvin Robinson was behind the cash register. His wife sat at the back of the store, by the bologna and cheese counter, dipping snuff.

Outside, Garvin Robinson's grandsons—Danny, Tommy, and Gary Baird—played in the fields near the highway. They greeted Moore as he entered Keener, the sun almost down behind the ridge of Sand Mountain. Moore asked them if they wanted the dog. Sure, they told him.

"6:50—boys adopt dog," he wrote in his diary.

He put on his shoes, entered the store, and looked for something to eat.

CHAPTER 6

The murder plans began to unfold even before the evening twilight. Less than two miles from the store, a gunman stood on an interstate bridge that was under construction and aimed toward U.S. 11. The visibility, though, was poor. The shot needed to come closer, especially in the night, somewhere near the highway, someplace certain. The killer knew the spot: the picnic area across from Harry Sizemore's dairy farm. A perfect ambush. The long straightaway from Hilltop Grocery to the picnic area, just more than a mile, provided a clear view of cars and pedestrians, and the black walnut tree and the slight curve in the road gave him protection. William Moore would never see him.

A salesman for the Provident Life and Casualty Insurance Company in Chattanooga saw the gunman on the hill. After passing Moore near Keener, he called the FBI, but FBI Director J. Edgar Hoover had already made his position clear: The bureau didn't protect civil rights activists. The state of Alabama didn't either. George Wallace had already informed Ku Klux Klansmen that they could commit any violence they saw fit to prevent integration.*

The gunman drove to the store, found a phone, and called WGAD-AM in Gadsden with a tip: A man walking south on U.S. 11 was about to be killed. The instructions were precise: drive about seven miles north of Reese City to find the story. The gunman was confident that WGAD would do as they were told. A Klansman who worked for the station was con-

* Wayne Greenhaw, *Fighting the Devil in Dixie* (Lawrence Hill Books, 2011), 101.

victed of disorderly conduct in September 1956 for warning a housewife, Gloria Weems Hei, about conduct that "we don't allow down South."

Then he called the *Gadsden Times*. Larry Keener, the newspaper's nineteen-year-old switchboard operator, gave the information to the newsroom. The gunman knew that the newspaper would also oblige him. The former exalted cyclops of the Gadsden Klan, Ace Williams, had warned the newspaper's publisher about the dangers of defying the Klan when the occupants of a car that belonged to his son, a University of Alabama student, had attempted to photograph a Klan welcome sign, smeared with paint, on the northern edge of Tuscaloosa.

The killer hung up and walked to the store parking lot, where the Baird boys played with their new dog. Sensing trouble before dark, the state made its final attempt to take Moore off the road. Ben Allen phoned Roy McDowell, the state troopers' investigator in Gadsden, and told him to find Moore and arrest him. McDowell was unaware of a law that allowed him to arrest Moore, so he phoned Cyril Smith, the new county judge. Smith didn't know of a law either.

Moore searched the shelves at Hilltop Grocery and found a can of corn and a pecan pie. He grabbed a copy of the *Gadsden Times* and handed $0.30 to Garvin Robinson. At the back of the store, Conola Robinson gave her evaluation of Moore from her easy chair.

"A tramp," she told her son, Bill.

Moore went outside, removed his windbreaker, and sat on a bench to eat his corn and pie. Some of the store's regulars were on the bench, most of them farmers. They asked him about his signs and his walk, and he told them that he was walking to end segregation and give Black people their rights. He said they were no freer now than they had been after the Civil War. The men in the black car were watching.

Around 7:00 p.m. Charlie Hicks, the midmorning disc jockey at WGAD, pulled out of his driveway in his Ford Falcon. His wife, Gail, and his two-year-old son, Chuck, rode along for Charlie's first attempt at covering news. The news director was away on National Guard duty, so it fell to Charlie, the new man at the station, to drive north on Highway 11 to find the man walking for civil rights. He had been hired only a few months earlier from a radio station in Sevierville, Tennessee, in the Great Smoky Mountains, where his in-studio performers included Dolly Parton, a then-unknown singer. It was about seven fifteen when Charlie Hicks found his story. William Moore was in the store parking lot with his integration signs.

"Where are you going?" Hicks asked him.

"I'm going to Mississippi and call on Governor Ross Barnett on the civil rights issue," Moore said.

"Are you going to walk all that way? You've got an awful long walk."

"I realize that."

"How are your feet going to hold up?"

He saw the bandages around on Moore's feet. Blood was seeping through his gray socks. He wondered how Moore could continue, especially with night approaching.

"This [Gadsden] is a dangerous town, and this is a dangerous situation," Hicks told him. "I don't think you need to be out here at night. Let me drive you to the motel down the highway."

D & J Truck Stop Cabins was only three miles south on Highway 11. But Moore refused.

"I'll be all right," Moore told him. "I don't believe the South is that way. I think a lot of this stuff is just made up."

Then Hicks turned on his tape recorder and began his interview.

"I intend to walk right up to the governor's mansion in Mississippi and ring the doorbell," Moore said. "Then I'll hand him my letter."

Roy McDowell arrived at the store around seven thirty. McDowell kept his engine running as he climbed out of the car and approached Moore and Hicks. Time was precious. It was already dusk.

"Get in my car," he told Moore. "I want to talk to [Hicks]."

McDowell asked Hicks's opinion of the situation. Dangerous, he told him. Very dangerous. Much too dangerous for him to stay out on the highway.

"I wanted to take him to a motel to get him off the road, but he doesn't want to do that," Hicks said. "He needs to go down to [D & J] and start walking again tomorrow morning."

McDowell agreed.

"That makes sense to me," he said. "I'm going to see if I can get him down to the motel."

On Hicks's way home, he rounded the curve by the black walnut tree, causing his headlights to flash onto the picnic area. A black Buick was parked there, with two men in the front seat. The driver's arm was hanging out of the front window.

"I hope they aren't waiting on [Moore]," Hicks told his wife.

She told her husband not to worry.

"I'm sure [McDowell] will take him in," she said.

The newspaper reporters were late to Keener. Bill Basenberg and Thom Wilkerson of the *Gadsden Times* passed the store as Moore was talking to McDowell. Basenberg, a twenty-year-old with only a few months of newspaper experience, drove his Volkswagen Karmann Ghia. He and Wilkerson saw the same scene as the Hickses as they passed the picnic area: a large man with an arm dangling out of the front window.

Moore was finishing his conversation with McDowell when Basenberg and McDowell sped past the store.

"I'm not here to harm you, only to keep you from getting hurt," McDowell said.

He asked Moore about his family. He told him about his father's family in Mississippi and about his father in New York.

"You know about the racial situation in Alabama, don't you?" McDowell said. "Why don't you call off this walk, at least for the night?"

"I can't," Moore told him. "I want to prove something, and I can't if I turn back."

Seeing the signs, McDowell asked him about the tear in the left corner. A Black man in Chattanooga ripped it, he said, telling him that it should have read "colored" instead of "black." The signs were enough for McDowell to arrest Moore. The Alabama legislature had passed a law in 1959 for situations such as these—conduct calculated to provoke a breach of peace, a statute designed to end civil rights disturbances. On August 16, 1960, the city of Gadsden used the law to arrest the Reverend Fred Shuttlesworth's three teenage children for refusing to give up their seats on the front of a Greyhound bus from Chattanooga to Birmingham. The state of Alabama employed it a year later when the Freedom Riders rode through Anniston,

Birmingham, and Montgomery. But Roy McDowell, in his fifth year as a state investigator, did not use it to arrest William Moore.

The state used other charges to arrest civil rights demonstrators. In 1962, Bob Zellner, a white member of the Student Nonviolent Coordinating Committee (SNCC), was arrested for conspiracy to violate the state trespass law during protests at Talladega College. On January 8, 1963, he was arrested by a state investigator and Al Lingo, the incoming director of public safety, on vagrancy charges as he walked through Huntington College in Montgomery. But McDowell didn't use any of those charges either.

Just before eight, Moore climbed out of McDowell's car. With the wind rising and the temperatures falling, he slipped a gray windbreaker over his blue sports shirt. He had two pairs of gray socks on his blistered feet, and the sweat from his green khaki trousers had chafed his legs. His shoes were in his cart. On his way out of Keener, he passed the San-Ann gasoline station across from the Baptist church. Carl Alverson, the manager, had seen the black car moving up and down the highway.

"He's asking for trouble," Alverson thought, "and he's about to get it."

Less than a mile from the picnic area, the driver of the black car backed out of Wendell and Betty Dowdy's driveway. From the front of the house, Betty Dowdy watched him ease back onto the highway, moving toward the picnic area. Now an average-sized man with his black hair combed straight back was driving the car. Perhaps he was wearing a cap. As the car pulled away, she caught a glimpse of the black Buick's license plate. The numbers on the tag began with "28"—the prefix for DeKalb County.

The driver headed south, moving slowly for about a half mile before turning across the highway. He parked under the black walnut tree, turned off the engine, and waited. The night was quiet except for the sounds of the green-and-white 1956 Ford with its noisy glasspack muffler approaching from the south. To the north, a Greyhound bus was preparing to climb the hill by Hilltop Grocery.

Seeing the Ford's headlights in the rearview mirrors, the men in the black car ducked in the floorboard. Hearing the car pass, they raised themselves onto the front seat, and the driver clutched his rifle, a Remington Nylon 66 that Simpson had bought recently for about $50. The magazine was almost full. The rifle had room for fourteen cartridges, and nine Remington long-rifle cartridges were loaded. Through the dark, the driver saw the sign on Moore's chest and called him over to the car. The driver leaned out of the car, clutching the rifle, so the cartridges fell into the park.

The first bullet entered the left side of Moore's head and passed through his temple. The second shot entered his throat and ripped through the back of his head. The impact thrust Moore forward, and he lay crumpled on the warning stripe of the highway, a bullet lodged in his shirt pocket. A pool of blood formed on the concrete and trickled into the edge of the park. The black Buick turned out of the park and sped away

Just before 9:00 p.m., the dispatcher from the state troopers' office in Attalla radioed McDowell at the Panorama Restaurant in Gadsden.

"That man you've been talking to up yonder," he said, "he's laying down in the highway, asleep."*

William Moore's body remained on the road for thirty minutes, until a man driving a 1956 Pontiac passed the picnic area before nine and saw a corpse on the warning stripe of U.S. 11.

"Hey," he said to his wife, "I saw a body on the other side of the road."

Until then, Willis Elrod, a twenty-four-year-old Gulf gasoline salesman from Birmingham, had not seen anything unusual on the road. He and his family—wife, Martha, and infant daughter, Sherri—had spent the day with relatives in Gaylesville, a small town near the Alabama-Georgia line. They were returning to their apartment in the Norwood section of Birmingham, north of downtown, where Willis and Martha had settled after marrying in 1962. They had passed only two or three cars after leaving Collinsville, and none of them, as Elrod told investigators later, appeared to be driving at high rates of speed.

The men in the black car had plenty of time to return home. It was around eight fifty when Willis Elrod saw Moore on the side of U.S. 11. Elrod turned his car around, eased into the picnic area, and shined his headlights onto Moore's body. A hit-and-run accident, he thought, seeing the blood on the highway. He drove across the road to Harry Sizemore's farm-

* *Los Angeles Times*, October 27, 1991, A-17.

house, about a hundred yards from the picnic area, a frame house among a grove of trees. Sizemore and his family—daughter, Cindy, and wife, Betty—were watching the *Red Skelton Show* when Elrod knocked on his door.

"A dead man's lying out here in the road," he told Sizemore. "It looks like he's been hit by a car."

Sizemore headed through his front yard and across the highway, flashlight in hand. Seeing Moore's body and the hole in his left temple, Sizemore said to Elrod, "This man hasn't been hit by a car—he's been shot."

Noble Yocum, the Etowah County coroner, examined the body. He found Moore's wallet and counted the bills and the change in his pants pocket: $50.15. Reaching into the pocket in Moore's sports shirt, he discovered the diary and the badly battered bullet that had passed through Moore's head. State and county investigators considered the diary, some tire tracks, and three cartridge cases to be their best clues.

Around 10:00 p.m., Yocum made a collect phone call to Moore's wife, Mary, at her trailer home in Binghamton. About two hours earlier, she had been on her knees in prayer, asking for protection for Bill, while the children completed their nightly routines before bed. She and the children were asleep when Yocum called collect.

"Where was your husband traveling?" he asked.

"Through Tennessee, Georgia, and Alabama," she told him.

"Where was his destination?"

"Mississippi."

He didn't tell her that Bill was dead. He wanted someone else, maybe a neighbor or a clergyman, to give her the news. She went next door, to the home of the Reverend Robert Drewry, the pastor of the Park Terrace Heights Gospel Church. She asked him to come to the phone, and Yocum told him that Moore was dead.

Overhearing their mother's sobs, Moore's three stepchildren—Shirley, fifteen, Marilyn, fourteen, and Danny, thirteen—rushed from their bedrooms.

"They've shot Papa," she told them.

Her first phone call was to Robert Moore.

"Mary," he told her, "we've got to keep this thing quiet."

Mary Moore, though, was too emotional for silence. Her moods vacillated between anger and sadness, and finally, anger prevailed—anger at the people in Alabama who killed her husband and allowed his accused killer to go free on bond, anger at the people in Binghamton who called her husband an atheist and an oddball.

"They never understood the man because they never had the guts to fight for what they believed in like he did," she said.

She was so angry, in fact, that she planned to go to Alabama after the funeral, anxious to see what kind of man would kill her husband.

"To him, people were people, and he was willing to give up his life to prove it," she said. "I am praying to God that his death bothers the conscience of every person in this country so that they may examine their hearts and see how much violence, misery, and suffering they are causing their fellow man."

William Moore with wife, Mary, examining his new book, *The Mind in Chains*. Moore paid $3,500 to Exposition Press in 1955 to publish his first book.

This 1962 road map shows the route William Moore took from Chattanooga to Keener, Alabama. This map is important because it is actually one of the few maps that shows Keener. This map also shows where the new Interstate 59 bridge was being constructed. Moore was killed just north of that bridge.

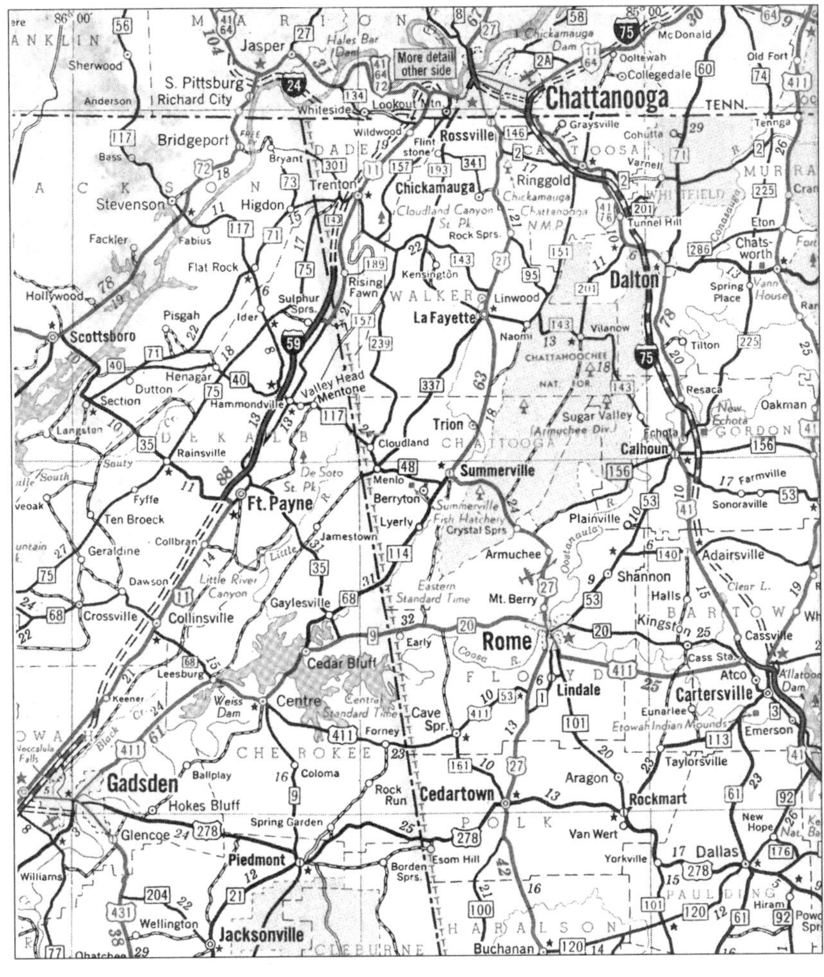

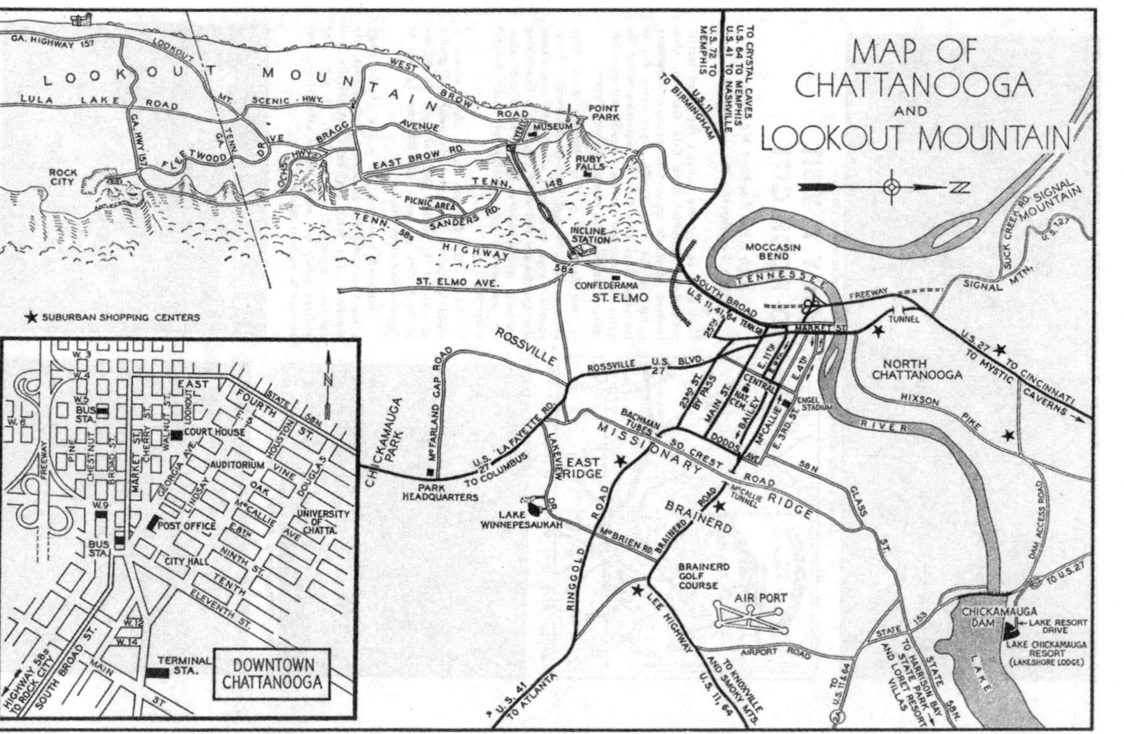

This is a detailed map of downtown Chattanooga in 1963. It shows the route Moore took out of Chattanooga to reach U.S. Highway 11. He walked off the Cummings Highway and turned left into a remote section of Tennessee, heading toward Wildwood and Trenton, Georgia.

William M. Beck (front left), Floyd Simpson's lead attorney, settles into his new position on the Alabama Board of Education. Governor George Wallace, Beck's longtime friend, is at the head of the table. After a thirteen-year absence from state politics, Beck became a force in Alabama again in the spring of 1963, using his alliance with Wallace to achieve the political influence he had long sought.

William Moore is shown in a publicity photo from the 1950s. In addition to *The Mind in Chains*, his 1955 autobiography, he also wrote an article for *Parade*, which was published on April 26, 1959. He wrote the article for *Parade* when he was working as a mental health activist. The article was titled "How You Can Help Ex-Mental Patients." Moore wrote, "We are now at the beginning of Mental Health Week, and therefore I am making this plea. Help me. Help all ex-patients fit into the wonderful outside."

William Moore roughhouses in 1959 with his three stepchildren, Marilyn, eleven, Shirley, ten, and Daniel, nine. This photo appeared in the *Parade* article.

Trenton, Georgia, became the last Southern town to officially rejoin the Union in 1945. This photo of the downtown square was taken around that time. Allison Blevins, the sheriff of Dade County, Georgia, drove William Moore from the square to Rising Fawn, Georgia, just north of the Alabama state line on the morning of April 22, 1963, after his appearance upset Trenton residents.

William M. Beck with Fort Payne leaders in the early 1950s, after he had returned home after serving as the speaker of the Alabama House of Representatives. The early 1950s marked the peak of Beck's political exile in the northeast Alabama hills because of his split with former Alabama Governor "Big Jim" Folsom.

Newlyweds Don and Paulette Whisenant pose for a photograph in the spring of 1962. One year later, the Whisenants passed the black car at the roadside park in Keener. They were the closest thing to eyewitnesses in the murder of William Moore.

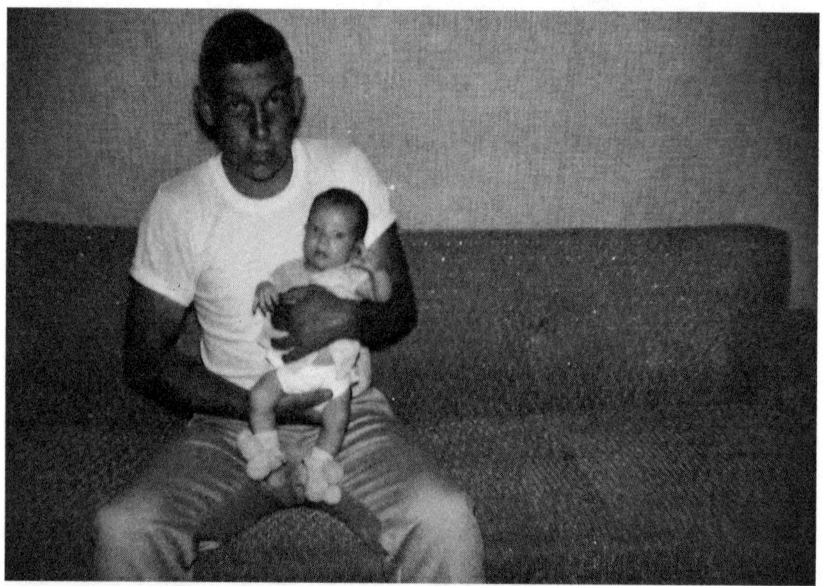

Don Whisenant holds his newborn daughter, Teri, two months after the murder of William Moore. Early that fall, he faced Ku Klux Klansmen as he entered the Etowah County Courthouse to testify before a county grand jury.

An aerial photo of Collinsville, Alabama, as it appeared when William Moore walked through town on the afternoon of April 23, 1963. At the top of the photo, U.S. Highway 11 stretches through the western edge of downtown.

Republic Steel, founded in Gadsden in 1903, was one of Gadsden's two primary industries for most of the twentieth century. The steel mill propped up Gadsden's uneven economy until it closed in the summer of 2000, when the city lost 1,600 jobs.

Goodyear Tire and Rubber Company, shown here in the mid-1960s, was long considered perhaps Gadsden's most prestigious employer. Families on Sand and Lookout Mountains and Little Wills Valley found prosperity after Goodyear President P. W. Litchfield announced on December 11, 1928, that he had decided to build the company's first plant in the South in Gadsden, spurning Atlanta and several other cities.

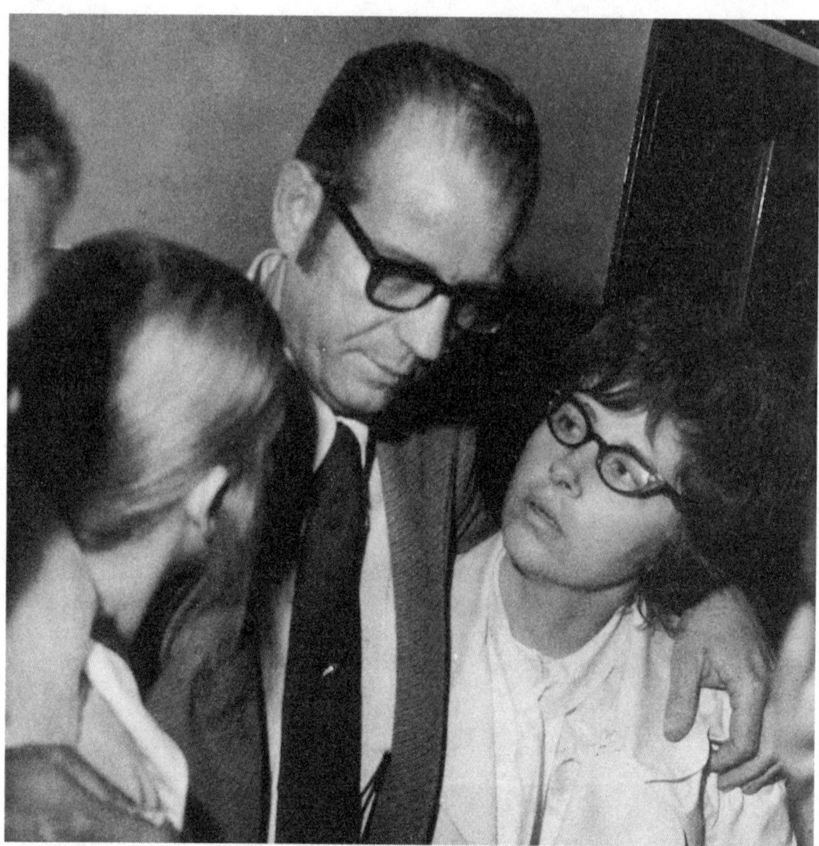

Former Ku Klux Klansman Aubrey Gene Arledge is surrounded by family at his 1974 murder trial. Arledge, forty, was one of three men accused of killing the Reverend Edward Pace, a Black minister who had recently moved into a white section of Gadsden, after Pace answered a knock at his door after returning home from Gadsden's Christmas parade on the night of November 26, 1973. His first trial ended in a hung jury. He was acquitted in his second trial. His son, Ricky Gene Arledge, received a ten-year sentence and a third man, Bruce Bostford, was convicted of second-degree murder. Pace's murder caused schools to be closed during several days of racial unrest. Thomas Reed, the head of the Alabama NAACP, said at Pace's funeral that "Blacks should continue to abide by the law but sleep with one eye open."

Actors Virgil Frye (left), Marlon Brando, Paul Newman (center), and Tony Franciosa stand outside Republic Steel on August 23, 1963. The actors came to Gadsden to support the civil rights movement that arose after the murder of William Moore. The actors received such a hostile reception from the city that local movie theaters canceled upcoming movies starring Newman and Brando. Goodyear officials declined to meet with the actors, but Republic Steel officials consented. Said Brando, "We are simply here to see if we can help the racial situation."

Alabama state troopers arrest actress Madeleine Sherwood on the afternoon of May 19, 1963, in Keener, Alabama. She was one of eleven people who were arrested for attempting to continue William Moore's walk from the murder site. At the top of the photo, the branches from the black walnut tree are stacked on the edge of the park and the picnic tables have been removed.

PART II

THE DEMANDS OF A DEEPLY OFFENDED COMMUNITY AND STATE

CHAPTER 7

The news of William Moore's death reached the rest of America after midnight. A Birmingham radio station broke the news at around 1:00 a.m., broadcasting a report from Gadsden that Moore was killed on Highway 11. Around 2:00 a.m., Raymond Faisst, the special agent in charge of the Birmingham FBI office, heard the news and telephoned FBI headquarters in Washington, D.C. Faisst described Moore as a "pro-integrationist" in his initial report. He didn't know if he was Black or white.

"SAC Faisst understood that the victim had been shot and the body is in the local coroner's office," concluded a memo from C. L. McGowan, the FBI's civil rights section chief. "ACTION: SAC Faisst was advised to obtain additional details and furnish same to the Bureau by teletype."

At 3:56 a.m., about ninety minutes after his phone call, Faisst sent a report to FBI Director J. Edgar Hoover and agents in Knoxville, Tennessee, and New Orleans. Faisst's statement read, in part, "[Moore] reportedly had been carrying some sort of [sign] of pro-integration nature. Etowah County Coroner reportedly stated this was a civil rights matter. [Reporter] for Station WGAD, Gadsden, Ala. stated William L. MooreWM [white male] age thirty five from Binghamton, N.Y. was reportedly walking alone from Chattanooga, Tenn., to Jackson, Miss., to visit relatives."

The investigation was urgent, Hoover told Faisst, and he was prepared to provide the FBI's resources to authorities in Gadsden. Faisst was already familiar with local law enforcement officials after attending a banquet in Gadsden on February 11 honoring J. H. Snyder, the City Commission's choice to be the new police chief, as the city's Officer of the Year.

"Follow developments closely and keep bureau expeditiously advised,"

Hoover wrote. "As [a] police cooperation matter, offer appropriate local authorities cooperative services of identification and laboratory divisions and coverage of out of state leads. Contact appropriate racial informants and sources."

Later that day, Faisst and agents from New Orleans and Baltimore sent memos to Hoover. The New Orleans office reported that an informant in Jackson, Mississippi, a member of the media, could not find any information about Moore or his family in Mississippi. The special agent in charge in Baltimore said two members of the National Alliance of Postal Employees came to the FBI office and said they planned to send telegrams to President Kennedy and Attorney General Robert Kennedy protesting the murder.

Faisst informed Hoover there were no witnesses and no suspects. The case, though, was "being pressed vigorously," in his words, despite the turmoil among the chief investigators. Major William R. Jones, the head of the troopers' investigative division, was furious over investigators making too many statements to the media.

"For information of bureau, [the agent] advised that [a member of] Alabama Highway Patrol, Gadsden, Ala., had informed him on a strictly confidential basis that chief [Joe] Smelley, Alabama Highway Patrol, Montgomery, had asked Alabama Highway Patrol to spot check victim on his trip to insure that all was well and that there are now a 'lot of red faces.'"

Faisst, though, had not given Hoover the whole story.

Don Whisenant awakened on the morning of April 24 in the upstairs bedroom of his in-laws' home south of Collinsville to reports of the murder on the radio. Piecing together the news, he concluded that he and his wife, Paulette, had been the last people to see William Moore alive.

Don was a twenty-one-year-old gas station attendant, newly married with a baby on the way. The night before, he had finished his shift at Doc Cleveland's Gulf, the gas station operated by his uncle, Cleo Nelson, at the intersection of U.S. 11 and Alabama Highway 77 in Attalla. Just after 8:00 p.m., he and Paulette headed home in his 1956 Ford for their nightly drive through Little Wills Valley on U.S. 11. Approaching the Sizemore farm in Keener, they saw a car cross the highway, turn into the roadside picnic area, and park under the walnut tree. Don tapped his brakes, thinking the vehicle belonged to an Alabama highway patrolman who was looking for speeders. One of the taillights of the car in the roadside park blinked once, then again, then off. The other taillight, the right one, didn't work.

As the Whisenants passed the roadside park, they looked to their right to see who was in the car, a black sedan. They saw no one. They did, however, see a man about forty yards in front of them. He was pushing a cart along the side of the highway, walking toward the park. The headlights of their car glanced off the chrome of his cart as they passed him.

"He must be bringing some gas to the people in that car," Don told his wife. "They must have run out of gas."

Immediately after hearing the news on the radio, Don phoned his father, Doug, in Attalla to tell him about what he'd seen. He wondered if he should call the sheriff's office to tell a deputy about what he had witnessed.

"No," his father told him. "Stay out of it. Don't get involved. Keep your mouth shut."

There were no other witnesses. Don and Paulette Whisenant were the only ones who had passed the picnic area as the murder unfolded. Betty Dowdy, who lived less than a mile from the murder scene, was perhaps the only person to see the murderer. Almost everyone who had seen the car said a large man with his arm hanging out of the window was the driver. Betty, though, had seen an average-sized man behind the wheel of the black Buick, but her description was never sent to the FBI or included in newspaper reports. Instead, it was widely believed that the man driving was a large man, and Floyd Simpson was short and slender.

On April 24, President Kennedy mentioned Moore, though not by name, midway through a thirty-minute press conference.

"We had an outrageous crime, from all accounts, in the state of Alabama in the shooting of the postman who was attempting in a very traditional way to dramatize the plight of some of our citizens, being assassinated on the road," he said. "We have offered to the state of Alabama the services of the FBI in the solution of the crime. We do not have direct jurisdiction."

Robert Kennedy, preparing for his trip to Alabama, addressed Moore's death at a press conference in South Carolina, predicting that "other bloodshed" would follow. He attributed the prospect of more racial violence to the increasing unrest throughout the country, created by the protests in the South and elsewhere.

"It's not just in Alabama and South Carolina," he said. "We have it where I come from."

Joseph Dolan, the assistant deputy U.S. attorney general, became involved on April 26, requesting information the FBI had received from its informants. He wondered if the bureau's laboratory had found any evidence that was useful in its investigation, eager to provide information to the media. The case was national and international news, making front-page news coverage in London. On April 26, as the *Guardian* of London reported that two men had been arrested, Alistair Cooke, the newspaper's foreign correspondent, wrote an op-ed piece headlined, "The Last Diary of Willie Moore."

"The opportunit[y] for irony in the juxtaposition of Moore's death and the President's refusal to withhold federal funds for Mississippi are rich and will not be resisted wherever black men yearn for that 'equal protection of the laws' to which the United States Supreme Court and the conscience of the mid-century entitle them," he wrote. "But these are two stories and only mischic [sic] can come from playing one against the other."

The *Guardian* reprinted Moore's diary, calling it "as pathetic an epitaph as one could write." In Australia, the *Sydney Morning Herald* devoted twelve paragraphs to the news of Moore's death. "Race Murder of Postman," the headline read. The *Age* of Melbourne was more straightforward. "White, Against Color Bar, Shot Dead," it announced.

The *New York Times* referred to the killing as "barbarism." The *Binghamton Press Sun-Bulletin* called Moore "one of the genuine heroes of our time." The *Baltimore Afro-American* said his murder was "the first known and proven death of a freedom fighter since the non-violent revolution began with the Montgomery, Ala., bus boycott which catapulted the Rev. Martin Luther King to national prominence."

Anne Braden, the editor of the Southern Conference Educational Fund's newspaper, *The Southern Patriot*, found that reaction to Moore's death "produce[d] some interesting insights into the very complex questions involved in Negro-white relations in America." Braden and her husband, Carl, had been active in the movement for years, once buying a house in suburban Louisville, Kentucky, for an African American couple, Andrew and Charlotte Wade, an act that ended with crosses being burned on the Wades' front lawn and the house being dynamited in 1954.

"To the average Negro-on-the-street, Moore became a saint," she wrote. "[A] Southern Negro student leader called him a nonviolent John Brown; and the Negro press played up the story of his death more prominently than any event I recall in recent years, including the murder of Emmett Till in Mississippi in 1955. Nor do I remember any happening about which their correspondents have written with as much feeling."

She sensed so much optimism among Blacks, in fact, that she believed there was now an opportunity for whites and Blacks to work together for equal rights.

"Negro reaction to the Moore killing shows that the door is still open for a joint effort of Negro and white to change America," she wrote. "But white people concerned for this effort should face the fact that suspicion and donut and disillusion with the white world run deep among Negroes now making a stand for freedom, and the death of one selfless man is certainly not going to erase it all."*

NAACP Executive Director Roy Wilkins called Moore "a hero and a dramatic symbol of concern of millions of Americans for the abolition of color-line injustice." A judge in Philadelphia said Moore and other freedom marchers are "the engineers in a new race for space—a race for a place in space which has too long been denied the Negro in his aspirations for a full economic and cultural life." In Northern Rhodesia, six people—two whites, two Blacks, and two Indians—started a memorial fund for Moore.

"It seemed to me," said an *Afro-American* reporter who knew Moore, "that he represented an idea so powerful that I could not bear to get too close to him for too long."

Many editorialists in the Deep South were critical of Moore's walk ("Moore's mission was ill-advised," wrote the *Birmingham Post-Herald*. "Fu-

* Gazette and Daily (York, Pa.), May 21, 1963, 19.

tile it was at best"), but the *Delta Democrat-Times* of Greenville, Mississippi, the newspaper of moderate editor Hodding Carter, a Pulitzer Prize winner for his views on race, considered his journey to be Christlike.

"For Baltimore postman William Moore, whatever his past history or present mental condition, above all was driven by an emotion which has always motivated the best of men in our world's history: love of his fellow man," the *Delta Democrat-Times* wrote. "Not race or creed, but common humanity impelled William Moore on his way with his message to a governor that was never delivered. He was struck down by a man or men who has another quality all men share in greater or lesser degree: a callous disdain for the sanctity of their fellow men. It is not sacrilegious to say that William Moore's murder was a symbolic crucifixion which all of us should note well. He was harming no man. He was breaking no law. He was simply walking to see the governor of Mississippi with a plea for greater tolerance, greater democracy, greater love than we now possess or exhibit. For this, apparently, he was killed by men whose bestiality finds a kindred spark in all of us all."

P. D. East, the maverick publisher of the *Petal Paper*, a pro-integration newspaper in Petal, Mississippi, gave the most emotional tribute of all. He believed that Moore's murder was even more significant than the protests in Birmingham and the prospect of more confrontation during the integration of the University of Alabama.

"But with all that is happening in Birmingham, the dogs, the water, the night sticks, with what is most likely to happen in Tuscaloosa, all of it does not equal the murder of a man near Attalla on the night of Tuesday, April 23rd," East wrote. "It may be that my evaluation is slanted; I know that, and I admit it, but there is considerable personal identification in the matter of this man's murder.

"Handwritten in ink, across the top of a sheet of 8½ x 11 paper were these words: 'P.D.—Provided I make it to Jackson, I'll try to meet you if, for you, it's safe to do so. All this is uncertain. Keep up the good work. Bill Moore.'"

East and Moore had been friends since East's appearance at Harpur College in the spring of 1961. They exchanged letters for the next two years, and East published many of them in his newspaper.

"I often wondered what sort of fellow he was," East wrote. "I noted quickly that he was of an unusually peaceful nature, that his concern for the rights of others was born of a deep conviction. In short, Bill Moore was anything on this earth but a phony."

Charles and Grace Cagle drove from Birmingham to Gadsden to confirm the identity of their nephew. The officers thought the Cagles were "nice Christian people," especially when the Jesus poster on Moore's cart offended them. The poster was "the thing that upset them most," said Tony Reynolds, the chief deputy.

Charles was a railroad conductor, and Grace was one of Robert Moore's older sisters. Bill had written them about two weeks before his walk, informing them that he would stop by their house on Thirty-Ninth Street South on his way to Mississippi. They told him not to come.

The newsmen came, too, and Grace Cagle didn't want them either, refusing to open her screen door when they gathered on her front porch.

"Too much has been said about this already," she said. "We don't want to read any more about him. If you men will grant my request and his family you'll print nothing more about him. He wasn't, uh, responsible."

William Moore was major news for more than a month. Newspapers in New York City and Los Angeles, a radio station in Saint Louis, and *Newsweek* were among the media that phoned the *Gadsden Times* in the days after Moore's death. Gadsden residents were increasingly sensitive to how the national media portrayed their city. Reports in the Binghamton and Baltimore newspapers emphasized the city's shame over the murder and the hope that people of the North didn't believe people in Alabama were as vicious as Moore's killer.

A woman stood on Broad Street, in the city's downtown business district, and collected donations for roses that were to be sent to Mary Moore. A card had already been prepared.

"It's a lonesome road," read the inscription. "He wrote his own sign. He did not stand behind another."

Another local woman recommended a day of prayer. A Gadsden carpenter, J. A. Walker, believed there was good reason for repentance, suggesting a new reason for the murder that the local newspapers and authorities had neglected to mention.

"That wasn't a racial thing," Walker said. "It was pure damned meanness."

Gadsden, though, had its limits. The city retaliated after Joaquin de Alba's editorial cartoon in the *Washington Daily News*, depicting Moore's body sprawled on a lonely highway, a sign lying next to him. In the background was a road marker with one sign pointing the way to Gadsden and the other pointing toward Jackson, Mississippi. In the foreground were two mountaineers wearing cowboy hats and holding shotguns. The cartoon's caption read, "I Hear It Ain't Safe to Walk the Streets in Washington."

Five days after the murder, the *Gadsden Times* reprinted De Alba's cartoon on the front page with its rebuttal.

"This cartoon appeared on the front page of a Washington D.C. newspaper the other day, giving graphic evidence of how vindictive is the treatment of the South by fellow Americans north of here, and how quick their judgment.

"Gadsden is pointed out as the death place. As a matter of fact the deed was committed 19 miles from downtown Gadsden.

"There is, however, a lesson to be learned even from this bit of revolting illustrated reporting, and this is how important it is to preserve the good, true image of the South and Gadsden.

"The South is no different than the rest of the nation in its reaction to the slaying of William L. Moore of Baltimore, near Keener; and a Baltimore Evening Sun reporter, who made The Gadsden Times his headquarters the last three days, saw it first hand—by the treatment he received and by witnessing the shock of the people over the murder—how biased and unrealistic is the opinion of the South by newspapers and other news media in the East and North.

"And the cartoon still hasn't changed anything—'It Ain't Safe to Walk the Streets in Washington.'"

Things hadn't changed in Gadsden either. Local leaders had always rallied to protect Gadsden's image when labor and bootleg liquor troubles cropped up, using its full resources to preserve its traditions. William W. Rayburn, the chief prosecutor in the William Moore murder investigation, was deeply familiar with how Gadsden had handled its potential public relations crises. His father, an attorney and judge, had protected the city during the labor troubles of the late 1930s, the most volatile situations to face Gadsden until the William Moore murder. William W. Rayburn, the new Etowah County district attorney, was about to show that he had learned his father's lessons well.

CHAPTER 8

Gadsden, Alabama, population 58,000, was in economic and legal turmoil in the months before William Moore's death. The city was on the verge of bankruptcy in 1962, when Gadsden leaders announced in January that the city had a $647,000 deficit—the equivalent of $6.6 million in 2024. Unemployment reached 18 percent in 1961, after the city lost 2,100 jobs with the closing of textile mills, pipe shops, and the air force depot. A year later, unemployment was still nearly 15 percent.

"Let's Face It!" read a newspaper advertisement during the 1962 gubernatorial election. "Ladies and Gentlemen of Etowah County, we have a problem!!! We can't conceal this by hiding our heads in the sand and saying all is well, because . . . it directly affects the lives of 20 of every 100 of us, thirteen of this 20 directly affected are minor children. We know by now you know we are referring to our unemployed situation."

Gadsden was classified as a depressed area by the federal government, qualifying for federal aid under Public Law 87–27, known as the Area Redevelopment Act. Lines at food surplus commodity centers were "the longest in Alabama," as one Gadsden resident put it. To bolster local leadership, Frank Helderman, the publisher of the *Gadsden Times*, proposed a new form of government. Even the county school system was in disarray, finding itself in need of $120,000 with six weeks left in the 1962 academic year.

City government and city law enforcement were also chaotic. For months, the city had been unable to decide on a police chief. The City Commission chose one candidate and the Civil Service Board another. With the city also paying a retired police chief almost $500 a month, Gadsden had three police chiefs on the city payroll. Meanwhile, city policemen were near revolt. A teenage girl, Sandra Nell Lankford, who escaped from jail the previous fall, made a series of explosive allegations against the Gadsden Police Department, causing the city to form a committee and the state attorney general, Richmond Flowers, to intervene. Lankford's charges included an officer having intercourse with her in the jail's laundry room and a policeman taking nude photographs of her in jail.* J. H. Snyder, the acting police chief, charged officers in March 1963 with fifty-three violations of the civil service code. One of the officers responded with countercharges against Snyder.

Labor violence, though, was the area's most persistent problem, and it flared with its usual savagery in 1961 and 1962. A Birmingham grand jury indicted twenty members of a local union, Teamsters No. 612, for threats and violence, among other things, during their strike at Bowman Trucking. Finally, after the driver of a Bowman truck was nearly killed by a bullet from a high-powered rifle, the National Labor Relations Board ordered local Teamsters to stop "throwing rockets, bottles, or other objects, missiles or materials at occupants of vehicles."

Six days before William Moore's murder, Cecil Beach, the director of the Gadsden Public Library, addressed the city's self-esteem in a newspaper editorial. The headline was, "The Enemy Within . . . Could It Be Us?"

> In recent days our city has been beset with turmoil, trouble and tribulation as one unpleasant situation after another has been revealed. As each new episode is brought to light, some rush hurriedly to fix the blame, while others move just as quickly to disavow and disown any responsibility whatsoever.
>
> Amidst all confusion of charge and countercharge, where and upon whom shall we fix the blame?
>
> Pogo, that wise possum philosopher of the Okefenokee swamp may have come pretty close when he said, paraphrasing Oliver Hazard Perry, "We have met the enemy, and not only is he ours, he may be us."
>
> Those words come so near to the truth that they sting. Let us face the facts that what is wrong is not the fault of others. . . . If there is gaffe it is because we permit it. If there is immorality it is because we condone it. If there is laxity in government it is because we indulge it by not taking part. If there is vice it is because we wink at it. If there is ignorance it is because we tolerate it.

* *Gadsden Times,* March, 31, 1963, 1; *Gadsden Times*, April 4, 1963, 2.

Life for Black residents was even worse.

"Gadsden is a living hell," one said.

Gadsden's law enforcement had long been known for sanctioning violence and crime. The city's reputation as the nation's toughest labor town was established in 1936, when Sherman Dalrymple, the new president of the United Rubber Workers of America, came from Akron, Ohio, to address a mass labor meeting at the Etowah County courthouse and talk to Goodyear Tire and Rubber Company management about the recent dismissals of two union leaders. The mass meeting was on the night of June 6. An angry crowd of more than two hundred gathered at the courthouse, including Goodyear supervisors and employees who threw eggs and tomatoes at Dalrymple. The sheriff, Robert Leath, intervened, leading Dalrymple and his wife out of the meeting and out a back door, where a mob was waiting. The mob beat Dalrymple so severely that he was nearly killed. Leath's response to the beatings was to tell Dalrymple, "The people are up in arms and I won't be responsible for your safety." Dalrymple and his wife left Gadsden after he was denied the chance to obtain medical treatment. Sherman Dalrymple returned to Akron, where doctors informed him that he had a severe concussion, keeping him in the hospital for a week.

The violence escalated in the summer of 1937. Three members of the United Rubber Workers of America tried to kill Jimmy Karam, a former Auburn University football star and leader of the Etowah Rubber Workers Association, a union of Goodyear employees. Early on the morning of June 18, 1937, a theater was bombed in downtown Attalla, just north of Gadsden. The next day, state police officers arrested three men, all United Rubber Workers, for attempting to bomb Karam's car.

A month later, a group of clergymen, educators, and writers came to Gadsden to investigate charges of violations of workers' civil liberties. H. C. Nixon, a professor of history and political science, was among the first to arrive in Gadsden, but he discovered that his reservation at the Morris Hotel was no longer available. Others in the group, from New York and Chicago, received similar information when they attempted to register. Even the Reverend A. M. Freeman of Birmingham, cochairman of the group, was denied a room. They also discovered they were unwelcome by Gadsden city leaders, who believed the group's purpose was to "besmirch" the city's reputation.

"This group of outsiders who seek to pass judgment upon our citizens are evidently provided funds from outside sources whose interest most certainly is not in the interest of our people and our city," said George Vann, the president of the Gadsden City Commission. "Why is it that this group is devoting its attention to this Southern city and overlooking the opportunity of investigating the conditions in the north and in the east? What is behind this, we ask? This is a question worthy of thought."

The group responded with a statement.

"We have heard but one side of the controversy and we have high hopes that our earnest invitations to public officials will be accepted so that we may know their problems and attitudes, too. More impressive than the detailed, specific testimony of several witnesses to alleged denial of civil rights to beatings of rank-and-file employe[e]s of Gadsden industrial plants, as well as outside union organizers, has been the obvious attitudes of those witnesses who have come before us. Again and again they have shown more vividly than their words could describe, their fear that their lives were endangered by their testimony before us. We come to Gadsden wondering whether the statements of some of the union men and women were correct that that was a serious situation in Gadsden or on the other hand whether the conditions had been greatly exaggerated. The attitude of these men and women who have come to us has shown beyond any further doubt on our part that there is something definitely seriously wrong in Gadsden. There is a tense situation. There is fear. There is a lack of confidence in the forces of law and order on the part of some."

Something was, in fact, seriously wrong in Gadsden. In March 1944, Raymond McMurray, an African American private from Chicago, was stationed at Camp Sibert, an army chemical training facility near Gadsden. Gadsden police accused him of attacking a white woman in a residential neighborhood despite uncertainties about whether he had been in Gadsden at the time. The incident caused such an uproar among residents that McMurray, a twenty-year-old member of the 166th Chemical Company at Camp Sibert, was moved twice for "safekeeping," as authorities put it, first to the jail in Anniston and then to the Jefferson County jail in Birmingham. On the way to Birmingham, McMurray, unarmed and handcuffed, was shot nine times by Fay Boman, the new police chief of Gadsden, and Jack Fisher, the Gadsden chief of detectives, as Sheriff O. P. Reagan drove south on U.S. 11. Louis E. Burnham of the Southern Negro Youth Congress described the shooting as an act that "ranks with the most dastardly crimes in the annals of Southern police terror."* A Black leader in Gadsden went to Washington, D.C., to convince the War Department to investigate the activities at Camp Sibert.† The leader, too afraid to identify himself to local reporters, said it was the fourth time Boman and Fisher had shot a Black soldier. Burnham issued a lengthy statement that described the murder and requested the U.S. War Department and the Department of Justice to investigate the murder.

"This is not the first instance in which Negro prisoners have lost their lives at the hands of law enforcement officials in Gadsden, Ala.," Burnham said. "In fact this is the fourth time in recent memory that the same officers have been responsible for the murder of Negro prisoners who were being held under arrest.

"And the citizenry of G[a]dsden is now being treated to the indecent spectacle of leading citizens publicly and brazenly congratulating Fay Boman, chief of [police], for having done a brave deed. As though he had been responsible for the annihilation of an enemy unit on the battlefield!"‡

Officials from the War Department went to Gadsden in the spring of 1944 to investigate a confrontation that involved heavyweight boxing champion Joe Louis, welterweight champion Sugar Ray Robinson, and white military policemen. Louis and Robinson were part of a boxing team at Camp Sibert that fought exhibitions to entertain soldiers. As Louis and Robinson prepared to leave camp, they found a long line at the segregated bus depot. Louis headed toward the white terminal to call a taxi, but a military policeman (MP) ordered him back to the Black depot.

"Why do I have to go back to the other side?" Louis asked.

* *New York Age*, March 25, 1944, 1.

† *Afro-American* (Baltimore, Md.), April 8, 1944, 16.

‡ *Black Dispatch* (Oklahoma City, Okla.), April 1, 1944, 5.

"Don't you know your color?" the MP said.

"I got a uniform on, same as you, and we're fighting the same war," Louis said. "I don't stand being discriminated against."

The MP took a golf club and jabbed it into Louis's ribs.

"I'll do more than touch you, n——," the MP said.

Robinson jumped on the MP's back as Louis prepared to swing at the policeman. Some officers threatened to take Louis and Robinson to the camp jail, but the commanding general intervened, and Louis and Robinson were freed. After an army investigation, Jim Crow practices on military buses were abolished. But reports of abuses to African Americans in Gadsden continued.

In the early spring of 1946, a Black prisoner, LeRoy Hampton, was taken from the jail in Guntersville and driven across Sand Mountain and on to Boaz, about twenty miles south. He was turned over to a state trooper, who drove Hampton to the Gadsden city hall. In Gadsden, Hampton was beaten by officers in an attempt to force him to confess to a robbery. Hampton's attorney, W. C. Rayburn, the Guntersville city attorney, said Gadsden officers "administered a severe beating about [Hampton's] head." He found Hampton in "very bad shape" and requested medical treatment.

"This is the second time that it has been brought to my attention that prisoners have been beaten and burned to force confession of guilt," Rayburn said.

Fay Boman was 6 feet 2½ inches and 230 pounds, and he used his size and muscle on the white and Black residents of Gadsden who crossed him. One was Swann Colwell, a Gadsden real estate owner and hardware store owner who had questioned the city's enforcement of its thriving bootleg liquor traffic. Colwell was so incensed that he had sent a letter to Governor James E. "Big Jim" Folsom, accusing local state patrolmen of escorting bootleggers through the county. Finally, Boman faced his accuser at his office on September 17, 1948. A police detective, Ned Simmons, attended the meeting, which began with Boman locking the door to his office.

"He told me he was going to 'beat the hell out of me,'" Colwell said. "He knocked me out of a chair and beat and kicked me."

Colwell called for help, but no one came. Finally, Boman opened his office door and ordered Colwell out of the building. With Colwell still on the floor, Gadsden Mayor Herbert Meighan entered the police chief's office. He said nothing. Boman justified the attack because Colwell had called him a liar. His penalty was a twenty-day suspension by the Gadsden Civil Service Board for conduct unbecoming a police officer.

But Colwell's concerns were substantiated less than six months later, after two sheriff's deputies resigned. One of the deputies, Robert D. Goode, said he was forced to resign because he was unable to work "under conditions enforcing prohibition laws." Two weeks later, a grand jury was called for "a general investigation of the sheriff's department." The grand jury ended after Sheriff Ira Ballard resigned. His successor, Cecil Folsom, the brother of Governor James E. Folsom, said his department was "going to clean up the county with respect to prohibition violations and violations of all other laws as well." The corruption, though, became more blatant and vicious.

Federal liquor agents arrested one of Boman's detectives, Carl "Red" Clements, and his brother in 1956 for possession of 120 gallons of white whiskey, 120 cases of beer, and 1 case of bonded whiskey. The arrest came months after a former deputy sheriff—"still regarded as 'the best chief deputy this county ever had in some circles,'" the *Gadsden Times* reported—was arrested on April 23 as the U.S. Treasury Department investigated the county's moonshine whiskey operations.

Circuit Judge Virgil Pittman called a grand jury on April 1, 1957, telling the jury that Gadsden had been gripped "by a cancerous and evil thing." For weeks, Public Safety Commissioner Cecil Weatherbee had received anonymous phone threats.

"You dirty bastard, keep your nose out of our business," one caller told him.

The calls became so frequent that Weatherbee appointed a Gadsden policeman to guard his home. Finally, late one night, an assassin fired bullets at Weatherbee as he stood in his kitchen, reaching for a paper towel. The policeman who had guarded Weatherbee's home escaped an assassination attempt when he left for a vacation in Virginia only hours before bullets were fired into Weatherbee's home. Weatherbee responded by shuffling police personnel, returning three detectives to the uniform division. Nine of the 13 witnesses summoned to the grand jury refused to testify, but the results came swiftly: a prostitution ring was operating in Gadsden, and the city's illegal liquor traffic was still thriving, according to the grand jury report.

"It has been charged that law enforcement has broken down," Boman said. "This must be clarified at once. The police department is on trial and we are asking [for] a fair trial."

Weatherbee, though, was powerless to pursue organized crime. The authority was with Boman and the police department.

"The police commissioner cannot investigate bootlegging, prostitution, gambling, or corruption in office or organized crime, except through the police force over which he has no disciplinary power," he said. "Whether it is functioning properly and has full confidence of the public depends on the police department."

Pittman's special grand jury adjourned that week with no indictments. He promised, though, that the grand jury would be recalled if investigators found enough evidence to believe an indictment was possible. Later that month, the owner of several small Gadsden hotels and a former mayoral candidate were among eight people indicted on prostitution charges.

The Etowah County grand jury resumed its investigation into Gadsden's city government on February 19, 1959, examining charges of irregularities in finances and inventory and equipment, primarily city-owned cars. The grand jury charged Homer Doss, the former director of the Gadsden Revenue Department, with sixteen counts of embezzlement, claiming he had misappropriated almost $4,000 from taxes that the city collected from movies and wrestling matches. Only a year earlier, Doss had been named Gadsden's "Man of the Year" by the Civitan Club for his work in civic and service club programs. After his indictment, he proclaimed his innocence, saying he would not "take the rap" for anyone. That fall, Wright dropped the charges against Doss, saying he couldn't obtain a unanimous verdict from a jury.

Hugh Sparrow of the *Birmingham News* provided the most explosive allegations. On the day the grand jury resumed, Sparrow wrote a front-page report that said jurors were prepared to examine anonymous charges that a "plush gambling casino continues to do business in the heart of downtown

Gadsden" and that the county's multimillion-dollar bootlegging trade had become more active. The grand jury asked Sparrow to appear. He told them that his information came from the same anonymous letter that was sent to Charles Wright, the circuit solicitor who was leading the grand jury.

The grand jury issued a report that attacked Sparrow's reporting.

"There have been newspaper articles in certain out of town newspapers concerning rumors of gambling casinos in downtown Gadsden frequented by higher-ups of the city. The Grand Jury attempted to substantiate this theory and had before it Mr. Hugh Sparrow, a reporter for *The Birmingham News*, who wrote such articles. Mr. Sparrow was unable to furnish any facts other than rumors to support this story. This Grand Jury resents such unsupported publication of charges without basis of fact."

Two days later, Sparrow countered with a rebuke of the grand jury.

"The recent Etowah Grand Jury shied away from reports of gambling, vice, etc., in its investigation of Gadsden's city government," he wrote. "Members instead tried to get from this reporter the source of information about the existence of a hot gambling spot supposedly a favorite with higher-ups. And, failing, they retorted with criticism in the jury's written report to the court. But that didn't prove there was no gambling, no vice, no bootlegging, no whatnot—naughty or worse—within the confines of Gadsden."

Sparrow, in fact, found plenty of corruption in some of Gadsden's busiest areas. He found, too, that the Etowah County grand jury was more interested in protecting Gadsden's image than the crimes.

"State taxed liquor is plentiful in Gadsden," he said. "But it's hard on the pocketbook. The worst brand of cheap state taxed whiskey is peddled, over the counter or otherwise, for $5 a pint. And it's said that here 'white lightning' of the almost forgotten bootleg era never made its exit from the devious illegal channels of Gadsden and its environs. It's said to be a million dollar bootleg paradise and well should it be. Served with an 'instanter' subpoena, which means immediate appearance before the grand jury, this reporter faced a barrage of questions. From their report, it seems, jurors were mainly interested in knowing the source of information about the gambling casino near downtown Gadsden which was supposed to have quite a few big shots as chief patrons. . . . It happened that both Solicitor

Charles Wright and this reporter received the same copy of a lengthy anonymous typewritten document giving the supposed lowdown on the city hall situation.

"Among those choice items was this: 'In addition to irregularities in the City Hall involving public funds, there is a bootlegging ring, a syndicate that controls the call girls and the prostitution racket. There is considerable gambling going on, bookies, etc. There is a gambling den on —— Street that is being patronized by —— himself, where all night high stakes gambling games are carried on.'

"It took very little inquiry to spot this house. Neither was it difficult to get the name of the reported king of the prostitution and call girl syndicate. . . . This reporter was convinced that the jurors were more concerned in knowing the source of the information than the information itself."

In the early morning hours of August 17, a Sunday, Sheriff Dewey Colvard and his deputies arrested six men on gambling charges at a house in downtown Gadsden. Two of the arrestees lived on Turrentine Avenue, where many of Gadsden's wealthiest residents resided. Colvard and his deputies seized two poker tables, some poker chips, eight dozen decks of playing cards, some checks, and less than a fifth of whiskey.

"I'm starting a crackdown," Colvard said. "I wouldn't be at all surprised if there are more raids."

The arrests were made at 802 Chestnut Street, a block behind the county courthouse.

With his health deteriorating from an enlarged spleen and cirrhosis of the liver, Fay Boman looked like a man in the final months of his life. There was an attempt to remove him from office in 1958, but he survived. When he died on September 22, 1959, the *Gadsden Times* eulogized him in a front-page story that began, "The man J. Edgar Hoover called the best police chief in the South has died."

The Gadsden Police Department made news in more dramatic ways after his death. In the late summer of 1960, Gadsden received its introduction to civil rights, creating a mob scene at the Gadsden bus station, accusations of police brutality, and a $9 million lawsuit. The Reverend Fred Shuttlesworth's children—Patricia Ann, seventeen, Ruby Fredricka, fifteen, and Fred Jr., thirteen—were returning to their home in Birmingham after six weeks at a youth workshop at the Highlander Folk School in Monteagle, Tennessee, the social justice training school near Chattanooga. As their bus left Chattanooga, the children took seats at the front of the bus, the area reserved for white passengers. The driver ordered them to move to the back, even though segregation on interstate bus travel had been outlawed since the U.S. Supreme Court ruled in 1946 that it violated the commerce clause of the Constitution. Approaching Gadsden, the Shuttlesworth children were still at the front of the bus, and the driver radioed authorities about the children's actions.

Five city policemen and a mob of about fifty were waiting at the Gadsden bus terminal. Someone in the mob said, "Get those [expletives] off the bus, or we'll throw them off." The children were jailed overnight on charges of conduct calculated to provoke a breach of peace. Their father, the state's best-known civil rights leader, posted bail after a night of harassment that included Gadsden police denying his initial attempts to free his children. Shuttlesworth accused the Gadsden police of slapping Ruby Fredricka and trying to choke his son. He likened the police's treatment to Gestapo tactics, citing Gadsden officers following him through the city as he attempted to post bail.

On August 18, 1960, two days after the arrests, Martin Luther King Jr., the nation's civil rights leader since his role in the Montgomery bus boycott in 1956, sent a telegram to U.S. Attorney William Rogers.

"Children were asked to move to the rear of the bus for segregated seating at Chattanooga, Tenn.," King wrote. "They refused. At Gads[d]en, Ala. driver called police and had children arrested. Were subjected to police brutality in jail. These facts confirmed. Forthright action by your office most necessary in view of obvious intent by some persons, and private agencies to continue denial of civil rights for the Negro and his equal protection and justice under law."

Most of all, there was fear among the white residents of Gadsden—fear of school integration, fear of the sit-ins at downtown lunch counters, fear of African Americans taking the better jobs at Goodyear, fear of the labor unions.

"Gadsden, Ala. USA, just 140 miles north of Montgomery, has come to have something in common with an oppressed and furtive Russian satellite town," wrote Allen Rankin of the *Montgomery Advertiser* on March 11, 1954, during labor violence at Bowman Trucking, one of the area's leading businesses. "A subtle poison of tension and fear seeps through the place."

Trucks were dynamited on local highways, causing Ralph Bowman, the owner of Bowman Trucking, to threaten to leave Gadsden. He claimed city and county officials failed to protect his truckers because "their election is coming up in September and they won't risk offending the powerful labor vote here."

John Thomas, the city's Ford dealership owner, said he received five hundred harassing phone calls after his appeal for law and order at a city commission meeting. Angry readers phoned Frank Helderman until 3:00 a.m., after his newspaper published an editorial that called for nonviolence and described the bombings as un-American. One merchant refused to give his identity to Rankin because he didn't "want any bombs in my basement." Even the city's policemen seemed too scared to confront the corruption. Alabama Senator Bruce Henderson said during his 1954 gubernatorial campaign that Gadsden was "under the stranglehold of 175 gangsters who frustrate the law and shield the real criminals who poison the cattle, dynamite the trucks, and frighten the local law enforcement authorities."

In this climate of fear, the Ku Klux Klan was prepared to thrive. The Klan was revived in Gadsden in 1947, when a crowd of about five hundred gathered at the Etowah County courthouse for a meeting of local Klansmen. The Klan frequently held Saturday night motorcades through downtown and the African American section of Gadsden, at the foot of Lookout Mountain. On the night of March 5, 1949, some photographers from the Gadsden Engraving Company took a shot of a Klan procession on one of the city's main streets. Two robed Klansmen sat on the front of the lead car, their legs dangling on the bumper and an American flag waving behind the Klansman on the right side of the hood. Two robed Klansmen were in the car. One had removed his mask.

The driver of the lead car, a black late-model sedan, chased the photographers for six blocks, nearly causing a head-on collision before ending their pursuit. The photograph of the lead car was published twice in the *Gadsden Times*, including a close-up view of the Klansman in the passenger seat, his face visible as he directed the driver through the downtown streets. The reason for the chase became evident to those who examined the photograph. The caption beneath the enlarged photograph read, in part, "Presumably the man beside the driver, unmasked above, was a guide familiar with the streets of this area." Some believed the Klansman in the passenger seat was Fay Boman.

"I have seen the photographs of the Saturday night episode from which the engravings were made and I firmly believe one of the individuals pictured is employed by the police department," a Gadsden resident, Clyde Townley, wrote in a letter published in the *Gadsden Times*.

A Klan motorcade followed a similar route on the night of October 20, 1956, traveling through town "unescorted [and] running traffic lights to prevent a break-up of the line," the *Gadsden Times* said. The newspaper, though, tried to downplay the incident, saying, "as long as the KKKK carries out its affairs beneath the cross it so boldly displays, there is no cause for alarm." Less than three months later, on the night of January 13, 1957, another motorcade, this one estimated at twenty cars, drove to the East Side Drive Holiness Church in south Gadsden to make a contribution.

In Boman's final months as police chief, the Klan held a raucous gathering in downtown Gadsden on a Saturday night in the spring of 1958. The rally became rowdier as they reached the town's most famous landmark, the 21-foot monument of General Nathan Bedford Forrest riding with Emma Sansom, the fifteen-year-old girl who showed him where to cross a rain-swollen creek after a Union officer, Abel Streight, had burned a bridge.

"This is to protest, however feebly, the meeting of the Ku Klux Klan at Moragne Park on Saturday, March 29," Dr. Jack Brock wrote in a letter to the editor of the *Gadsden Times*. "I was not there. In fact, I was in Alabama City at the Spring Festival political rally. But I have been informed that the loud and long blowing of auto horns was quite upsetting to patients in the nearby hospital. I am not Catholic. I am not Jewish. I am not a member of the Negro race. I am a physician, and I must speak up and voice my objection to this unnecessary noise, or I would be derelict in my duty to my patients."

The Klan was so influential by 1959 that its exalted cyclops, James "Ace" Williams, arranged a meeting with Frank Helderman. Helderman's son, Frank Jr., found himself in a dispute between some University of Alabama students and Klan leaders in Tuscaloosa, home of the National Knights of the Ku Klux Klan. The controversy surrounded photos of a Klan welcome sign on U.S. 11 on the outskirts of Tuscaloosa. Some students in Helderman Jr.'s car had defied the Klansmen's orders to not photograph the sign. Already angry because paint or battery acid had damaged their sign, the Klansmen gave chase but could not catch the students.

Ace Williams arranged a meeting at Frank Helderman Sr.'s office after Klansmen traced the license plate number to Helderman Jr. Some newspaper reports, quoting Frank Helderman Jr., said Robert Shelton, the head of the U.S. Knights of the Ku Klux Klan, was also at the meeting. Others reported that "intimidation and harassment" were issued by Klan officials. On April 28, 1959, Frank Helderman addressed "misleading" reports, as a headline in the *Gadsden Times* put it.

Frank Helderman Jr., a junior at Alabama, said he had loaned his car to a friend on the night of April 23, 1959, when the Klansmen guarding the sign had seen the students take a photograph, according to the *Gadsden Times*.

"I had been informed that his son's car had been reportedly seen at the location of the sign," Williams said. "I visited with Mr. Helderman to discuss this and this only. The meeting was completely friendly and harmonious and at no time were any threats of intimidation, reprisal or harassment made to Mr. Helderman."

Helderman called the meeting a "goodwill visit" by Williams. He and Williams denied that Shelton, soon to be the most powerful Klan leader in America, was at the meeting. Days later, Shelton also denied he was at the meeting, although he admitted he had received a phone call from Helderman, who apologized for the mistakes in the newspapers.

"I regret that my son's name has been connected with an incident that could bring embarrassment to the University of Alabama," Helderman said. "Had he been involved in the incident at this time, or at a later time, I think that he should be punished according to University regulations."

The story was a lie. Frank Helderman Jr., soon to be an executive at his father's newspaper, had been a participant. He had helped another student, another aspiring journalist, secure photographs of the Tuscaloosa Klansmen in front of the damaged sign. The Klansmen had chased Helderman's car but had not caught them. Four days later, Williams assured Frank Helderman Sr. there would be trouble if his son continued to defy the Klan. Frank Helderman Jr. took the threats seriously, refusing to drive his car for a week.

Three months later, on a Friday night in late July, the Klan placed similar signs on Gadsden's northern and western city limits. Frank Helderman Sr., perhaps appeasing the Klan, published a photograph of the sign near the Gadsden Country Club on the front page of the Sunday newspaper.

> REALM NATIONAL ALABAMA,
> U.S. KLANS, KKKK INC.
> GADSDEN KLAVERNS
> NOs. 01 & 8
> WELCOME YOU

The Klan sign was splattered with battery acid from water pistols, as the students in Tuscaloosa had done, and a photograph of the damage was published on August 3 in the *Gadsden Times*, along with a request from a local Klan representative to not "smear the sign with paint or other materials."

Perhaps sensing the inevitable, the city started bracing for school integration with a plan so audacious that Juanita Jelks, a member of the Gadsden NAACP, told Martin Luther King Jr., the rising star of the civil rights movement, that the Black residents of Gadsden "need help from all sources of strength, spiritual, mental, and financial." More than 350 Black families and 54 homeowners were moved from their residences near downtown and sent to the predominantly Black sections of the city, at the base of Lookout Mountain. Most of the families willingly relocated. Some, though, were physically removed from their homes and their furniture placed on the streets. The city of Gadsden referred to it as a "slum clearance" program, but the city's Blacks, using the terminology of the late 1950s, called it a "Negro clearance." A Black dentist and a retired pastor were among four defendants who filed a lawsuit against the city. The case made it to the Fifth

Circuit Court of Appeals, but the judge denied a rehearing in a ruling on September 4, 1959. On November 7, the U.S. Supreme Court rejected the appeal, saying the plan did not constitute segregation.

The Klan planned a more dramatic stand: Burning crosses were to be placed along the major highways of northeast Alabama, another display of the Klan's resurgence, a development attributable, in part, to Robert Shelton's alliance with the new sympathetic governor, John Patterson. An attack on a synagogue in downtown Gadsden on the night of March 25, 1960, delayed its show. Hubert Jackson Jr., a sixteen-year-old junior at Etowah High School in Attalla, threw a Molotov cocktail into Temple Beth Israel, where the dedication of a new annex was being celebrated. Jackson shot two members of Beth Israel when they rushed out of the temple—one in the hand and the other in the leg and chest, in the most violent attack on a U.S. synagogue at the time. Jackson told police that he "passionately hated Jews" and that he had been a Nazi sympathizer since he was seven. Among his possessions were a Nazi battle helmet and the red Nazi armband that he occasionally wore to school.

After the bombing, Gadsden leaders introduced a city ordinance that attempted to limit hate literature. On the afternoon of the bombing, anti-Semitic and racist literature had been distributed at the Etowah County courthouse. A Gadsden attorney, George Hawkins, condemned "men in high places" who ignored Nazi sympathizers who "roam about to intimidate and terrorize." Hawkins said other innocent people would be hurt if Gadsden leaders permitted such activities.

"Many of us have waited in vain for someone to expose the real reason why this 16-year-old defendant could have found himself in a climate which led him to believe that his act of terror was the proper thing to do," Hawkins said.

Protestants and Catholics worshipped with members of Temple Beth Israel in an interfaith service, but the peace was only momentary. The Shuttlesworth children passed through late that summer, and Klansmen burned crosses at local schools in early September. On May 14, 1961, after the Freedom Riders bus was burned in Anniston, the streets in Gadsden were filled with rumors that another bus of riders was on its way. Mark Mashburn, the Gadsden public safety commissioner, eased worries by saying, "I have talked to a number of colored people, and they don't want trouble any more than we do."

But trouble came for Gadsden police in the summer of 1962, when African Americans tried twice to integrate the city swimming pools. Each time, the police intervened, and the pools were closed. Then, that fall, six African American students tried to integrate Gadsden High School. I. J. Browder, the Gadsden superintendent of education, ordered them to return to Carver High School, the city's high school for Blacks, and dismissed their attempts as "a maneuver to get publicity."

Change, though, had already begun. In May, three Black leaders filed a lawsuit in U.S. District Court against the city of Gadsden, charging that "every segment, unit and division" in the city denied African Americans equal opportunities for employment and access to public facilities. The mayor, the police chief, and the fire chief were among the defendants. Four months later, Goodyear hired its first African American tiremaker, Lorenza Thomas. In the late fall, the first sit-ins were held at the courthouse coffee shop and at the downtown lunch counters. On November 24, four police officers arrested fifteen Black teenagers at the lunch counters of Woolworth Drug Store and W. T. Grant in downtown Gadsden.

More sit-ins were held on November 27 and 28 at three downtown department stores, but the greatest fears among whites in Gadsden had already been realized. An "outside agitator," Frank Holloway, was in town to organize the sit-ins. At twenty-three, Holloway was a veteran of the movement. In 1960, he had participated in the demonstrations of the department stores in Atlanta, sharing a jail cell with Martin Luther King after his arrest. In 1961, he was among the Freedom Riders who rode from Montgomery to Jackson, Mississippi, where he was arrested at the Greyhound bus station. He was a member of the executive committee of the SNCC when he arrived in Gadsden in the fall of 1962 to hold workshops on nonviolence, conduct voter registration drives, and organize selective buying campaigns. Lack of money was among his biggest challenges.

"You know actually these are some real wonderful people," Holloway wrote SNCC Executive Secretary James Forman on November 6, 1962. "They really believe in giving until it hurts. But they just don't have it to give, you probably know this from my last report [concerning] the employment problems here."

Three weeks later, police arrested sixty-two protesters, including Holloway, during the sit-ins at the downtown lunch counters. More than forty of them were convicted and received $50 fines or fifty-five days in jail. In his final days as the juvenile judge, William Rayburn sentenced the juveniles to indefinite probation.

The nation's top civil rights leaders—Martin Luther King Jr., Ralph Abernathy, and Wyatt Tee Walker—came to Gadsden in early December for meetings with leaders of the local movement. King went to the city jail, where he spoke for thirty minutes with Joseph Faulkner, the city's SCLC president and one of the protesters who was arrested during the sit-ins. The city was still so thoroughly segregated that Lorenza Thomas was ordered to the basement at Goodyear when the white workers had their company Christmas party.

The threat of integration in public schools and public accommodations was lurking, though, and the Klan retaliated, even using Thom Wilkerson, the *Gadsden Times*' rookie columnist, to send a message to those who tried to interfere. In the early spring of 1963, as William Moore was preparing for his walk to Mississippi, Wilkerson printed portions of a letter the Klan was circulating through Gadsden.

"For years, we have complacently watched as the federal government has taken more and more of our basic liberty . . . our states rights. Our voices have been weak as we watched our federal government take over our sister states, one by one, cramming integration down our throats. [President Kennedy must know] we are still a potent force, although downtrodden."

In Gadsden, with a police force in disarray and labor violence as savage as ever, with grand juries appearing more interested in protecting the city's fragile image than justice, and with a newspaper that printed its propaganda, the Klan and its sympathizers were about to unleash their power again.

CHAPTER 9

William W. Rayburn was only three months into his first term as Etowah County district attorney, and he was already responsible for the murder case that he regarded as the most important in the history of northeast Alabama. At thirty-five, he was a veteran of local and state politics after serving as the county and juvenile judge for seven years. Three years before the murder of William Moore, in a packed courtroom in which he refused to allow African American spectators, he made a maudlin pitch for the loyalties of Gadsden and Etowah County residents during the trial of the three Shuttlesworth children.

"I have a sentimental attachment to this county and city, and I love its people," he said. "We do not need this kind of racial trouble."

The desire for political power ran deep in the Rayburn family. In his youth, William W. Rayburn received political lessons from his father and grandfather, who counted governors, judges, and legislators among their friends. His grandfather, W. C. Rayburn, was a member of the Alabama House of Representatives and the permanent chairman of Alabama's Seventh Congressional District. His father, Wightman Melton Rayburn, had written *Rayburn's Alabama Jury Charges*, a guide that had been used by judges and lawyers since its publication in 1926. Local newspaper reporters who wrote about the promise of William W. Rayburn noted that he was believed to be distantly related to Sam Rayburn, the flamboyant speaker of the U.S. House of Representatives.

He was born in 1928 in Montgomery, Alabama's capital, where his father was an assistant attorney general during Bibb Graves's first term as governor. Graves, a member of the University of Alabama's first football team and a graduate of Yale Law School, had been elected with the endorsement of the Ku Klux Klan. He was also an officer in the Ku Klux Klan until 1928, his second year in office. Charlie McCall, Graves's attorney general and W. M. Rayburn's boss, was also a member of the Ku Klux Klan until the fall of 1927, when he sent a letter of resignation to the exalted cyclops of the Montgomery Klan. McCall and W. M. Rayburn had been classmates at the University of Alabama and belonged to the same military unit at the beginning of World War I.

After leaving office in 1931, Graves made another bid for governor in 1934. W. M. Rayburn was Graves's campaign manager in Etowah County, where Graves won by more than 400 votes in the Democratic primary and 125 votes in the runoff. The National Labor Relations Board came to Gadsden during the height of the labor troubles of 1937, and W. M. Rayburn was a defender of the local interests, serving as attorney for the Etowah Rubber Workers, an organization of about one thousand Goodyear employees. During a hearing on October 20, a witness, Ted Morton, told the board that he was summoned to Rayburn's office for a meeting with the president of the Etowah Rubber Workers, U. M. Gilbert. Gilbert told Morton that the association would make the remainder of Morton's car payments if he gave favorable testimony during the hearings. Rayburn agreed to the payments, Morton said, after he returned to his office.

The testimony stung W. M. Rayburn, causing him to announce his disapproval from across the courtroom.

"Look this way," he told Morton.

Walter Wilburn, the trial examiner, told Rayburn that he would have a chance to cross-examine the witness.

"I just wanted to see the color of his eyes when he said that," Rayburn said.

As Graves prepared to leave office in January 1939, he appointed W. M. Rayburn to fill the unexpired term of a circuit judge who had died in office. At forty-five, W. M. Rayburn settled into a career in the judiciary, raising a son and a daughter in a stylish, white frame house near downtown Gadsden. In the late 1940s, while William W. Rayburn was away at the University of Alabama, W. M. Rayburn and W. C. Rayburn were part of a delegation from Alabama that went to Jackson, Mississippi, to convince

Governor Fielding Wright to come to Birmingham for a statewide rally against President Truman's civil rights program, the start of the Dixiecrat movement. Three years later, in the fall of 1951, W. M. Rayburn died, and Governor Gordon Persons appointed Virgil Pittman, the head of the Etowah County Bar Association, as the new judge of the Sixteenth Judicial Circuit.

Following the examples of his father and grandfather, William W. Rayburn attained power at an early age. In the early summer of 1955, William W. Rayburn, then a twenty-seven-year-old lawyer, was named the county and juvenile judge. He quickly showed that he had his father's and grandfather's political acumen, establishing himself as an advocate for the area's most cherished causes. The trial of the Shuttlesworth children was his chance to prove that he had the pedigree to ascend to political heights that neither W. C. nor W. M. Rayburn could attain, and he would not squander it. The Shuttlesworths' attorney, Len Holt of Norfolk, Virginia, made a motion to desegregate the courtroom, but Rayburn denied it. Perhaps positioning himself for future political campaigns, Rayburn delivered a soliloquy to the overflow crowd that addressed the most emotional issues in Gadsden — race, Communism, and economics.

"We have enough economic and other kinds of trouble without stirring up other types of trouble," he said. "The Communists are seeking to divide us and we cannot and shall not let them succeed."

Two months after the Shuttlesworth trial, he announced his bid to become the district attorney for the Northern District of Alabama. The local press pegged him a "rising political star" at thirty-two. He wrote letters to the state's leading politicians—Governor John Patterson, U.S. Representative Albert Rains, and Alabama's U.S. Senators John Sparkman and Lister Hill—asking for their support, but only Patterson, an arch-segregationist, offered a public endorsement. After he was beaten by Macon Weaver, a lawyer from Huntsville, he abandoned his plans to run for the state attorney general, settling for the Etowah County district attorney's office.

Rayburn's handling of the William Moore murder case was an opportunity to solidify his commitment to his pledge during the trial of the Shuttlesworth children. His first moves included a recommendation to Governor Wallace that he offer a $1,000 reward for the arrest of Moore's killers, citing a provision in the Alabama Code. Wallace announced the reward the day after the murder, calling the killing a "dastardly act."

"I note with a great deal of satisfaction that Gov. Wallace has complied with my request," Rayburn told the local press.

The Whisenants were unable to identify the murderer or any accomplices, but they confirmed the model of the car that Hicks, Basenberg, and Wilkerson had seen—the 1950 black Buick. A DeKalb County sheriff's investigator provided another clue: Floyd Simpson owned a .22-caliber rifle. He had seen it hanging over the fireplace in Simpson's store. Simpson owned the car, and he had the same kind of rifle as the murderer. A chief suspect had been identified only a few hours into the investigation.

"We have reason to believe at least two persons were involved," said W. R. Amos, the Attalla police chief. "We think the killers came from outside Etowah County."

Late on the morning of April 25, Felton Yates and George Geer changed into civilian clothes at the courthouse before driving north on Highway 11. Without their police uniforms, they slipped through the courthouse entrance without being recognized by reporters, some from as far away as Baltimore. At the store, Yates asked Simpson for the rifle. It was in full view of the officers, hanging over the fireplace near the front door. Simpson retrieved it reluctantly and headed down the front steps, escorted by the deputies. Outside, a crowd began to gather, perhaps fifty or so people. Many wondered why he was a suspect. Some had seen Simpson at the store on the night of the murder, and others believed they already knew the identity of the killer. Their confusion turned to anger when they realized he was about to be arrested and taken to Gadsden.

Yates and Geer handcuffed Simpson, and Geer put him in the back while half the population of Collbran tried to make sense of what they were seeing. As the sheriff's car headed south on U.S. 11, Lucille Simpson ran after the car and onto the highway. Watching the car fade into the distance, she yelled, "My husband had nothing to do with it."*

Arriving in Gadsden, the deputies saw reporters clustered near the en-

---

* *Daily Press* (Newport News, Va.), April 26, 1963, 10.

trance of the courthouse. Geer removed the handcuffs and walked Simpson through a door at the side of the courthouse, taking him to the jail on the third floor. Geer entered Simpson's name on the blotter and gave the charge to the officer at the front desk: "Suspicion," he wrote.

The case remained one of J. Edgar Hoover's immediate priorities. Faisst sent a memo after the arrest, giving his boss a description of the chief suspect. A state lawman provided the initial details, offering the information "in strictest confidence," as Faisst put it.

"[Simpson] runs a small store near Collinsville in DeKalb County, which is not too far from where the shooting occurred," Faisst wrote. "Simpson has the reputation of being an extreme segregationist and is the owner of a Nineteen Fifty black Buick which is registered in DeKalb County and therefore would have the prefix Two Eight on its license tag. [The informant] advised that Simpson was the owner of a Twenty Two caliber rifle and at the present time the state ballistics men are examining the weapon and the three empty shells which had been recovered near the scene of the shooting. It being noted previous information indicated only two empty shells recovered."

Authorities refused to identify Simpson after the arrest. They did not name the second suspect either. After finishing his postal route on April 24, Gaddis Killian drove down the western slope of Lookout Mountain and returned to Collbran. The men at the store told him state and local policemen were looking for him, and he drove to Gadsden to turn himself in to the sheriff's office.

Harold Richards, the newly elected sheriff of DeKalb County, informed the FBI that Killian was now in custody. Moments later, Faisst sent a memo to Hoover about Killian.

"[He] reportedly has the reputation of being an ardent segregationist as well as Simpson," he wrote.

Lucille Simpson and Lorene Killian, Gaddis's wife, told reporters that their husbands were part of the investigation. But both were confused. Neither Simpson nor Killian had left Collbran after 4:00 p.m. on the day of the murder, their wives said.

"Gaddis couldn't have done it because he was home by four o'clock, and he never left anymore," said Lorene Killian.*

More unusual developments surfaced on April 24 and 25. An organization known as the Soldiers of the Cross, headquartered in Colorado, held a conference at the Bellevue Hotel in Washington, D.C. An FBI agent described the meeting in a memo: The Soldiers of the Cross recruited guerrillas from around the country to eliminate Communism in America. The murder of William Moore was discussed at the conference, according to the agent. A member of the Soldiers of the Cross had "worded his remarks concerning the Moore incident in a manner so that his organization might receive credit for Moore's liquidation, although he made no claim that the organization was directly responsible," the agent wrote.

The murderer, in other words, thought Moore was a Communist.

"In this regard he allowed room for thought that unassociated individuals with relative anti-subversive interests had performed this service to society," the agent said.

After the conference, another memo about the organization was sent to the FBI offices in Birmingham and Washington, D.C. A representative of the National Education Organization in Washington, D.C., claimed to have more information: The Soldiers of the Cross had discussed the murder at a recent meeting in Denver. The organization, he said, consisted of "fifty guerrillas around the country to stamp out Communism." Each member had been selected to kill a Communist, the memo said, and the FBI's informant indicated that one of the members had murdered William Moore. The guerrillas from the Deep South were known to be especially violent, the informant said.

The *Gadsden Times* sought credit, too. Wilkerson and Basenberg informed the *Times*' readers on April 25 that sheriff's deputies were about to wrap up the investigation because of tips they had given authorities. Late

* *Daily Press* [Newport News, Virginia], April 26, 1963, 10.

that night, as state and local officers were finishing their questioning of Gaddis Killian, six policemen rushed from the jail and headed to DeKalb County, apparently acting on a tip. Around 10:30 p.m., Colvard announced that Gaddis Killian had been released.

"He's a sick man," Colvard said. "He's claustrophobic and can't abide being locked up."

Bill Beck, the lead attorney for Killian and Simpson, had already begun to display his new political muscle. He was a tall and imperious man, about six feet three and 220 pounds, with a booming voice that he used to intimidate. As a high school football coach in Collinsville, he had used that voice to motivate his players. After becoming a lawyer in Fort Payne, he had used that voice to pressure rival lawyers and judges, even clients. During World War II, he had used that voice to frighten marine recruits on Parris Island, South Carolina. His ascension in the Marine Corps was soon to become part of DeKalb County political and military lore. At the age of forty, he left his position as county judge and enlisted as a private. In less than a year, Beck was promoted to sergeant. Months later, he was named master sergeant.

After the war, he was elected to the Alabama House of Representatives and became the Speaker of the House, a position he attained with the help of the new governor, James E. "Big Jim" Folsom. He now had political strength to go with that booming voice, and he intimidated more people. Bill Beck understood the application of power, but he intimidated so many people that he soon found himself in political exile, despite an ambition so deep that his tireless campaigning from one end of the state to the other caused his weight to drop to almost two hundred pounds.

"From the shores of Mobile Bay to the hills of TVA [Tennessee Valley Authority], big and friendly ex-Marine Bill Beck, speaker of the House of Representatives, is running hard for Governor," the *Alabama Journal* reported in November 1948, almost two years before the next election. "Beck lives in northern DeKalb County in Fort Payne. With a 'tally-ho, Leatherneck' Beck has recently been known to drive plumb down to Mobile with an AFL [American Federation of Labor] boss to carry out a beachhead landing on Lieut. Gov. Clarence Izner's preserve, the state Chamber of Commerce. Izner is an announced candidate for governor."

Beck was trampled, though, in the 1950 gubernatorial election, finishing tenth in a fifteen-man field, collecting barely more than 10,000 of the 402,000 votes. He came home to Fort Payne, tried to run for mayor, and was routed again. He was confined to the political wilderness of the northeast corner of the state for thirteen years, forced to settle for being the area's preeminent lawyer. He was almost sixty, his gray hair thinning but his ambitions undiminished. Suddenly, though, Bill Beck became a force again in Alabama. The election of George Wallace had revived his career, thanks to some favors he had performed in the early years of Wallace's career.

Their friendship began in the late 1940s, after Folsom's support had made him Speaker of the House. Folsom, however, was a progressive governor from north Alabama, the state's first major politician to express moderate views on race. The state's political power was in the southern part of the state, where Wallace resided in the Barbour County village of Clayton. A man who wanted to be governor, as Beck did, needed alliances with legislators from south Alabama and Birmingham, the state's wealthiest and most politically powerful regions.

Beck's split with Folsom began in the late summer of 1947, only months after he had been elected Speaker of the House, favoring a state income tax amendment that the governor opposed. The amendment received strong support in Birmingham because it would boost teachers' salaries, and Beck agreed that an increase in taxes was needed.

"Gawd Almighty," Folsom said, after learning of Beck's disloyalty, "now Bill's gone and got ambitions."*

Beck spotted similar ambition in Wallace. He was, as he was to recall years later, the first person to tell Wallace that he should seek higher political office. Their relationship was solidified after Beck discovered Wallace, then newly married and a young father, was having financial struggles.

"George, what the hell are you putting your family through that for?" Beck asked him.

---

* *Montgomery Advertiser and Alabama Journal*, November 28, 1948, 3-B.

The Wallaces lived in an apartment in downtown Montgomery above a drugstore.

"Because I can't afford any better," Wallace told him.

Beck made sure Wallace could afford better. He arranged for Wallace's twenty-year-old wife, Lurleen, to receive a job as a clerk, allowing the Wallaces and their infant daughter, Bobbi Jo, to move out of the apartment. He had rescued the Wallaces from those dismal circumstances—"a rat- and cockroach-infested apartment," Beck was to recall—and the favor was never forgotten, especially when Bill Beck needing rescuing, too.

Not that Bill Beck found himself in financial distress upon his return to Fort Payne. He lived in a stylish frame house in the center of town and occupied a law office in perhaps the best spot in town, across from the entrance to the county courthouse. He was the town's leading lawyer, the scoutmaster of Boys Scouts Troop 24, and the owner of the Northeast Alabama Bus Lines. He made regular appearances in the local newspaper, announcing his latest accomplishments in law, education, and civic affairs, usually accompanied by a photograph of his firm and scowling countenance. Every summer, he spoke at the Fourth of July picnic in Sylvania, a crossroads village on Sand Mountain, holding on to leftovers of his former political base, his ambitions still unfulfilled.

All his life, Bill Beck had been unwilling to concede to circumstances that seemed overwhelming to most men, and he was not about to quit now that his career in elective politics was finished. In his youth, he had left school in the fourth grade to help on the family farm. Failing to graduate from high school, he was forced to take an entrance exam to Newberry College in South Carolina, where he was recruited to play football and baseball. Later, he earned his teaching certificate after graduating from Jacksonville State Teachers College and became a football coach at Collinsville High School. In 1929, he married the former Vera Isbell, daughter of John Isbell, the U.S. attorney for the Northern District of Alabama. John Isbell taught law to his new son-in-law at night, and his lessons allowed young Bill to pass the bar exam in 1932. Bill and Vera moved from Collinsville to Fort Payne that spring, and Bill started his law practice at the firm of Isbell and Beck. Long before his split with Jim Folsom, Beck had gone and found ambition. He founded the county's first Boy Scout troop, with his wife serving as a den mother. In 1936, he ran for mayor of Fort Payne, believing he had acquired the proper standing in the community with his law practice, scouting activities, and new membership in the Baptist church. He received only 16 of the 778 votes. The loss only strengthened his resolve. He spoke at community picnics on the mountain and oversaw the installation of Fort Payne's new telephone system, waiting for his next opportunity. In 1938, he won a runoff to become the county's representative in the Alabama legislature. Two years later, Governor Frank Dixon named him the county judge, a position he held for four years. For the rest of his life, many residents of DeKalb County continued to refer to him as "Judge Beck." He had aspired for more than a career in the judiciary, though, and the political fires of his youth still smoldered as he approached sixty. With the inauguration of George Wallace on the bitterly cold afternoon of January 14, 1963, Bill Beck quickly renewed his quest for power in Alabama, and he reached for all that was available.

Three months after Wallace's inauguration, Beck was the vice president of the Alabama Bar Association, the vice-chairman of the Alabama Board of Education, and the chairman of Judson College, a women's college west of Montgomery. He was also lobbying Wallace for a new junior college on Sand Mountain, to be built on the border of DeKalb and Jackson Counties in a remote area known as Powell's Crossroads. For the cause of segregation in the Deep South, he was the most important figure in the defense of Floyd Simpson, the accused murderer of William Moore, an internationally known martyr. Bill Beck now had the political platform that he had wanted since he announced his candidacy for governor in 1950.

In that booming voice, Bill Beck announced his return on April 26, 1963, when he entered the Etowah County jail.

"I want to see my client," he said.

Upstairs, Simpson and William W. Rayburn, sitting in a dayroom outside the jail, could hear him.

They knew that voice, too.

CHAPTER 10

Lucille Simpson and Simpson's brother Morris drove to the Etowah County jail on the morning of April 26 to tell Dewey Colvard what she tried to inform his deputies as they drove away from the store: Her husband was innocent. Her meeting with Colvard lasted forty-five minutes, and then she and Morris returned to Collbran to pack some clothes and cigarettes for Floyd's weekend in jail, where he would celebrate his forty-first birthday the next day.

On the night of April 26, the top criminal investigators in Alabama and Etowah County held a meeting at the Etowah County courthouse around ten thirty, about four hours before Roy McDowell's flight to the FBI Laboratory in Washington, D.C. Among them were five of the state's fourteen investigators, William W. Rayburn, and Al Lingo, the head of the Alabama Department of Public Safety. Bill Kovach, a reporter for the *Tennessean* of Nashville, watched investigators enter the conference room. He was told one of the men was Ace Williams, a former Ku Klux Klan leader who now operated a bail bonding business near the courthouse. Kovach identified him as "a one-time active member in the North Alabama Ku Klux Klan" in his front-page story the next morning.

Kovach's description had lacked some of the more notorious details of Williams's final years in the Klan. Ace Williams had been the head of the Etowah County Klan on Mother's Day 1961, when Bull Connor gave Klansmen fifteen minutes to beat the Freedom Riders at the Trailways bus station in Birmingham before sending in the police. Williams's appearance at the Birmingham Trailways station earned him a trip to federal court, where he invoked the Fifth Amendment when asked if he was a Klansman and if his name had appeared on a Klan voting ballot that was produced by John Doar, the U.S. assistant attorney general for civil rights. He later testified that he had been in Birmingham on the day of the beatings and had voted on a Klan ballot.

Rayburn carried a .22 rifle into the meeting. Investigators had taken Simpson's rifle and a rifle belonging to Gaddis Killian to Huntsville for examination, but Killian's rifle was eliminated as the murder weapon.

"No comment one way or another," a smiling Major William R. Jones, the head of the state troopers' investigative division, said when reporters asked him for updates.

Waiting for the meeting to end, Kovach gathered details of the murder, none of which were reported in the local media. He discovered that many now believed the murderer or someone affiliated with the murder had made anonymous phone calls to WGAD and the *Gadsden Times*. The WGAD news director told Kovach that the caller said there would be a good story on Highway 11 and then gave a tip for how the station could confirm the information.

"And if you want to check on it, you can call the police station," the caller said.

The meeting ended around midnight, and McDowell headed for the Birmingham airport, about a one-hour drive from the courthouse.

"We should know something by tonight," Lingo said after the meeting.

In Birmingham, McDowell boarded Eastern Airlines flight 552, scheduled for departure at 2:10 a.m. He arrived at Dulles Airport in Washington, D.C., at 7:10 a.m. and went immediately to the laboratory's entrance at Ninth Street and Pennsylvania Avenue, about a mile from the U.S. Capitol.

As the FBI prepared for his arrival, Faisst sent a memo to Hoover, expressing confidence in the investigation.

"State authorities are still holding suspect Floyd Simpson, owner of the rifle, as they have witnesses who placed him in area where shooting occurred and they feel certain he is involved in murder," he wrote.

Robert Zimmers, the FBI's forensic analyst, examined the evidence and prepared the report, making detailed drawings of the two bullets and three cartridges. The bullets were Remington brass-coated "Golden" shells, and the cartridges were .22-caliber long-rifle cartridge cases. Zimmers concluded that the bullet found in Moore's shirt pocket had "no marks by which it would be possible to identify the weapon firing it." He gave the same analysis of the bullet taken from Moore's head.

"However, general rifling [characteristics] on both bullets from [the] body of Moore are alike and are same as our test bullets from Simpson's gun, indicating that gun of same type taken from Simpson used," he wrote.

Hoover sent a synopsis of Zimmers's laboratory report to W. R. Jones. He considered the results to be inconclusive: There were similarities between the cartridge cases from the scene and the ballistics tests from Simpson's gun, but they weren't enough to provide sufficient identification in his estimation.

"However, general rifling on bullets from body same as on tests from Simpson gun indicating Simpson gun is type of weapon used," he wrote.

William Moore's body arrived in Binghamton on a train from Gadsden around three thirty on the afternoon of April 26. The workers at the Erie Railway freight station removed their caps and stood in silence as employees loaded the pine box that contained his corpse into a hearse. The funeral was held the next afternoon at three o'clock at the William R. Chase Funeral Home in Binghamton, where a crowd of more than two hundred wedged into the tiny chapel.

A crew from CBS came to film the ceremony for its documentary, *Death of a Mailman*. Governor Nelson Rockefeller sent George L. Hinman, one of his advisers, and a Republican National Committeeman, John Lindsay, a U.S. congressman from the east side of New York City, also attended. The service was integrated with civil rights activists from around the country, mainly from Baltimore and New York.

"I received a telephone call [on April 24] from some people in Baltimore who were Negroes," Mary Moore said. "They wanted to come to the service but were afraid they wouldn't be welcome. I told them they would be welcome. He [William Moore] would want them there."

The Reverend Drewry conducted the service.

"What's involved here is a historical epic," he said.

Drewry and another minister, the Reverend Marlin Ballard of the Universal Churches of America and a representative of the Fellowship of Reconciliation, compared Moore's death to the crucifixion of Christ.

"We feel that Bill Moore's sacrifice, accomplished by one man alone, emulated what Christ did two thousand years ago," Ballard said.

Two Black ministers, the Reverend Latta Thomas of Elmira, New York, and the Reverend Archie Ijames of Indianapolis, were among the six hundred people who came to Binghamton for the funeral. During the service, Ijames sat on a step inside the funeral home, near Hinman and Lindsay. He was among the hundred or so people who walked to Vestal Hills cemetery for the burial. He put a rose on Moore's grave as the crowd went away.

"One of the benefits of the crucifixion was that it dramatized just how deeply entrenched human evil had become," Thomas said. "Someone has described us as a group of people who can drink a cup of coffee over morning headlines without too much disturbance. Therefore, it is a great service that someone, even at the risk of losing his own life, has dramatized that evil today. Mr. Moore has done that."

Rayburn made his first mistake on the afternoon of April 27. He phoned the FBI laboratory, seeking clarification on the ballistics report, but he pressed too hard in his attempts to have Zimmers say Simpson was the murderer. Zimmers was firm: The rifle cartridges found at the murder scene appeared to have been fired from Simpson's gun, but he would go no further.

"I can't prove it, but it's my opinion that they were fired from his gun," Zimmers said, according to Rayburn.

The conversation outraged J. Edgar Hoover. He was angry that Rayburn had pressed Zimmers for an opinion, and he was even more furious that Zimmers gave it. All communication between Rayburn and Zimmers was over.

"It is absolutely wrong for our laboratory personnel to orally amplify official findings," he wrote in a memo on April 30.

Hoover stuck to the findings in the forensics report. Nevertheless, Rayburn prepared to issue a first-degree murder charge against Simpson, even though he admitted to FBI officials that the killer might still be free. He based the warrant, in part, on Simpson's black Buick being at or near the scene before the murder. He believed Simpson's two conversations with Moore on the day of the murder were another reason to charge him, along with his refusal to take a polygraph test or discuss what happened after 4:00 p.m. on the day of the murder.

In a memo to Assistant Attorney General Burke Marshall on May 2, Hoover wrote, "Mr. Rayburn has advised that he will readily admit Simpson may not have been the man who actually pulled the trigger; however, he and investigators are convinced that Simpson knows something about the murder and they are proceeding with their investigation directed toward Simpson's involvement."

It was also clear from the beginning that investigators knew that a third person was involved. In a memo to Hoover on April 30, Faisst informed his boss about a conversation he'd had with Rayburn: Three witnesses had seen a man from DeKalb County in Simpson's car "about the time of the murder or shortly before." The man had not been questioned yet, but he would be arrested and held on an open charge if authorities found him. Hoover relayed the same information to Marshall in a memo on May 2. But no one else was arrested.

With the newspapers filled with reports of SNCC's and CORE's plans to come to Gadsden, Rayburn told Faisst that he was so pessimistic about the case that he wondered if he could obtain a conviction even if he had a signed confession from the murderer and his accomplices.

"Rayburn states persons interviewed to date by investigators have indicated they do not believe in killing, but are against such marches as that of [the] victim and are incensed that more marches are contemplated," Faisst said. "Rayburn feels these marches would have a definite effect on his case to point of making him lose same."

Still unsure he had the right suspect in jail, Bill Rayburn filed first-degree murder charges against Floyd Simpson. Dewey Colvard phoned the jail and gave instructions to change the open charge against Simpson to a first-degree murder charge. The court reporter was unavailable on weekends, so the charges wouldn't be official for another day, until early Monday.

"Right now, I don't expect charges to be brought against anyone else," Colvard said after his call to the jail, "and I don't care to comment further."

State and local officials said the secrecy was directed by "the state capitol in Montgomery," apparently George Wallace. State law denied bail in capital murder cases, but Beck filed a writ of habeas corpus, allowing Simpson to go free on $5,000 bail.

Beck was in a defiant mood when he met the press after Simpson's release on Monday.

"What the hell do you think an attorney is for, if not to get his man out of jail?" he snapped. "But I'm in no hurry to get Simpson out of jail. There is a lot more they don't have against him than they do have against him."

By now, Simpson had two attorneys—Beck and Roy D. McCord, the best-known lawyer in Gadsden. McCord's wife, Ethel, and his secretary had been instrumental in Simpson's release. Both signed his bond, with McCord using their power of attorney.

McCord, like Beck, was a former member of the Alabama House of Representatives. His record as a legislator, though, was tainted by allegations of corruption. He encountered trouble in February 1939, when he was accused of soliciting a $2,000 bribe on a controversial milk control bill—a charge that was later dropped by the House of Representatives in a 71–27 vote. Beck, then in his first year as a legislator, was among McCord's defenders, making such an emotional plea for his innocence that the Speaker of the House rebuked him.

He remained active in politics after leaving the House of Representatives, regularly serving as a delegate to the Democratic National Convention. He solidified his record as a segregationist in 1956 during a campaign for a seat as a delegate at the Democratic National Convention. He had been among the few candidates to answer a state Citizens' Council questionnaire on segregation. Question no. 4 was, "Do you here and now deny the Negro vote?"

"I don't understand this question," McCord replied. "I don't think Negroes ever should have been allowed to vote."

More recently, McCord had been one of two attorneys to represent the city in its battle with the Civil Service Board over the selection of the police chief. In the William Moore murder case, though, he was the secondary attorney. Beck, with his connections to Wallace, was the lead attorney and doing all of the talking for Simpson.

Simpson appeared before reporters after his release, smiling as he stood between his attorneys.

"He won't answer any questions, so don't ask any," Beck told them.

Beck, though, was ready to talk. He had found his villains—the newspapers and the Northern activists—and he was eager to attack both.

"I think they ought to indict the newspapers," he said. "This is all stirred up in the North by a bunch of outsiders. This is all stirred up by the newspaper. This is no different than any other killing.

"If this has been some boy murdered, there wouldn't be anything said. They just blew this into something big up North."

Moore's signs had aroused the emotions of newspapers and the residents of the North, in Beck's estimation.

"This man had signs on about eating at Joe's," he said, "and maybe nobody wanted to eat at Joe's."

The handling of the case had been erratic from the start. State and local investigators had worked intensely until Simpson's arrest and Gaddis Killian's release on April 25. They had done little since then, relying on the results of the FBI's ballistics report to finish their investigation. Wilkerson assured *Gadsden Times* readers that "no citizen could ask for more diligence than these men have shown," but the investigation was incomplete.

An officer confided to Kovach that lawmen believed someone else was involved in the murder.

CHAPTER 11

J. Edgar Hoover was about to give Bill Rayburn a harsh lesson on the dangers of being too aggressive with the FBI. Hoover believed Rayburn had been overzealous in his initial interpretations of the laboratory results, and he drafted a letter on May 9 to Rayburn to inform him that he was damaging his credibility with the FBI. He sent the letter to Rayburn on May 9 to tell him how he should have interpreted his phone conversation with Zimmers.

"With reference to your telephone call to the firearms examiner, Mr. [Zimmers] has advised me that because at the time of your call you had only the telegraphic summary, he undertook at your request to explain the meaning of the similarities noted between the cartridge cases and test cartridge cases from Simpson's gun since such meaning was being set forth in detail in the Laboratory report then in the process of preparation. As stated in both the telegraphic summary and in the above complete Laboratory report, and as stated in Mr. [Zimmers's] telephone conversation with you, these similarities noted were not sufficient to support an identification, but rather merely suggest the possibility that Simpson's gun may have fired these cartridge cases. Mr. [Zimmers] further advises that at no time during the oral discussion with you did he intend to convey that it was his expert opinion that these cartridges were, in fact, fired from Simpson's gun, for obviously such a statement of expert opinion constitutes an identification and, as mentioned above and as reported, the similarities were not considered sufficient by Mr. [Zimmers] to support an identification of Simpson's gun as the specific gun firing the cartridge cases."

Rayburn also knew that he lacked evidence. He told Zimmers in a letter on May 6 that "if we have a case against the accused Simpson, such a case will have to be based on the amount of evidence we have been able to secure thus far." By Rayburn's count, he had three important pieces of evidence—Simpson's gun, Simpson's car at or near the murder scene, and Simpson's admission that he had spoken with Moore twice on the day of the murder.

His case against Simpson was even weaker after his call to Zimmers. Hoover made no promises that Zimmers would be available to appear before the grand jury. Requests for expert testimony, he wrote, were granted in the order they were received. The FBI also had a policy: For Zimmers to testify, he would have to be the only forensic expert to testify. No member of the state laboratory—neither William McVay nor Robert Johnson—could be summoned.

McVay and Johnson were more definitive about the ballistics. They agreed the cartridges had been fired from Simpson's gun, even though the bullets' markings were not sufficient to support an identical match. But if Rayburn wanted the prestige of the FBI at the grand jury trial, he would be unable to summon Johnson and McVay.

Hoover gave Rayburn another requirement: If Zimmers testified, he would tell the grand jury only what was in the laboratory report.

"Any testimony relative to the expert's findings will, of course, be identical in the meaning as set forth in the above [laboratory] report," Hoover wrote.

Four months before the grand jury met, Bill Rayburn already knew the FBI firearms examiner's testimony, perhaps his strongest witness, would be inconclusive.

Bill Beck also knew the case against Simpson was weak. He gave a description of the killer to Bill Basenberg, who was filing stories from Gadsden for the *Binghamton Press*.

"The person who did this is either a religious fanatic or a racial fanatic, and Floyd Simpson is neither," Beck said.

Floyd Simpson was, in fact, no religious zealot. The local church, Gravel Hill Baptist Church, was between his store and the two-story frame house that belonged to Annie Brandon, Simpson's mother-in-law. But he rarely attended church because of the demands of his new business. He was, however, a hardcore segregationist and a longtime Klansman, though he was restrained compared to some of his fellow members. As one acquaintance said in later years, "He could be in a crowd of three and you wouldn't notice him." He was also considered rigidly conservative and "a man who was not to be messed with," as someone who worked with him said years later.

"Floyd Simpson did not do this awful thing," Beck said. "I've known him too long to suspect him of this. It's not because I'm his lawyer that I say this: I just don't believe he did it."

Basenberg did not include Beck's comments in any of his reporting for the *Gadsden Times*, perhaps because his editors found them to be too explosive or too critical of the local investigation. The interview was only the beginning of Beck's campaign to strengthen the reputations of Floyd Simpson and DeKalb County. In a telephone interview with the *Binghamton Press*, Beck described Simpson as a respected member of the county. He was a combat veteran from World War II and the Korean War, he said, who had continued his military service as a sergeant in the Alabama National Guard.

"We don't have a segregation problem in this area—DeKalb County," Beck said. "We have a population of about forty-five thousand whites and four hundred or five hundred colored people. We get along well. We don't worry about each other. The colored people are just as well off as the white people. They have as good, if not better, schools, than the whites. The greater percentage of the colored people are property owners. In this county, we have less than 1 percent illiteracy. We have nine accredited hospitals in this county of forty-five thousand people. It is one of the most progressive sections in the country. And one other thing: We have less crime in this section of the country than any other section."

DeKalb County, though, had one accredited hospital, DeKalb County General Hospital in Fort Payne, and it was only twelve years old. The county was infamous for its production of moonshine and bootleg whiskey, a trade so lucrative that even a former sheriff, W. R. "Samp" Evans, and his wife were arrested for selling confiscated liquor out of the county jail.* Dog-fighting, cockfighting, and snake-handling churches were still

* DeKalb County Sheriff Wyatt R. (Samp) Evans and his wife, Junie, were indicted by a federal grand

among the activities on the mountains. Race relations were so tense that even Fort Payne Mayor Fred Purdy's recent announcement that he had requested a loan from the federal government to build fifty low-rent houses for senior citizens became another threat to white supremacists.

"Remember, Federal Money is Involved, and by accepting Federal money, the City of Fort Payne Housing Authority would build and construct these homes throughout our city of Fort Payne and if our Colored senior citizens applied for admission to one of these homes, they have the federal government to back them up in their demand to move into these homes and live right on your street or mine," Guyton Tutor wrote in a letter to the *Times-Journal.*

Bill Rayburn knew federal officials wondered if he was serious about prosecuting the case, but he assured the FBI that he was sincere. After only four months in office, he had already acquired a reputation as an aggressive prosecutor. His first major case as district attorney was the rape and murder of an eighteen-month-old girl. A fifty-six-year-old motel handyman was charged with killing the child and burying her in a creek near the motel. Before the trial, Rayburn asked potential jurors about the death penalty: "Do you believe that the Bible in any of its parts taught that capital punishment was contrary to the teachings of the Bible?"

He requested a special grand jury, and Circuit Judge A. B. Cunningham granted the motion. The special grand jury returned an indictment about a month after the murder. The trial was to begin two months later, in late May. On May 31, three months after the murder, the jury of twelve men found the handyman guilty and recommended that he die in the electric chair.

Rayburn had campaigned in 1962 on the pledge of "firm, vigorous and aggressive prosecution of all criminal cases." He was so vigorous in his prosecution of cases during the spring grand jury that his work had resulted in 123 years in prison terms, including two life sentences. But there

jury in September 1950 for selling moonshine and bonded whiskey out of the county jail. The Evanses were accused of reselling liquor to bootleggers that had been seized during raids. The Evanses were acquitted after almost a dozen bootleggers testified during the trial in Gadsden in November 1951.

was no urgency in the William Moore case. Rayburn chose to waive the preliminary hearing because "the state didn't want to tip its hand," as he put it. Beck and McCord approved. They said they needed more time to present their case, and the fall grand jury session, scheduled for September, was fine with them.

Rayburn wavered after the state's largest newspapers criticized his approach, saying he might request a special grand jury "whenever I feel it becomes necessary." He reiterated his stance days later with a new stipulation: Investigators were still working on the case, and he believed it was his responsibility to cooperate with law enforcement officers.

Even Thom Wilkerson, once troubled by the murder, seemed threatened by the possibilities of the trials to come.

"Condemned from without in the murder of William L. Moore, an integrationist from Baltimore, the state now comes under the caustic scalpel wielded by an outraged nation," he wrote on May 3. "Alabama admits the murder of Moore was atrocious. More significantly, Alabama admits it is Alabama. It need not make excuses for what it is. Alabama admits that the crime shall not go through its courts as a tuft of wind through a sea shell.

"Moore nurtured a belief which has not died with him. Man cannot believe in America unless he believes in its 50 states. We fight side by side, not as separate entities. When you condemn Alabama, you condemn our country, as well."

CHAPTER 12

James Farmer, the executive secretary of CORE, announced on April 27 that ten to twenty white and Black members of CORE were heading for Alabama. He emphasized the thoroughness of the group's plans for a freedom walk, referring to the marchers as "disciplined" in an interview with Claude Sitton, the Southern correspondent for the *New York Times*. Having already reported on the violence of the Freedom Rides and integration of Ole Miss, Sitton understood the possibilities of their journey, saying "these and other developments indicated that the freedom walk might grow into an anti-segregation protest similar to the freedom rides, with all of the implications of potential violence and Federal-state controversy this would entail."

Marvin Rich, the community relations director for CORE, said the march was needed to give Alabama and America a chance to redeem themselves.

"William Moore traveled through this country to express his hopes for equality and justice and he died," he said. "This was a failure for the people of Alabama and the people of America."

On May 1, an integrated group from CORE and the SNCC—five white and five Black marchers—began retracing Moore's walk from the Greyhound bus station in Chattanooga. A crowd of about one hundred gathered for the start of their journey around 9:00 a.m. on May 1.

"We want to hold America's attention for a while yet on the hope and belief of William Moore," said Richard Haley, CORE's lead representative. "So we must reiterate this man's simple yet profound purpose: To express the ideal of human brotherhood by a peaceful walk across the American countryside."

They walked single file through the streets of downtown Chattanooga and around the foot of Lookout Mountain, the lead marcher wearing replicas of Moore's signs.

"I hope all of you all's legs cramp," a white man said.

"Hope you stop a .22," yelled another.

Leaders of the Chattanooga Klan instructed their members not to intervene since Alabama state officials had already promised to arrest the marchers at the state line.

Nevertheless, Chattanooga police and Tennessee highway patrolmen monitored the marchers until they reached the Georgia state line. The only incident came when a handful of gravel was thrown.

Early that afternoon, eight Black walkers gathered near downtown Attalla, the city of 8,200 that bordered Gadsden to the north. Aware that the walkers were planning to resume Moore's walk, Felton Yates, the Etowah County chief deputy sheriff, drove to the murder site in Keener, about ten miles northeast of Attalla. He was in Keener when the sheriff's dispatcher radioed him at twelve forty-five that afternoon with the news that the marchers were in Attalla. Among them were Diane Nash, who had participated in the Freedom Rides, and Paul Brooks, the Fisk University student who was now making good on his vow to come to Alabama to resume Moore's walk.

At 12:55 p.m., the marchers approached the intersection of U.S. 11 and Attalla Boulevard. One was wearing a sign that read, "Love Thy Neighbor—Thou Shall Not Kill." As he pulled beside the marchers, Yates waved his hand out of his patrol car and said, "All right, just hold it right there." He stepped out of the car and made the first arrest, informing the lead marcher, "Give me that sign, boy, and get in that car." The charge was "conduct calculated to provoke a breach of peace."

At the Alabama-Georgia line, the marchers had a message waiting for them: An effigy of William Moore was swinging from a tree.

"EAT AT JOE'S," it read.

The campaign to make Moore an unsympathetic victim had already begun. The Etowah County Sheriff's Department announced it believed the poster of Jesus on Moore's postal cart was among the reasons for the murder. On the front page of the *Gadsden Times* on May 3 was a story headlined, "Officials Hold Moore's Poster." The lead paragraphs of the story read:

> The religious significance in the murder of Baltimore integrationist William L. Moore, 35, is traceable to an obscene poster of Jesus Christ which Moore carried with him to his death on April 23 on U.S. 11 about 13 miles north of Gadsden.
>
> The poster bears a drawing of the head of Christ. It measures about 8 inches by 10 inches. It says that Christ is "wanted for vagrancy, sedition, anarchy, conspiracy to overthrow an established government," according to Chief Deputy Tony Reynolds. The poster is now under lock and key as state's evidence.
>
> Reynolds said the poster describes Christ as "an alien, a Jew. Alias—Prince of Peace. Habits—Known to associate with common people. Trade—Carpenter." Further, it says scars or marks on body made by the law including citizens of the community.
>
> The poster is printed in black and white.

The *Birmingham News*, the state's largest and most influential newspaper, joined in, publishing an exclusive interview with Simpson on May 3, the day the marchers arrived at the state line. Simpson arrived at Beck's office wearing a coat, dress shirt, and tie.

"I am emphatically denying any part in the slaying of William L. Moore," he said. "I had no reason to slay him, and my interest in him was merely as a curious individual. I wanted to talk to a man who apparently had no belief or faith in God, as I had never talked to a man of this character."

Simpson described his first encounter with Moore as a discussion of "religion, integration and inner-marriage questions." He admitted calling Moore over to the front of his store, where several people questioned Moore about his walk. The second encounter, he said, was about five hours later in Collinsville.

"Gaddis Killian and I drove to Collinsville in my car for the second conversation with Moore," Simpson told Hopper. "Killian wasn't around when Moore passed through Collbran, and he was just as curious as I was."

It was around 3:30 p.m. on April 23 when Simpson and Killian saw Moore walking on the south end of Collinsville, about ten miles from the store. There were no arguments during either discussion, he said. Moore, in his estimation, appeared to enjoy giving his opinions.

"I returned to Collbran after that, and I haven't seen him since," Simpson said.

The rest of the interview focused on two subjects—religion and Simpson's suspicions that Moore was a Communist. Moore's views on religion seemed vague to Simpson and Killian, and the poster on his cart confirmed their beliefs that he was an atheist. When asked about the poster, Simpson recalled only one portion of the caption—"Jesus Christ, son of a carpenter." But the meaning was clear to him: The poster was "low-rating Christ," he said.

He also suggested Communism when he said he believed Moore was part of a subversive organization.

"I don't see how anybody could believe in such a thing as inter-marriage between the white and Negro races unless he was being paid for it," Simpson said.

Simpson was untruthful, though, when *Birmingham News* reporter Jack Hopper asked him about his involvement in racial issues. He said he didn't belong to any segregationist organizations, and he had no interest in segregation or integration.

"I have never taken any part in any racial difficulties nor indicated any interest in these type problems," he said. "We just don't have them around here."

They had them on the afternoon of May 3. A crowd of two hundred to three hundred whites followed the marchers as they moved toward the Alabama-Georgia line. Some threw rocks and eggs over the head of the lone Georgia state patrolman assigned to protect the marchers. Then, as the marchers broke for lunch, a white teenager bolted through the crowd and punched Robert Zellner, a white member of the SNCC, in the head. Allison Blevins, the Dade County sheriff, helped him to his feet as the teenager passed through the crowd, but neither Blevins nor the Georgia state patrolman chased him.

Passing the stream of Confederate flags at the Georgia Game Park and the alligators and five-legged animals at Deer Park just before 2:30 p.m., the marchers found an even more carnival-like atmosphere at the Alabama line. Rounding a curve and walking single file down a hill, they saw cars and spectators jammed on both sides of the highway, leaving barely enough room for the marchers to make it to the state line. Near the top of the hill, a youth from Alabama sat on the bumper of his car, parked among the wild onions on the shoulder of the highway.

"You won't make it," he shouted at the marchers. "Georgia may take it, but Alabama won't stand for it."

Spectators hung from an empty advertising billboard on the Alabama side of the Alabama-Georgia border. Behind the billboard, more spectators were in a pasture. At least two thousand people, maybe more, had gathered, according to the FBI estimates.

Al Lingo directed traffic, bullhorn in hand, waiting to issue orders to the marchers. Many of the participants and bit players in the William Moore murder were gathered. A station wagon from WGAD-AM was parked along the state line. Nearby was a man in his mid-forties wearing a fedora, waiting for the marchers and hecklers to come down the hill. The local lawmen and state troopers allowed Gaddis Killian a prime view of the proceedings.

Agents from the Atlanta FBI observed a leader in the Chattanooga Dixie Klans—believed to be Imperial Wizard Jack William Brown or his brother Harry Leon Brown—in a green Cadillac with a Tennessee license tag. Birmingham agents saw Kenneth Adams, the head of the Dixie Klans in Anniston, Alabama, who had orchestrated the burning of the Freedom Riders' bus on Mother's Day 1961.

Lingo had already informed Raymond Faisst of the Birmingham FBI how he would handle the situation: He would welcome the marchers to Alabama as individuals. But if they insisted on coming as demonstrators, he would arrest them on charges of breach of peace. He planned to give them one minute to make up their minds.

"Do any of you not understand?" Lingo asked the marchers as they arrived at the state line.

They understood. No hands were raised.

"Get the goddamned Communists!" a white man yelled after Lingo gave the order.

"Throw the n—— in the river," someone else yelled.

"Kill him! Kill him! Kill him!" shouted a woman wearing pink plastic curlers.

A minute passed, and state policemen arrested the marchers. Three of them—Zellner, Zev Aelony, and Eric Weinberger—dropped to the pavement, causing the Alabama state troopers to use their electric cattle prods on them.

"Stick him again! Stick him again!" an elderly, toothless man yelled from the pasture.

To the FBI agents in the crowd, the spectators sounded hysterical.

"Hang them!"

"Lynch them!"

"Low white man! A dog and a fox got better sense than you."

Some observers in the pasture climbed over a fence and ran toward the marchers. As the highway patrolmen made their arrests, the spectators surged toward the marchers, but the officers managed to repel the crowd.

The patrol cars made a U-turn and sped toward the DeKalb County Jail in Fort Payne. With the excitement of the day over, the crowd was content to savor the possibilities of the marchers crossing the state line without protection. Many agreed that the troopers prevented the murders of the marchers.

The threat of violence remained as night fell. Claude Sitton of the *New York Times* passed on a news tip to authorities: A mob was headed to the DeKalb County Jail to remove the marchers by force. No mob arrived at the jail, but a representative of the SNCC was concerned enough to call the jail late that night to check on the marchers' safety. No marcher, though, was allowed to come to the phone.

The harassment continued, even in jail.

"The other prisoners have been aggravating them something awful," a guard said.

With the marchers in jail and more on the way, DeKalb County began to rally around Floyd Simpson. On May 6, just below the fold, the *Fort Payne Times-Journal* announced on its front page a drive for Simpson's legal defense fund.

> **Fund Raising Underway for Simpson**
> Jack Killian is heading a fund raising campaign to raise money for Floyd L. Simpson, charged with the first degree murder of William L. Moore of Baltimore, Md.
>
> Workers in the campaign said that the money would be given to Simpson to help him bear his expenses during the legal fight which is expected to ensue.
>
> Several points in DeKalb County have been established as collection stations for this purpose.

Madeleine Sherwood, a forty-year-old actress whose Broadway credits included *Cat on a Hot Tin Roof* and *Sweet Bird of Youth*, left New York on May 13 in a 1955 Studebaker station wagon, a donation to CORE. She was accompanied by Nelson Barr, a twenty-six-year-old sculptor, Peter de Rome, a jeweler from Tiffany's, and Bob Kaye, a poet and truck driver. They drove nine hundred miles in twenty-three hours, arriving in Chattanooga ready to fulfill SNCC Director James Forman's promise to hold demonstrations at the DeKalb County Jail in support of the jailed marchers. The FBI began monitoring the station wagon as soon as it arrived at a minister's home in Chattanooga on May 14. After two days of training, Sherwood and her friends drove to Fort Payne to hold a vigil for the marchers at the DeKalb County Jail. They discovered that the marchers had been moved twice, from the jails in Fort Payne and Gadsden to Kilby State Prison in Montgomery. Virgil Pittman, the judge who had overseen Floyd Simpson's release from jail and would oversee the grand jury hearing in September, signed the order that sent them to Kilby.

In Keener, the Sizemores were already preparing for the arrival of Sherwood and ten other protesters. Harry's father, Ernest, told the state to cut down the black walnut tree at the murder site so the protesters would be unable to determine where to begin their walk. On the afternoon of May 19, a Sunday, a procession of fifteen cars left an African American church in Gadsden around one, their headlights on and driving slowly along U.S. 11, as if they were headed to a funeral. With the tree and the picnic tables gone, four African American motorists drove into DeKalb County and turned around after realizing they had gone too far. The state troopers arrested them for making illegal turns. A crowd of about one hundred huddled around James Peck, who led the ceremony. He and Broadway actress Madeleine Sherwood began the service by placing a wreath on a funeral stand near the area where Moore's body was found.

Standing on the stump of the tree, Peck gave some opening statements about Moore.

"Bill was a genuine idealist," he said. "He worked for brotherhood all of his life."

The Reverend E. W. Jarrett of the Galilee Baptist Church in Gadsden was the next speaker.

"We are gathered on this spot of ground to commemorate the gallant stand taken by William Moore, who died but not in vain," he said. "His death has shown the world the ugliness of segregation and the so-called Southern way of life. They crucified Jesus. They shot William Moore. But his voice is still heard. It has bridged the North and the South. It tells us and those yet unborn that we are determined to be free—not yesterday, not tomorrow, but now."

Barr was the final speaker. He was a native of Chattanooga, the only white protester who was familiar with segregation in the South. The other whites were activists from the North, mainly from New York and New Jersey.

"I have come down here to make amends for the way this thing has been going for the last two hundred years," Barr said. "If Christ was on this earth today, I'm sure he would be killed just like William Moore."

The march began at about 3:20 p.m. The protesters and many in the crowd, still dressed in their church clothes, linked arms and sang "We Shall Overcome," the civil rights anthem. When they finished, Peck picked up the memorial wreath that had been next to the tree stump and laid it by the warning stripe of the highway, where Willis Elrod found Moore's body.

The officers made no move during the service, directing the traffic on U.S. 11. But R. P. Hooks, the stumpy commander of the Gadsden state trooper office, gave his first order as the marchers moved next to the shoulder of the highway, lining up single file.

"If you walk on the highway, we'll have to arrest you," he said. "Don't get over that white line."

The marchers sang "We Shall Overcome" again and began to walk. They stayed on the grass, never crossing the white line, but the song and the sight of an integrated march were too much for Hooks. After taking five steps, the marchers were arrested.

"You're under arrest for violating the law of the state of Alabama," Hooks said. "Come right over here and get in these cars."

State policemen issued breach-of-peace charges, but the marchers lay in the grass when the officers tried to arrest them.

"I don't know why you people want to be so stubborn," Hooks said.

CHAPTER 13

There was fighting in Gadsden all through the spring and summer. There were billy clubs, nightsticks, and cattle prods. There were fights in the Black section of Gadsden and the white section, sometimes with guns. There were squabbles in the stores downtown, on the courthouse lawn, at the swimming pools, and on the steps of churches. The Blacks who filled the churches unleashed their frustrations with complaints such as, "I'm sick of the white man—I want him off my back." The white people sang "Dixie" in the streets and heckled demonstrators with taunts of "Go back to Africa, n——."

Mostly, they fought in courts, in jails, and in city buildings that were used when the cells overflowed. There were $1 million lawsuits against Martin Luther King and against ABC radio. Demonstrators were sentenced to months of hard labor but usually suspended the sentences after torturous conditions in jail. When Gordon Harris, a twenty-five-year-old from Rochester, New York, was arrested by state troopers in Keener on May 19, he was placed in solitary confinement for thirteen days. He was not allowed to sit in his cell or call his lawyer or relatives.* At a court appearance on May 24, he refused to plead guilty and was denied a lawyer. He was warned that he would receive a lengthy sentence if he continued to proclaim his innocence, but he was unmoved. On June 5, Cyril Smith, the county judge, found Harris guilty and gave him a six-month suspended sentence. Before releasing him, Smith warned Harris to stay out of the Alabama courts or "he'd get the works."†

* *Rochester (N.Y.) Democrat and Chronicle*, September 3, 1963, 13.

† *Rochester Democrat and Chronicle*, June 6, 1963, 15.

Demonstrators gave affidavits describing beatings by Gadsden policemen, Etowah County sheriff's deputies, and Alabama state troopers, mostly with cattle prods. One demonstrator, William Douthard, known as "Meatball," recalled being arrested by Al Lingo and driven to a shopping center, where he was surrounded by police cars. The officers took turns jabbing him with nightsticks and cattle prods before releasing him.

"There are a number of additional affidavits and statements from other persons in Gadsden who were physically assaulted by state troopers and whose homes were broken into and ransacked after the occupants had been thrown out," Farmer wrote in a letter to Assistant U.S. Attorney General Burke Marshall. "Such a reign of terror as has been visited upon men, women and children in the Negro community of Gadsden by Alabama State Troopers has seldom been matched in the annals of the contemporary civil rights struggle."

The newspapers fought, too. Bob Farrell, the vice president of the *Brooklyn Daily Eagle*, fired the first shot in his "Man About Town" column on May 3, claiming Gadsden "embraced more hate than any square mile I ever visited." He based his opinions, he wrote, on his experiences in Alabama during World War II, when he edited the newspaper at a military base. His credibility was questionable, though, because of several grammatical and factual errors. He misspelled Gadsden—"Gasden," he called it in his column—and he had written about Camp Sibert, where soldiers made chemical weapons at a 37,000-acre center near Attalla. Instead, he had been more than 250 miles south, at Fort Rucker near Dothan. Nevertheless, he told his readers that he knew "the town of Gasden [to be] a bigoted, backward and very corrupt one."

Perhaps Bob Farrell believed no one in Gadsden would see the column, but a Gadsden resident, Maurice "Speedy" Shannon, did, and he delivered it to the *Gadsden Times*. The *Times* printed the entire column on June 2 and a story that gave the newspaper's opinion of Farrell's work. A banner headline ran over the story.

Gadsden Most Lied-About City in U.S.
By MARY HOFFMAN

Times Staff Writer
Since the murder of integrationist William L. Moore on April 23, only 13 miles from here, Gadsden has become the most lied-about city in the nation.

The crime was deplored in private by our law-abiding citizenry and in public by more than one editorial in The Times.

No responsible person has condoned it.

But in their loathing for the South, the hate-mongers have had a Roman holiday. With a great air of virtue, they have condemned the entire South as a section of evil and lawlessness, never hesitating to employ falsehood for their purposes.

The most vicious parade of lies The Times has seen to date is Bob Farrell's "Man About Town" column of May 3 in The Brooklyn (N.Y.) Eagle, which was brought to the attention of the newsroom by Maurice (Speedy) Shannon, 331 Hollywood Road.

Farrell's malice is more dangerous than other writers' because of his "I've lived there and I know what I'm talking about approach"—though every detail of his twenty inches of copy is an easily-proven lie.

Farrell had been right, however, when he predicted that Communism would be used to make William Moore more unsympathetic.

"Many will say, 'It's a communist plot. Moore was a communist,'" he wrote. "That's the way they satisfy themselves over an incident like this. It's always a communist plot when our flag is dipped in blood and shame."

In a story that ran next to the reprint of Farrell's column, the *Gadsden Times*, with the help of J. Edgar Hoover, offered evidence of Moore's ties to Communism. Using Moore's poster as the link to Communism, the *Times* cited a passage from Hoover's book, *Masters of Deceit*. Bill Basenberg referred to Hoover's book as "an expose of the Communist Party from its inception to the present." In chapter 23, section 6, titled "Communism: A False Religion," Basenberg found a reference to the poster on the front of Moore's cart.

Hoover tells of tactics used to influence clergymen. "One cartoon published in The Worker, and a Communist newspaper shows a sketch of Christ in the form of a wanted criminal. The caption reads: REWARD for Information Leading to the Apprehension of—Jesus Christ: WANTED—for Sedition, Criminal Anarchy, Vagrancy, and Conspiracy to Overthrow the Established Government."

Hoover continues: "When tactically expedient, the Communists even liken themselves to the early Christian martyrs suffering persecution for attempting to aid mankind."

The reaction in Gadsden to Farrell's column was swift and furious—so furious that virtually every state politician in Etowah County called for a federal investigation. Two local legislators, State Senator George Hawkins and State Representative Ollie Nabors, prepared to introduce a bill in the

Alabama legislature, requesting intervention from the Federal Communications Commission (FCC).

Hawkins wanted the FCC to pursue possible charges against Ferrell. Nabors asked the *Brooklyn Daily Eagle* to retract the column and put the retraction in a prominent part of the newspaper. Gadsden Mayor Lesley Gilliland joined in, sending a telegram to the FCC that made the formal request to investigate Farrell.

"The article is false in every instance and is the most vicious example of irresponsible news reporting we have ever witnessed," Gilliland said.

The Alabama legislature unanimously adopted a resolution on June 4 that requested the *Brooklyn Daily Eagle* to retract the column. The *Eagle* responded with a lengthy editorial on June 7 headlined, "Depravity in Alabama."

> Recently, our columnist and vice president, Robert W. Farrell, wrote a column on the murder of William L. Moore, a Baltimore mailman murdered in Gadsden, Alabama, en route to Birmingham to become a Freedom Rider. Farrell called Gadsden bigoted, backward and corrupt. He did commit one geographical error in identifying Gadsden, referring to it as near Camp Rucker, when he meant Camp Sibert. This was a natural mistake, because Farrell was stationed at both camps during the war. In fact, while at Sibert, in Gadsden, he was a member of the Counter-intelligence Corps assigned to the investigations in Gadsden itself. So he knows how backward, corrupt, and bigoted the city is, as well as the state.
>
> What Farrell could not do, because no one has the eloquence to properly describe the situation, is to tell our readers how thoroughly depraved is the Alabama mentality when it defends the assassination of a man like Moore and perpetuates the flaunting of God-given constitutional rights.
>
> The Alabama Legislature demands that The Brooklyn Eagle retract the Farrell statement.
>
> We do not retract. We reiterate. We say that column is an understatement as regards Gadsden in particular and Alabama in general. . . .
>
> Gadsden Times, please copy if you dare.

It dared. On June 16, the *Gadsden Times* fired back with Mary Hoffman's reply, along with a reprint of the *Brooklyn Daily Eagle*'s response to her article on June 2 and an *Eagle* editorial about New York residents' fear of using their city parks.

> Dear Mr. Farrell:
>
> So you have learned to spell Gadsden.

That, at least, is a step in the right direction.

But now you are off on six other tangents, all in the wrong directions.

It's because of your temper, I think.

If you'd simmer down a bit, you'd write more objectively, more coherently and certainly more accurately. . . .

An interesting juxtaposition of editorials in the same issue that caused your Open letter makes your case for innocence pretty thin.

True, your lead editorial is headlined "Depravity in Alabama" and ends with one of those childish "print if you dare" bits.

Well, we dared.

We also dared print the editorial that followed. This one offered a fascinating sidelight on the precious liberty denied the citizens of New York City, of which Brooklyn is a borough—freedom from fear.

Your citizens from all parts of the city, according to the editorial, are afraid to use their own parks "because of the threat of muggers, young toughs, addicts, drunks, derelicts, rapists and sex perverts."

. . . How much more depraved can you get?

I'm sure we have our full quota of similar undesirable characters, but they must be in jail. Our children play in our parks and walk the streets unmolested.

At least they always have.

Outside agitators spewing hate and stirring up discord can certainly change the picture overnight.

Mr. Farrell, if you will courteously refrain from trying to solve our problems by remote control, it will be my greatest pleasure to give yours a wide berth.

Hoffman said she considered her response to Farrell "the end of this little skirmish." But it was not the end. Farrell replied five days later, still defiant.

"I have no axes to grind, seek no favors and don't give any where they are not deserved," he wrote. "I owe your city no apology. You are a city of 'sin' and have been one for many, many years. I repeat. Your city is backward, corrupt and bigoted."

A Black leader confirmed Farrell's depiction of Gadsden.

"The stories," he told a Canadian journalist, "are not lies."*

The demonstrations began in Gadsden on June 10—the day before George Wallace attempted to block the enrollment of Vivian Malone and James

* *Kingston (Ontario) Whig-Standard*, July 22, 1963, 7.

Hood, a recent graduate of Gadsden's all-Black Carver High School, with his "Stand in the Schoolhouse Door" at the University of Alabama.

About twenty-five protesters, mostly teenagers, attempted to integrate downtown lunch counters and theaters, but the lunch counters closed without incident. Jim Allen, the state's recently elected lieutenant governor and a former Gadsden lawyer, was in his hometown to observe the start of the demonstrations.

"Whatever the colored people may be gaining by federal decrees, they are losing in public relations and human relations with the white people of Alabama," he said. "The colored people have far overstepped their legal rights in the carrying on of private businesses. For example, at one of the local picture show theaters in the downtown area, instead of being satisfied with asking admission for themselves, they have formed a heavy phalanx of children and are seeking to prevent white people from entering the theater. They are definitely breaking the law."

The next day, with the country's attention on the confrontation in Tuscaloosa, the protests were larger, with about thirty participants in sit-ins at five downtown lunch counters and the coffee shop at the Reich Motor Hotel, Gadsden's largest hotel. On June 12, the arrest of a Black woman for using abusive language to an officer caused three hundred demonstrators to march to the county courthouse. Sheriff's deputies arrested two people, dragging them into the county jail. The marchers returned for more protests, but burning sulfur was dropped among them, scattering the crowds and ending the day's activities.

The demonstrations lasted two weeks, causing Martin Luther King Jr., the Alabama state troopers' riot squad, and U.S. Department of Justice officials to come to Gadsden. On June 13, about three hundred protesters gathered at the Gadsden city hall and on the Etowah County courthouse lawns before marching through both buildings. Later that day, Bill Rayburn sought an injunction that prohibited marchers from blocking the entrances or aisles of businesses, streets, and sidewalks. Judge A. B. Cunningham issued the injunction as soon as he received Rayburn's request. It was presented on June 14 to Marvin Robinson, a CORE field secretary from New Orleans, and Bernard Lee, an SCLC representative from Atlanta. Robinson said he "definitely would break the injunction." The city braced for confrontation.

A hotel installed locks on doors that were usually open. A downtown drugstore removed the tops from the stools at its lunch counter. A variety store covered its stools with paper bags and decorated its lunch counter with merchandise. Police officers stood at downtown street corners, wearing helmets in anticipation of the violence to come.

"We're going to give [the merchants] hell," Robinson said. "We'll use the works."

Richmond Flowers, the Alabama attorney general, filed an injunction that prevented the marchers from disrupting the flow of traffic in and out of the city. Later that day, Robinson stood on the balcony of the Gadsden city hall and told the demonstrators that they would remain there until city leaders met with them. About 450 demonstrators were arrested the next day, many of them children who had gathered for protests at a downtown variety store. Police arrested another 250 for lying on the courthouse lawn and in the streets. Sheriff's deputies, Gadsden police officers, and civil defense workers used electric cattle prods to make some of their arrests. More deputies were dispatched to the Black churches to arrest ministers who had been instrumental in the local movement.

Colvard decided the situation was more than he could handle, summoning Lingo and his riot squad. Lingo and sixty-five of his troopers arrived around midnight. They found a ready-made battlefield on the courthouse lawn. Demonstrators arrived around 9:00 p.m. to protest the day's activities. At 3:00 a.m., Lingo and the riot squad moved in from the west side of the courthouse. The city and county policemen moved aside except to restrain spectators. The riot squad used cattle prods and beat the demonstrators with clubs. Three riot squad members met a woman trying to walk up the courthouse steps and drove her into some bushes by the front sidewalk. As dawn broke in Gadsden on June 19, the state troopers patrolled the streets in silence.

"It was brutal as hell," a local law enforcement official told Hedrick Smith of the *New York Times*. "There was no need to club those people."

A local doctor, J. W. Stewart, treated about thirty demonstrators, according to Smith's report in the *New York Times* on June 20. One had a three-inch gash down the middle of his forehead.

"I can't help it if these people ran into each other," Lingo said.

❖

Hedrick Smith's report was buried near the bottom of page 18 in the June 20 editions of the *New York Times*. His story was only ten paragraphs, but its impact was substantial. The details were shocking: troopers swinging billy clubs and using cattle prods on protesters who hadn't moved fast enough, the crowd fleeing in terror as the riot squad beat Black men and women to the ground. City leaders responded by defending local law enforcement officers and the community.

"We are proud of the people of Gadsden and the way that they have responded as a whole in the crisis which we are going through," Gilliland said.

Smith's reports and other news stories so wounded the city's fragile image that the Gadsden City Commission instructed Roy McCord to prepare a $1 million lawsuit against the next wire services that filed erroneous news reports on the demonstrations. Movement leaders responded by informing a crowd of about two hundred at Grant Chapel to continue the demonstrations and not fear the state troopers. As the meeting ended, a procession of about one hundred cars, transporting whites from a National States Rights Party rally near Keener, drove past the church, honking horns.

Flowers arrived on June 21 to assess conditions. After meeting with Gilliland, Pittman, and Police Commissioner Joe Hubbard, he denounced the demonstrations and the Black residents who participated in the protests.

"The white people here are the ones who are being wronged now," he said.

Flowers said activists from outside the city were manipulating local residents. Where were the local Black leaders? he asked. Why weren't the parents of demonstrators keeping their children at home and out of trouble? State troopers responded by using cattle prods during the arrests of fifty protesters at downtown businesses.

That night, Martin Luther King Jr., accompanied by Birmingham attorneys Oscar Adams and W. L. Williams Jr., came to Gadsden to speak at Galilee Baptist Church. Forty state troopers guarded the church, questioning white motorists who passed through the Black neighborhoods near the base of Lookout Mountain. About six hundred gathered inside the church to listen to King as the thirteenth consecutive day of demonstrations ended.

"I hear they are beating you!" King said.

"Yes, yes."

"I hear they are cursing you!"

"Yes, yes."

"I hear they are going into your homes and doing nasty things and beating you!"

"Yes, yes."

"Some of you have knives, and I ask you to put them up," King said. "Some of you may have arms, and I ask you to put them up. Get the weapon of nonviolence, the breastplate of righteousness, the armor of truth, and just keep marching."

King reiterated his message to white clergymen in his "Letter from Birmingham Jail": Immoral laws are not laws at all.

"It is not against the law to break unjust laws," he said. "We will break unjust laws."

Cunningham countered by saying he would not uphold the recent U.S. Supreme Court ruling in *Gideon v. Wainwright*, the landmark decision that required legal representation for defendants who were unable to afford a lawyer. Cunningham informed Black leaders that he would not provide a lawyer to anyone who defied his injunction. The court, he said, wasn't required to appoint a lawyer in contempt cases.

John Nolan, Robert Kennedy's thirty-five-year-old administrative assistant, was sent to negotiate a truce between the city and the demonstrators. As a former marine and a war hero in Korea, he had the credentials to influence Gadsden's political and business leadership despite his ties to the Kennedy administration. Six months earlier, Nolan had negotiated with Fidel Castro to obtain the release of 1,100 American prisoners from the Bay of Pigs invasion.

When he arrived in Gadsden, he sensed a tension that reminded him of his war days in the Punchbowl, the South Korean valley where he had been a rifle platoon leader during three weeks of combat that killed about three thousand and wounded another five thousand.

"I have been around where the casualties were a lot heavier than they were in Gadsden, but the temperature of what was in the air was, I thought, as high in Gadsden as it was in South Korea and the Punchbowl," he was to say years later.

Conditions were worse in Gadsden than what federal officials had encountered during negotiations in Birmingham. Biracial meetings were possible in Birmingham. In Gadsden, though, Nolan was forced to meet separately with Black and white leaders. There were virtually no meetings between the two groups. After two days of negotiations, however, Stewart, the Black doctor who had treated the marchers' wounds, was sure leaders had made progress. A white leader told him, "You've won a moral victory. Now the problem is how to implement it and save face on all sides."

Sensing victory, the demonstrators stayed home on June 21, after twelve days of protests. Their optimism lasted until the second day of negotiations. Nolan could offer Black leaders only two concessions—the immediate integration of the city buses and the delayed integration of only a few lunch counters at a time to be determined. Gilliland refused to consider a biracial committee.

"We've got to go back to marching," said Bernard Lee of the SCLC. "That's all we can do. This just didn't come close to what we wanted."

The marches and the police brutality resumed on June 24. Black leaders sent a wire that day to Robert Kennedy, informing him of the beatings by policemen. The attacks were so violent, they said, that "we cannot assure that counter-measures may not be taken by those who have been and still are being beaten."

Even Judge A. B. Cunningham approved of the most inhumane tactics—the shocking of demonstrators with electric cattle prods.

"[The cattle prods] only gave them a little bit of a shock," he said.*

A secretary for a Black lawyer scoffed at Cunningham's insensitivity.

"That's not true," she said. "Those prodders left scars on their bodies, on their legs, backs, all over."

* *North Bay (Ontario) Nugget*, July 30, 1963, 27.

The demonstrations appeared to erode the last of the sympathies for William Moore and his cause among the white residents of Gadsden. In his column on June 20, Thom Wilkerson gave his views on equality, writing that one of the basic truths in life was "no man bemoans his 'inequality' to others unless he knowingly is unequal to them." He also dismissed the civil rights movement as a Communist plot.

"When I consider the wealth of propaganda the Communists are feeding their followers on the American racial demonstrations, it makes me sick and leaves a starchy taste in my mouth," he wrote. "Perhaps this is what Premier Nikita Khrushchev meant when he said he intended to take over the United States without firing a shot."

A week later, Wilkerson referred to Moore as "integrationist-atheist William L. Moore, a Baltimore, Md., postman who was slain 13 miles north of Gadsden on the night of April 23."

The murder had been the lead item in his column headlined, "Justice Dept. Pledges Its Assistance." Four days earlier, the FBI arrested Byron de la Beckwith in Greenwood, Mississippi, for the murder of Medgar Evers, the NAACP field secretary in Mississippi, charging him with violating the Civil Rights Act of 1957 before turning him over to the police. J. Edgar Hoover offered the FBI's cooperation to local authorities, including the use of the bureau's facilities, as he had done in the William Moore case.

Perhaps wondering if the federal government would also intervene in the Moore case, Wilkerson wrote the Civil Rights Division of the Justice Department to clarify its role in the murder.

"Information available to this department regarding this regrettable incident discloses the violation of state law only," replied John L. Murphy, chief of the General Litigation Section of the Department of Justice. "Consequently, this department has no jurisdiction to take any action."

Martin Luther King Jr. had told reporters at Galilee Baptist Church that one of the goals of the demonstrations was to awaken whites in Gadsden to the "new Negro." Mary Hamilton's appearance in the Etowah County courthouse on June 25 offered perhaps the starkest evidence that Gadsden's intimidation tactics had been ineffective. Hamilton was a former schoolteacher from Lebanon, Tennessee, a twenty-eight-year-old who had been raised in Iowa and Colorado. She had joined the civil rights movement in

1961 during the Freedom Rides demonstrations in Jackson, Mississippi, where police arrested her and subjected her to an assortment of tortures, including unnecessary vaginal exams. Two years later, she participated in the protests in Birmingham and Gadsden and was arrested again. In Jackson, the prosecuting attorney had addressed her as "Mary" instead of "Miss Hamilton," part of the South's racial caste system. She decided to protest the next time she received such treatment in court, and her opportunity came when Bill Rayburn called her by her first name as he opened his questioning.

"Mary, I believe you were arrested by—who were you arrested by?" he asked her.

"My name is Miss Hamilton," she said. "Please address me correctly."

"Who were you arrested by, Mary?" Rayburn asked.

"I will not answer a question until I am addressed correctly," she replied.

Neither Hamilton nor Rayburn conceded. At the peak of the confrontation, Hamilton's attorneys, Norman Amaker and Charles Conley, objected to Rayburn raising his voice to Hamilton, saying his yelling violated her civil rights. Cunningham fined her $50 and sentenced her to five days in jail. He said she would receive another twenty days in jail if she refused to pay the fine.

The demonstrations resumed on June 27, when police arrested about fifty marchers downtown and fifty-two more in the Black section of Gadsden. John Nolan returned to negotiate an informal truce. Civil rights leaders received almost none of their original demands—a biracial committee and integration of restaurants, schools, and recreational facilities—but they had integrated the city bus lines. They also received the withdrawal of Al Lingo and his state trooper riot squad. Three days later, on July 1, the truce was official.

"There's a lot of hope," Dr. J. W. Stewart said. "If we can continue progress along these lines, there will be no need for further demonstrations."

Stewart and other Black leaders believed they needed more time to integrate the schools, restaurants, and parks. They were hopeful, however, about the integration of lunch counters. Black leadership also believed negotiations might resolve their remaining issues now that whites appeared willing to meet. But their optimism lasted only a few days. The truce ended on July 10. The Gadsden Freedom Movement, a coalition of local civil rights leaders led by Marvin Robinson, issued a statement: "After two weeks of attempts at negotiations, no positive steps have been taken toward the elimination of segregation and discrimination. It is now felt that much time has been wasted, and it is now necessary to renew demonstrations."

The jails were already full from the arrests in June, brimming with song and the anthem of Gadsden's summer. From the courthouse sidewalks, the passersby could hear prisoners singing it from the jail on the top floor.

"Oh, freedom," they sang, "oh, freedom."

As the truce ended, Bill Rayburn braced federal authorities and William Moore's hometown for the outcome of the grand jury hearing. Bill Basenberg, the local reporter who had been hired by the *Binghamton Press* as a special correspondent, was his messenger. On July 11, Rayburn told Basenberg that "there is a strong possibility that more arrests will be made in the future." He said more ballistics tests were being conducted at the FBI lab in Washington, D.C., and that the findings were "a very important factor in our case." The demonstrations in Gadsden, though, were still hampering his search to find Moore's killer.

"The freedom marchers who tried to continue Mr. Moore's walk have done irreparable harm to our investigation," he said. "I suppose they thought they were doing the right thing, but they have only hindered our efforts to capture the killer. That man was shot down like a mad dog. This will not be tolerated by the people of Alabama. Certainly some people disagreed with his viewpoints, but he was a human being with a right to express his opinions. His killer will be tried and he will receive the punishment that is due him."

Again, Basenberg's story appeared only in the Binghamton newspaper. There were no reports in the *Gadsden Times* that more arrests were coming in the William Moore murder investigation.

On July 15, Rayburn and another county official told the FBI there was more investigative work to be done, but the demonstrations had caused the investigation to stall. Local attitudes, clearly against the protests, had reinforced Rayburn's opinion of his case after Simpson's arrest: He was unlikely to convict the murderer, even if he had a confession.

"These men advised as a result of this, this case has received no continuous attention, as all personnel have been tied up on demonstrations and cases arising [from them]," according to an FBI memo. "[A local official] and Solicitor Rayburn advised they sincerely desired to prosecute to the fullest extent of the law the person or persons responsible and fully intended to do so; however, their efforts to do so were being continuously thwarted by these demonstrations."

Signs of change were coming quickly, so quickly that white leaders were now on the defensive. More than fifty Black students attempted to transfer to white schools on July 18, but Gadsden education officials rejected their transfers because they were not accompanied by their parents. Robinson later led about forty Black students to the city schools administrative building in another integration attempt, but a deputy sheriff turned them away, refusing to allow them to step on the front porch. On July 19, six Black students, accompanied by their parents, applied for transfers to white schools. Three days later, six more students met with Gadsden School Superintendent I. J. Browder after applying for transfers. Sensing momentum, activists made plans for the largest demonstrations of the summer, sending out a notice that "D-Day" was near. More than two thousand were ready to participate.

Tales of police brutality in Gadsden reached Congress on July 26. Appearing before a congressional hearing on civil rights in Washington, D.C., James Farmer opened his remarks with an assessment of the police practices in Gadsden.

"As a matter of fact," he told the House Judiciary Committee on Civil Rights, "I just returned from Gadsden, Ala., and I saw the necessity for strong legislation to prevent police brutality."

He informed the committee how city policemen beat the demonstrators, some so savagely that the prisoners bled. Seeking help from federal authorities, Marvin Robinson and other civil rights leaders went to the office of the local FBI agent, Robert Moran, but their requests for intervention were ignored. Later, Farmer submitted materials to the committee that described conditions in Gadsden, including his letter to Burke Marshall about Moran's apathy about the beatings.

"Immediately after the beatings, while the men were in jail, another CORE field secretary, Miss Mary Hamilton, reported the matter to an FBI agent in the locality, a Mr. Moran," he wrote. "At that time the physical evidence was crystal clear, with open wounds on the bodies. Mr. Moran, I am told, however, for reasons better known to himself, declined to go to the jail to view the physical evidence and interview the victims and the perpetrators of the violence. Upon his release from jail, Mr. Robinson went by Mr. Moran's office. Although the wounds had healed by this time, the scars were still visible. Mr. Moran's response as he examined the scars, according to the reports I have received, was an apparently incredulous 'no stuff?'

"There are a number of additional affidavits and statements from other persons in Gadsden who were physically assaulted by State Troopers and whose houses were broken into and ransacked after the occupants had been thrown out."

One of the affidavits was from James Foster Smith, sixteen. Smith said he had been participating in a "stand-in" at the restaurant in the Etowah County courthouse on June 17. He left the restaurant to go to the whites-only bathroom. Tony Reynolds, the chief sheriff's deputy who picked up the cartridges fired from the rifle that killed William Moore, followed Smith into the bathroom.

"[Reynolds] began kicking and slapping me," Smith said. "Before this, he had told another officer to stand on the outside so no one else could get in. There were two whites inside and they told Reynolds that they would be a witness for him. Reynolds threatened to kill me the next time he saw me."

On August 2, Alabama's white supremacists countered with a United Americans for Conservation Government rally in Birmingham, where a crowd of five hundred, including five members of the Jefferson County legislative delegation, heard former Birmingham Mayor Art Hanes appeal for contributions to Floyd Simpson's legal defense fund. The members of the legislative delegation, including Alabama Representative John Hawkins, applauded after Hanes suggested that white Alabamians form a "solid wall . . . around the schools when the Negroes try to" enroll in September.

A solid wall of Black marchers moved toward downtown Gadsden around twelve thirty the next afternoon. The procession stretched for more than a half mile. About 1,200 marchers approached Broad Street, clustered in twos and threes, as the injunction allowed. Four clergymen were at the front, followed by the male marchers. The women and children were next, with women holding babies at the rear. The Alabama state troopers, including Al Lingo, were waiting for them, along with Gadsden police officers and Etowah County sheriff's deputies. After a mile, the policemen ordered the marchers to disperse.

"We won't turn around," the Reverend L. A. Warren told policemen.

Demonstrators accused law enforcement officers of using cattle prods and aiming shotguns at them—charges a sheriff's deputy later denied. One demonstrator, Eric Rainey of the SNCC, watched a state trooper knock a woman to the ground and shove her baby from her hands. Police made more than 1,200 arrests, but the total dwindled to 680 after juveniles were released.

"They're going to be charged with violating that injunction, every one of them," Colvard said.

The demonstrators filled the city and county jails. More accommodations were needed at the Gadsden Coliseum and Camp Gadsden, a convict camp on the east side of town. The prisoners were taken in cattle cars to the camp, with state troopers escorting them along U.S. Highways 431 and 278. A Klan cross burned in the night, and the troopers stopped at the rally in an open field, where the troopers taunted them with threats of Klan lynchings.

When the day was over, local and state police officers had completed one of the largest mass arrests of demonstrators in U.S. history.

On August 22, Mary Hamilton drove to the Birmingham airport to pick up actors Marlon Brando, Paul Newman, Tony Franciosa, and Virgil Frye. Wearing sunglasses, an open-collared shirt, and a beard that he had grown for a movie still in production, Newman arrived in a playful mood, teasing newsmen who questioned him.

"At least one of us ought to come down here as a Northern beatnik," Newman said. Brando, Franciosa, and Frye were more formal and subdued, dressed in coats and ties for their appearance at church that night in Gadsden. A crowd of three hundred gathered at Union Baptist Church. Policemen watched the service from inside the church, many with their pistols visible.

Newman appeared nervous to some of the reporters at the church. One of the people in the crowd, Mildred Williams, was to recall years later that Newman cried through most of the service. Brando, however, gave a long and spirited speech, filled with encouragement.

"It doesn't matter whether you're jailed or beaten or discriminated against," Brando said. "It doesn't matter whether we run you into a street or blister your feet. It's not going to help one bit because it's on the move. Civil rights is a wave that's going to sweep the country.

"All of the unknown heroes and unsung heroes of civil rights are not written about as heroes. But you are the heroes of this country. This is a grassroots democratic movement. It is by the people and for the people. It is the first time since the conception of this country that such a movement has been found."

With the March on Washington for Jobs and Freedom six days away, Brando told the crowd that fifty-six of his fellow actors were about to head to the largest civil rights rally in American history. Brando considered chaining himself to the Lincoln Memorial in protest, but the actors regarded his idea as too radical. Instead, he waved a cattle prod that he received from a policeman as evidence of the brutality to the nation's civil rights activists.

"We're all going to talk about civil rights [in Washington]," Brando said. "We're all going on television because this country is ignorant. People say, 'What the hell is this Yankee doing out here? It's none of his business.' It's everybody's business. As a Yankee, some of what I am is lost. Some of what Bull Connor has is lost. But we're all in one country together."

The actors found out the next day what Gadsden thought of white men who meddled in their affairs, no matter how famous they were. Mayor Leslie Gilliland, Police Commissioner Joe Hubbard, and Public Works Commissioner Hoyt Warsham refused to meet with them. Gilliland, a stumpy, bespectacled man who was less than a year into his first term, promised to arrest them if they broke any of the city's laws. He, Hubbard, and Warsham issued a joint statement accusing the actors of using Gadsden to create attention for themselves.

"We do not intend to meet with these people at all," they said. "We feel they are serving no purpose in Gadsden except to create trouble and chaos.

The only reason they are here is for the publicity they will get out of the trouble and chaos which they are creating.

"All of the trouble which we have had in Gadsden has been created by outside rabble-rousers coming in here and using our Negro people for their own gain. We have nothing but contempt for people such as these movie stars who are here, and the quicker they leave and go back where they came from, the better we will all be."

Newman called the trip "an attempt to find the pulse of a feeling." City leaders and businessmen were so annoyed by the actors that a theater owner canceled Brando's newest film, *Mutiny on the Bounty*, scheduled to open the next week. Martin Theater owners announced that they were also pulling *Hud*, Newman's latest film, nominated for seven Academy Awards.

"Are we creating turmoil by being here?" Newman asked the reporters from Gadsden.

"Yes," they said.

"Why is it agitating to be curious?" Newman asked.

The actors tried to meet with executives from Gadsden's two largest employers—Republic Steel and Goodyear—but had little success. A. C. Michaels, the plant manager at Goodyear, said he was busy. He was in a meeting when the actors dropped by, and he said he was unable to meet with them because they had not made an appointment. At Republic Steel, they managed a meeting with the public relations director, Ray Glenn, but they agreed not to divulge any details of their discussion.

"We had an interesting conversation on civil rights here and elsewhere," Glenn said. "It was our understanding that the subject matter of our conversation would go no farther than between us, and I see that Mr. Brando has respected that."

After a two-hour meeting with the Reverend John Sparks, rector of the Episcopal Church of the Holy Comforter, the actors left town. Their trip inspired African American boycotts of white merchants advertising back-to-school specials on their store windows on Broad Street.

"They were very nice to me, and I hope and pray we can find a reasonable way to work out the differences which exist," the Reverend Sparks said.

Brando, Frye, and Franciosa returned to California after the meeting with Sparks. Newman flew to New York, where he and his wife, actress Joanne Woodward, appeared at the Apollo Theater in Harlem for a fundraiser for unemployed workers who wanted to attend the March on Washington. A crowd of three thousand heard performances by Tony Bennett, Billy Eckstine, and Thelonius Monk, among others. When Newman and Woodward went onstage, he told the crowd about what he and the other actors had encountered in Gadsden.

"It is pathetic that the Negroes have no place to negotiate other than in the streets," Newman said. "The white officials simply will not talk to them."

Sparks's plea for reasonable solutions was becoming increasingly difficult, with local sensibilities heightened by the possibility of school integration in other parts of the state and the conviction that the city had been mistreated by the media. The *Gadsden Times*, McCord said, had done "a wonderful job in carrying factual news." But the reporting by other dailies "is contributing to the race problems in Gadsden," he said.

ABC Radio made the first mistake, attributing two statements by Brando to Gilliland: African Americans were "the heroes of this country" and that the civil rights movement was a grassroots campaign that would sweep the nation.

"I'm fed up with this sort of thing," said Gilliland, announcing plans on August 26 to file a $1 million lawsuit against ABC.

More than 250,000 attended the March on Washington the next day. Standing in the Lincoln Memorial, Brando described the treatment that Blacks received from Gadsden policemen and Alabama state troopers, calling it "indescribable tortures seen previously only in Nazi Germany." He showed reporters a cattle prod that state troopers used on the demonstrators.

"There is nothing so symbolic of this spirit of oppression than this—a cattle prodder," Brando said. "They call it a 'hot stick.'"

Police had "whipped and beaten and slashed" some of the demonstrators, he said. He had seen their scars. Others told him that police had forced more than 150 demonstrators to run two miles in the August heat, and many of them had collapsed. One, he said, was ordered to run barefoot over broken glass.

Mary Hamilton told reporters that Eddie Saunders, eighteen, had been forced to remove his shoes and socks and run from the jail to the Gadsden Coliseum. She said Saunders fell when blisters formed on his feet, then policemen prodded him with cattle prods and beat his head until he stood. A doctor at the Gadsden hospital was forced to cut the socks off Saunders's feet before he could begin treatment. Some of the blisters, said the doctor, were more than one inch in diameter.

"They were supposed to have walked from the jail to the coliseum," Dewey Colvard said. "Since they had already been marching, I didn't think a little more walking would hurt them."

CHAPTER 14

Robert Zimmers, the star witness, arrived in Gadsden on Southern Airways flight 107 at 8:18 p.m. on September 8, the night before the grand jury hearing. As the FBI firearms expert and examiner of Floyd Simpson's rifle, he was the most important of the three witnesses who were to appear in Virgil Pittman's courtroom. No suspense surrounded his testimony. Bill Rayburn had known for four months what Zimmers would say and that his testimony would likely mean the grand jury would not indict Floyd Simpson.

About three weeks earlier, J. Edgar Hoover and Bill Rayburn had resolved their differences over Rayburn's phone call to Zimmers about the lab report. Hoover referred to that phone call in his letter to Rayburn on August 16. At the bottom, he added a postscript in case Rayburn needed a reminder.

"NOTE: This is a situation where Rayburn contacted [Zimmers] directly by telephone in attempt to have the results of examination interpreted stronger than reported," Hoover wrote.

Rayburn apologized to Hoover in a letter on August 12, apparently enough to secure Hoover's commitment for Zimmers's grand jury testimony. Hoover allowed Zimmers to testify on two conditions: the prosecution would use no other firearms expert and Zimmers would testify for only one day. Neither was a problem.

"Please let me assure [Zimmers] that we will be through with his testimony on September 9, 1963," Rayburn replied on August 19. "Also let me further assure you that we understand and will abide by the condition that no other expert in the same scientific field will be used by the prosecution."

Rayburn informed Robert Johnson, a state of Alabama toxicologist, that his testimony would not be needed, even though Johnson was sure about the ballistics. Johnson had determined Simpson's gun had fired the shells found at the crime scene. Rayburn, however, chose the prestige of the FBI over the reputation of the state's lawmen. On August 19, after learning that Zimmers was available to testify, Rayburn sent a letter to Johnson, informing him he would like to have two experts appear before the grand jury, but Hoover had been emphatic about the conditions of Zimmers's testimony.

The grand jury met on the morning of Monday, September 9, with Alabama in turmoil over the integration of public schools in Birmingham, Huntsville, Mobile, and Tuskegee. The public schools in Gadsden and Etowah County remained segregated, though, with more than 17,000 white students and 3,400 Black students starting classes on the day of the hearing. The foreman was Robert Tinsley, whose father, Roe, had been elected twice to the Etowah County Commission. Robert Tinsley's family, in fact, was something of royalty in Gadsden. His maternal grandfather, Wesley Akridge, was a lieutenant under General Nathan Bedford Forrest during the Civil War. Such a lineage gave Robert Tinsley and his wife, Gladys, admittance into Gadsden's most prestigious social circles: bridge and canasta at the country club with the Agricolas, one of the area's original industrial barons; chairman of the Goodyear Ladies Golf Association spring fashion show; president of the March of Dimes' Council of Dance Clubs; and lunch at the home of A. C. Michaels, the Goodyear plant manager.

At 10:00 a.m., Robert Tinsley, sixteen other whites, and one Black gathered for Pittman's jury charge. The appearance of the Black juror was not unprecedented. An African American had appeared on a jury when DeKalb County Sheriff Samp Evans was found innocent in 1951 of selling liquor out of the county jail. Still, fewer than one hundred Blacks were available from a jury pool of more than six thousand, causing Pittman to rule a year later that there was evidence of systematic exclusion of Blacks from local jury rolls.

Pittman, though, had defended the county's race relations in 1959 before the fall grand jury.

"They are good," Pittman said. "There has been noticeable good sense by whites and colored in their relations. We are proud of every good fortune our colored friends enjoy. We should all move forward harmoniously.

Time and again, in criminal and civil suits, I have seen our juries give the benefit of doubt to colored witnesses. I believe this is a conscientious effort to deal justly regardless of color. There is one problem I should mention to you that does not involve interracial problems. Let me repeat: does not involve interracial problems. There are too many crimes of violence between the colored people, particularly homicides and assaults with deadly weapons. Many of our colored friends think the courts deal too lightly with these offenses, and they have asked that they be dealt with more sternly."

Pittman's remarks to the grand jury on the morning of September 9, however, indicated that he had observed a deterioration in the racial climate, so much so that he now believed an indictment in the William Moore case was difficult, perhaps impossible. Pittman asked the jurors to put aside their emotions, forget their views of integration, and not embarrass themselves or their hometown.

"We take particular pride in our Anglo-Saxon traditions and legal heritage," he said. "In the oldest and most respected English legal document, the Magna Carta, charter of man's rights, written 750 years ago, the idea of free and safe passage was guaranteed.

"There are times when personal feelings and personal 'drathers' concerning his purpose in being here must be curbed wherever they exist, and you must answer man's most sublime motivation—duty.

"In the words of the South's most beloved leader, Robert E. Lee, duty is the most noble word in the English language. This may well be one of those times when devotion to duty, to law, to even-handed justice must override personal or emotional reaction to the victim's activities and beliefs. He was, after all, a man, one of God's children, even as you and I." The investigators, Pittman said, had done their jobs. He considered their work in the case "prompt" and "diligent."

"If you falter, if public officials falter, there is a breakdown of law enforcement, and anytime that occurs the lives of all are in jeopardy," he told the jury. "The community, the state, the nation, yes, the world has its eyes on what we do here, and we are rightfully concerned with our reputation among friends and strangers.

"The measure of protection you will have for yourselves in the days ahead—for your wife, your daughter and your pastor, your friends—is the same protection you give strangers, even unwelcome strangers. Your safety is interwoven with their safety. Dare we give any person or persons outside of [a] trial jury of his peers the role of executioner? We do so at our own peril."

Pittman concluded with a final plea for jurors to do their duties: Don't shame yourselves before justice or Almighty God, he told them.

Rayburn directed the hearing in his father's former courtroom. He called only three witnesses—Zimmers, Charlie Hicks, and Don Whisenant. Hicks and Whisenant said they had not seen Simpson at the murder scene, only a car that looked like his 1950 black Buick. More damaging to Rayburn's case was Zimmers's refusal to say that Simpson's rifle had fired the bullets that had been taken from Moore's body.

Rayburn kept his promise to J. Edgar Hoover: He needed only one day for Robert Zimmers's testimony. The case ended on September 9, and deliberations began the next day.

With one of its members on trial, the Klan resorted to its traditional tactic of intimidation. Walking into the courthouse that morning, Don Whisenant saw members of the DeKalb County Klan near the entrance, a message to the witnesses and others involved in the hearing. Now that the Whisenants had their first child at home in Collinsville, a three-month-old daughter named Teri Lynn, they had more to fear than they did in the days after the murder. Another message, intended or not, was delivered two days later in the *Gadsden Times*. On page 5 was a photograph of Ace Williams. Dressed in a coat and tie, Williams was recognized for his appointment to Governor George Wallace's staff.

"J. H. (Ace) Williams, 309 Hoke Street, East Gadsden, has been appointed by Gov. George Wallace as an aide de camp on the Governor's personal staff with the rank of Lieutenant Colonel in the State Militia. A Gadsden native, he is the son of Mr. and Mrs. J. H. Williams."

Messages were being prepared in Baltimore, too. On September 10, as the grand jury began deliberations, the Baltimore chapter of CORE issued a statement about George Wallace's appearance on Friday at Goucher College, a liberal arts school in the suburb of Towson, where he was to participate in a televised panel discussion about civil rights.

"Bill Moore was a member of Baltimore CORE," said Edward A. Chance of CORE. "We feel that Governor Wallace is responsible for creating the atmosphere that made his death possible. We want to show our sympathy for those Alabamians who are being greatly damaged by Mr. Wallace's racism and irresponsible use of political power in the current school crisis in his state."

Tinsley announced the verdict three days later: Floyd Simpson was not indicted. James Perry, a staff writer with the *Gadsden Times*, informed Simpson of the ruling in a phone call to the home of Simpson's mother-in-law, Annie Brandon.

"Sure, I was worried," Simpson said. "Any normal person would have been when he's been falsely accused. . . . I'm not guilty. I still don't understand how they gee-hawed in the first place. I don't see how they thought I was guilty."

Simpson's attorneys—Roy McCord, Bill Beck, and Beck's oldest son, Morris—issued a joint statement: "It would have been quite a surprise to us had they indicted him, knowing the weakness of the evidence they had. The ballistics experts could not agree, especially the ones we had employed."

In their attempts to diminish the backlash from the national media, Etowah County officials vowed to find the killer.

"The Moore murder has not been written off the books," one said. "An innocent man has died, and his killer will be found. He will be found. We will not halt our investigations until the murderer is found and brought to [justice]."

Noble Yocum, the coroner, said, "This senseless [act] will not be tolerated. The killer will be found sooner or later. As far as I am concerned, the sooner the better."

George Wallace was at a televised debate in Baltimore when the news arrived early that afternoon. He presented the segregationists' viewpoint during the debate at Goucher College, along with Frederick Malkus, a

Maryland state senator. Members of CORE and the National Alliance of Postal Employees were among the fifty protesters, causing the state of Maryland to provide Wallace with police protection. Many of Wallace's remarks received laughter and applause, but he was booed when he said the recent March on Washington was led by Communists and perverts. Otherwise, Wallace's trip went so smoothly that CORE officials sent a telegram to Wallace after the debate, contrasting his treatment to the reception for Moore in Alabama.

"Protection was sadly lacking for our William when he was shot to death in your state for simply carrying a sign expressing his wish for equal rights for all," they wrote.

In Binghamton, Mary Moore was surprised by the verdict. She was surprised, too, by something James Peck had told her recently: The crime scene in Keener had been bulldozed shortly after the murder and the picnic table removed.

"I thought that when a murder happens, the area [a]round it is protected and roped off," she said.

She found other reasons for anger: No one from Alabama had contacted her since Noble Yocum called collect to inform her of her husband's murder. No one from Alabama had returned his belongings or told her about the grand jury's verdict. When she called, she was told she could come to Alabama if she wanted her husband's cart and other possessions.

"I wonder because of all the race troubles at this time, I wonder if everyone isn't biased," she said. "I say throw away all this bias. Let's get down to the fact that a man has been murdered.

"God keeps the books. He knows who did it. He says, 'Revenge is mine. I shall repay.' This person is going to meet justice, even if he doesn't meet it in these courts."

That night, a group of Klansmen gathered at the Modern Sign Company, a downtown Birmingham business owned by a Klan sympathizer. The meeting lasted for more than six hours. They made a bomb, using a fishing bobber as a timing device. The next night, they parked in an alley near the Sixteenth Street Baptist Church. In the early morning hours of September 15, they planted the bomb on the northeast corner of the church, underneath a staircase, and left with only one person, a laundry worker from Detroit named Kirthus Glenn, having seen them.

The bomb exploded at ten twenty-two that morning, killing four girls in the ladies' lounge, all of them preparing for their roles in the youth choir at the eleven o'clock service. At the crime scene, FBI investigators gathered pieces of the shattered fishing bobber, but the FBI lab never received them. Instead, the investigators determined that nothing of consequence had been found.

Like the William Moore case, the investigation was rushed—so rushed, in fact, that the state filed only illegal dynamiting charges, spoiling the FBI and local investigators' chances of prosecuting the bombers for murder.

"We certainly beat the Kennedy crowd of the punch," George Wallace said.

On September 16, Bill Rayburn sent a letter to Robert Zimmers, informing him of the grand jury's findings.

"As you probably know, the State presented all of the evidence that we had, including your own, and evidently the Grand Jury did not think that it was sufficient to return an indictment upon. As a matter of fact, besides your testimony to the effect that you could not positively say that the cartridges found at the scene of the crime were fired from Simpson's gun, we had the testimony of a witness who supposedly had seen the accused's car a few minutes prior to the crime. However, this witness could not say positively that it was the accused's—only that it was a car similar to the accused.

"Further, we presented another witness who testified that he had seen the accused's car an hour or so prior to the crime. However, he stated that the description of the man in the car was a large man. In particular, he noticed that he had a very large arm, and this description does not at all fit the physical description of the accused. Inasmuch as Mr. Simpson is a man of small or medium build."

An FBI memo summarized the laboratory report presented to the grand jury.

"The similarities noted suggest the possibility that Simpson's gun may have fired these cartridge cases but it would not be possible to eliminate other guns of the same type," it said.

J. Edgar Hoover expressed his approval at the bottom of the report.

"Certainly my conclusions," he wrote.

Playing his traditional role, Virgil Pittman was Gadsden's spokesman, offering the city's final official words.

"More investigative work must be done," he said. "This case will not be allowed to die on the vine."

Macon Weaver, the chief federal attorney for North Alabama, confirmed two days after the grand jury that the federal government would not pursue an investigation because it was "not within our jurisdiction." Gadsden's long summer was over. Its tormentors were gone, and the city would not give them a reason to return. The investigation was dead.

PART III
THE SEARCH

CHAPTER 15

Sand Mountain still looked a lot like the place I knew as a child when I began my search for William Moore's killer in the late winter of 2000. I saw the same kudzu-covered hills, rusted roofs of chicken houses, and fields of corn and cotton. I saw gas stations with church pews out front, sock mills, and snack bars where I had eaten ice cream as a child. I saw the same sandy soil and smelled the same fragrant mountain air.

The mountain, though, had caught up with the rest of society in many ways. Z. Z. Richey's store was closed, along with most of the other one- or two-pump service stations. The highways were wider and better paved, no longer chipped concrete or tar-slicked chert. Alcohol sales were legal, but moonshine was still made on Lookout Mountain and in the hollows below Sand Mountain. The Klan had been gone since the late 1970s.

Many of its sympathizers remained. One of them, Jimmy Dan Kilgore, once owned a coal business in Rainsville, near the former site of Z. Z. Richey's store. Kilgore and three other men from the mountain were accused of running a Black man from Chattanooga, Danny Adams, and his white wife off the road on February 16, 1980. Adams wrecked his car after the men led him on a high-speed chase across the mountain. When Adams left his car and tried to find his brother-in-law, a resident of the mountain, he was beaten. One of the men threw a rock at him, almost severing his ear. Another swung a shovel at him.

The men tried to call police because their car had hit a telephone pole in the yard of Marilyn Goolesby, whose sister was married to Adams. As Kilgore tried to use Goolesby's phone, he bragged that he had run the couple off the mountain and would have "killed the n——" if he had a gun.

"Why did he bring that white woman on Sand Mountain?" Goolesby heard Kilgore say. "We'll teach him. He'll never do that again."*

Before he was sentenced to twelve years and eight months for assault, Kilgore told Assistant U.S. Attorney Henry Froshin, "There are several Jimmy Kilgores, and you ain't got nothing on me."

On the afternoon of March 16, 2000, I was in Rainsville with Herman Kerley, the former principal at Douglas High School, the Black school in Fort Payne during segregation. He became DeKalb County's first African American administrator in 1965 when he was named the local director of Head Start, one of the Great Society programs created during President Lyndon Johnson's War on Poverty. I met him at his office, and he recalled what life was like for Black men on the mountain in the years when I passed the afternoons with the regulars at Z. Z.'s store.

"The Klan used to chase me all over this mountain," he said. "The FBI told me I needed to carry a gun for protection. The Klan followed me all the way home at night. They didn't like me having a white secretary."

He had been the closest thing to a civil rights leader in DeKalb County, once leading a group of Black high school students to downtown Fort Payne, where they integrated the DeKalb Theater. The Klan's influence was so strong in the 1960s that Kerley counted his boss, the superintendent of the DeKalb County schools, as one of its members. He had watched from afar on a summer night in 1964, when the Klan held a rally near his home in Collinsville to denounce the newly passed Civil Rights Act. Peering through a grove of trees, he saw many of his neighbors among the crowd of more than two thousand gathered in a field near a new interstate highway. The field, he said, was owned by a relative of one of the men who was at Floyd Simpson's store on the morning William Moore passed through Collbran.

"The Klan didn't bother me," he said. "I wasn't scared of them."

He wasn't scared of them, even though he had been warned by the brother-in-law of Floyd Simpson, whom he considered one of his closest white friends.

---

* *Birmingham Post-Herald*, April 28, 1981.

"For some of those people," he said, "hatred was a way of life."

On Highway 11, he passed telephone and utility poles with homemade signs that announced Klan meetings at Gravel Hill, the area that took its name from the Baptist church in Collbran. The Klan, he said, was infamous for tacking its signs and posters high on poles for greater visibility and so that no one could knock them down.

"Who was going to stop them?" he asked. "The sheriff? He was just playing in the band."

The most obvious difference since the Klan's departure in the late 1970s was the influx of Hispanics, who had migrated to DeKalb County to work in the chicken plants, causing a shift in the county's social order. Hispanics had become so abundant in the southern part of the county that Collinsville's population was almost equally divided among whites, Blacks, and Hispanics. Its high school soccer team was now among the regular contenders for the state soccer championship.

"The reason the attitudes have changed is they've found a new person to hate," Kerley said. "That's the Hispanics. The Hispanics are at the footstool where Blacks used to be. They're not accepted. They've accepted me over the Hispanic."

Kerley was a wiry and spirited man with a quick smile and a deep laugh, usually wearing a cap to cover his balding head. At sixty-four, he was widely known and respected for his years in civil rights, education, and religion. In the evenings and on weekends, he was the pastor of Pleasant Grove Baptist Church, near his home in Collinsville. Like other clergymen, he found religious symbols in the murder of William Moore.

"That's the way they did the Good Master," he said.

All of his talk about the Klan and race relations caused me to remember my childhood promise to solve the murder of William Moore. When I left Rainsville, I decided it was time to start my search. I drove toward Fort Payne, past the cutoff to Z. Z. Richey's old store, and down the eastern slope of Sand Mountain.

I decided my first task was to find Roy McDowell, the state's chief investigator.

A family ritual during my early childhood was to drive from my maternal grandparents' home on Sand Mountain to my paternal grandparents' home south of Gadsden. It was a fifty-mile ride down the mountain and through Fort Payne, Collbran, Collinsville, and Keener. U.S. 11 was an old road, narrow and mostly straight, a lonely lane that curled through Little Wills Valley, named after Red-Headed Will, a half-breed Cherokee chief. My sharpest memories of those trips were of the tiny railroad crossings at the foot of Lookout Mountain and the green-and-white signs with the state of Alabama logos that pointed the way to the picnic tables across the road—places like the roadside park where William Moore was murdered.

My father grew up on a farm in an all-white community near the Coosa River known as Smokeneck when Creek Indians lived there in the nineteenth century. The racial attitudes of my father and many of my Etowah County relatives confused me. My father was so angered by the riots in Detroit in the summer of 1967 that he fired our family maid, an African American woman named Viola, fearing I might be harmed by my only contact with a Black person. The next year, he enrolled me in the all-white private school that refused to admit the children of one of the state's leading civil rights activists, a decision influenced as much by segregation as academics. My mother was a native of the Sand Mountain, but I never heard her or my aunts give an opinion on race. They appeared uninterested in the turmoil on the mountain, the valley, and the rest of the country.

I thought of Keener as another poor farming town between Fort Payne and Gadsden, a "wide spot in the road," as my relatives called it. It had become more remote after state police officers left on the afternoon of May 19, 1963, with Madeleine Sherwood and the other ten demonstrators. Weeds and wildflowers covered the area where the picnic tables used to be, and a thicket of honeysuckle and vines grew where the black walnut tree had stood. The elementary school closed in the summer of 1964, three years after it was built, with only two teachers available for fewer than one hundred students. The opening of Interstate 59 around 1966 was more devastating to Keener, taking most of its traffic and eventually closing all of its businesses. The last of the general merchandise stores, a red frame building that had been open since the 1920s, closed in 1985, leaving Keener without a community store for the first time in more than a century. Hilltop Grocery, where William Moore had talked to Charlie Hicks and Roy McDowell, was turned into a house.

Race and a fragile economy still plagued Gadsden. Some of its issues were violent enough to cause unrest for months. Black leaders and others tried to rename a middle school named after General Nathan Bedford Forrest, the founder of the Ku Klux Klan, but the attempts failed until it closed because of school consolidation. In November 1973, two Klansmen killed Reverend Edward Pace, a fifty-nine-year-old Black preacher, when they fired at least eight carbine rifle shots after he opened the front door of his home in East Gadsden, across from the headquarters of the Gadsden Ku Klux Klan.

The Klan and the SCLC held marches through Gadsden in 1978 after policemen shot and killed Collis Madden, a twenty-seven-year-old Black man, for speeding away as sheriff's deputies tried to question him on suspicion of drunk driving. The autopsy by state toxicologists discovered fifteen to seventeen entrance wounds. The mortician at the funeral home counted forty to fifty bullet holes.

"Blacks are tired of being brutalized and killed for petty reasons," said Joseph Cole, the head of the Gadsden chapter of the SCLC. "This is the last straw."

Klansmen marched through downtown Gadsden with signs supporting city policemen and sheriff's deputies. Georgia State Representative Hosea Williams, a veteran of the civil rights movement, told an SCLC rally at the courthouse that "a movement will be mounted on Gadsden that will make Bull Connor in Birmingham look like a Sunday school picnic."

Williams wanted policemen to be indicted for murder, but an Etowah County grand jury cleared four policemen and two sheriff's deputies, saying the officers had acted in self-defense. The Alabama Bureau of Investigation and a federal grand jury also found no wrongdoing.

Chet Fuller, a reporter for the *Atlanta Journal*, attended a demonstration on May 11, 1978. Standing among the protesters, Fuller saw policemen wearing new riot gear. Their billy clubs were the longest he had ever seen. Several policemen taunted the demonstrators, looking for an excuse to use their sticks. One used a derogatory sexual term to try to provoke violence.

"Hey, you," the policeman said to a young Black woman. "I bet you can't pull a train."

The woman's husband ran toward the policeman. One of the demonstrators restrained him, but the policeman continued to heckle him, crouching as he brandished his stick.

"Come on!" the policeman yelled. "Come on!"

Finally, the man was dragged away.

"The problems are deep here," Fuller wrote. "They did not start with the shooting in January. It is obvious that the distrust between the races and the hatred are old sores that the shooting and the protests have caused to fester again."

Fuller, traveling through the South in a beat-up automobile and portraying himself as an unemployed Black man seeking work, found fear in Gadsden that he had not witnessed since the 1960s. Part of that fear was because of the Gadsden Police Department, which seemed to have several Klan sympathizers—"if not outright members," he wrote.

"Black people on my job scared to talk about [the Madden shooting]," said Mattie Dupree, a maid at a Gadsden hospital. "You'd think them days was gone, but they ain't. They got Black people over a barrel down here. Gadsden is rotten. It's a rotten town."

Fuller's opinion of the Gadsden Police Department was confirmed a few months later. The police chief, Charles Cary, told the *Wall Street Journal* in February 1979 that twelve members of his force were members of the Ku Klux Klan and others were Klan sympathizers.

"I've got some people here who hate n——," Cary said.

Cary said he was misquoted. Two months later, he resigned as police chief.

Gadsden finally integrated its fire department and changed the racial makeup of the police department in the 1980s after Black leaders filed lawsuits. Another lawsuit abolished the mayor-council government in Gadsden, and a seven-member city council with representatives elected from districts was created, giving Blacks and women their first opportunity to serve in government. In 1986, Gadsden elected its first Black city official, Robert Avery, a participant in the demonstrations that followed Moore's death.

“Every right we have won—even when it was obvious that the right thing for them to do was let us in—we had to go to court to get it,” said Joseph Faulkner, the executive director of the Gadsden chapter of the NAACP. “We can’t ever relax. They won’t let us.”

There was no relaxing even when Lawrence Presley, the county’s first Black county commissioner, died on January 10, 1993. The local Republican Party executive committee announced it planned to submit Ace Williams, the former exalted cyclops of the Gadsden Klan, as a candidate to fill Presley’s unexpired term. Williams, then in his early sixties, was the owner of a detective agency and a member of the Etowah County Republican Executive Committee. The executive committee withdrew his name, though, after his former ties to the Klan were revealed.

“Many, many long years ago, I had an affiliation,” he said. “A lot of us had an affiliation, but I never did anything I was ashamed of.”

By 2000, the city’s population had fallen more than 30 percent since the murder of William Moore, to 38,978.

My first stop was to the Gadsden Public Library. I wanted to dig through the telephone books and city directories to find out how many investigators and former lawmen were alive. I knew Roy McDowell, the state’s chief investigator, was still living. I had spoken to him a few years earlier about another civil rights case—the murder and rape of a pregnant white woman near Scottsboro in the summer of 1964. A posse had chased Johnny Beecher across Sand Mountain before a policeman in South Pittsburg, Tennessee, shot him in the leg, causing the leg to be amputated. Beecher’s surgery was performed in a prison hospital, where McDowell wrote Beecher’s confession after the surgery. Sedated with morphine, Beecher gave his approval by writing his initials.

Harry Sizemore was alive, too, still living in the farmhouse across from the murder site. Floyd Simpson, though, had died two years earlier at a nursing facility in Fort Payne.

I found McDowell’s phone number in a telephone directory at the library and drove back to Keener, stopping at Sizemore’s house before dark. No one was home, but I had better luck when I called Roy McDowell that night.

"Come on down tomorrow," he said. "Sure, I remember the case. I've got the file. I kept all my files."

McDowell lived near my grandparents' home in Southside. Like many associated with the William Moore case, he found a better life after the murder investigation. He retired in 1974 from the Alabama Department of Public Safety, where he had served for thirty years as a highway patrolman and investigator. As Dewey Colvard began his fifth term as sheriff, he hired McDowell as an investigator. Five years later, Bill Rayburn hired him as an investigator for the district attorney's office. In 1980, he was appointed sheriff. Seven years later, he retired after his second term as sheriff.

When I arrived, I approached the side of his home, and he instructed me to enter through the sliding glass doors. My first question was about the files.

"No, I don't have it," he said. "I thought I had that one, but I couldn't find it."

His memories of the case, though, were clear. He remembered the conversation in his car in the Hilltop Grocery parking lot as night descended, William Moore's tired, harmless face illuminated by the dome light of the Chevrolet cruiser, framed against the darkness. From somewhere on Highway 11 or the Hilltop Grocery parking lot, McDowell sensed the killer watching them from afar.

"This fella was a postman in Baltimore, and he was coming down the highway," McDowell said. "He was going to the governor's mansion in Mississippi, and he had pamphlets and a cart he was pushing. He was on U.S. 11, and it was the main thoroughfare. They didn't have no right to kill him. He wasn't hurting no one. There was no reason to kill him."

His involvement in the case began when Ben Allen, the longtime state investigator, called him from Birmingham earlier that afternoon.

"The director, Colonel Al Lingo, had called [Allen]," McDowell said. "They discussed it, and they said for me to go check on him. He [Allen] told me about this fella coming down 11 and pushing a little wagon. I went up there, and it was just getting dark. I stopped up there in Keener and asked him to get in the car. I had the dome light on. I always figured—and I figured I'd be right—that whoever shot him was watching him at the time he sat in my car."

He remembered Moore's expression: pleasant, highly agreeable, eager to talk about what he was doing in Alabama, and what he had encountered that day.

"He was as nice as he could be," McDowell said. "He was no problem with me. He was going to do what I asked him to do."

They talked for twenty minutes, maybe twenty-five, by McDowell's estimate. Moore told him that someone had been following him down U.S. 11—"harassing him" as McDowell put it. But no such treatment was mentioned in Moore's diary.

"I asked him where he was going, where he had been," McDowell said. "He'd had trouble that day. He told me about it. He didn't know who he was, but they were harassing him."

McDowell feared for Moore's safety as night was near, and he asked Moore to stop at D & J Truck Stop Cabins in Crudup, a community about three miles south of Keener. Unaware of any state law that allowed him to arrest Moore, he returned to Gadsden before 8:00 p.m. About an hour later, just before nine, McDowell was at the Panorama restaurant on Meighan Boulevard in Gadsden, sipping a cup of coffee, when the radio dispatcher relayed the news to him.

The next day, he drove north on Highway 11 to begin the investigation. He met Major W. R. Jones, the head of the Alabama Investigative and Identification Division, who came from Montgomery to lead the search for the murderer. Jones, McDowell, Allen, and another state investigator, Maurice Chambers of Huntsville, spent much of their time on Highway 11, canvassing the highway for clues. They received a tip about Floyd Simpson: His car and gun had been used in the murder. McDowell and Jones drove to the store in Collbran to interview him.

Entering the store, they saw the .22-caliber rifle hanging above the fireplace near the front door, positioned on two nails over the mantel.

"I didn't know [Simpson] from Adam's house cat," McDowell said. "We got the rifle out of his house, so we came back to Gadsden. [Major Jones] told me he'd get with the FBI and make arrangements to process the gun at the FBI crime lab in Washington. He told me he wanted me to carry the gun to the crime lab in Washington, and the FBI made arrangements.

"I went to Birmingham, got on a plane that night, and they made arrangements [with the FBI] to meet me at Dulles airport the next morning. When I got there, this agent knew exactly what he was looking for. He didn't have no trouble finding me. We went to the crime lab and he run ballistics on that gun."

McDowell and Robert Zimmers, the FBI's ballistics expert, spent much of the day in the lab, examining the gun and the shells found at the scene. The results were conclusive.

"He [Zimmers] told me that was the gun that matched the bullets we were trying to match up," McDowell said. "I said, 'How 'bout you calling down to Gadsden and tell them that?' He called Mr. Rayburn or Dewey [Colvard]. It was one of the two. I asked him to call the sheriff or the DA, and he did. He told them the same thing he told me. He said that was the gun that done it.

"He could almost tell by looking at the bullets before he completed the examination. They pretty well know what they're doing. They examine so many. He was fully convinced that was the gun that fired those hulls."

The phone call caused problems for everyone: It led to the disagreement between J. Edgar Hoover and Rayburn and sent Hoover into a rage about Zimmers's analysis of the rifle.

"I want the [carelessness] of our Laboratory staff to end," Hoover wrote in an FBI memo on May 2. "This mess will no doubt end in the full responsibility being placed on the FBI just because [Zimmers] couldn't [keep] his mouth shut."

McDowell was certain about the final hour of Moore's life: He had been the last person to talk to Moore. The murderer waited for their conversation at Hilltop Grocery to end, then eased down the highway, continuing to stalk Moore as he approached the park. He parked the black car, waited for Moore to pass, and shot him from the car.

"Later on, the grand jury met on it," McDowell said. "I have never been able to figure it out. Apparently, somebody on that grand jury didn't like the racial business, one way or another, and didn't indict him. I didn't think there would be no trouble."

The state's chief investigator seemed so sure about how William Moore had been killed. So why was the murder still unsolved after almost forty years?

"No doubt in my mind [the killers] were riding up and down the road," McDowell said. "I'm sure they saw him talking to me. I figured that."

I returned to Keener to try to find Harry Sizemore again. This time, he answered the door. He did not invite me in, though, because he and his wife, Betty, had come home only minutes earlier from Birmingham, where they had visited their daughter and grandchildren. I told him why I wanted to talk to him, and he told me to come back next week, giving me a day and a time.

"Just come back then, and we'll talk," he said.

When I returned, I knocked on his front door, and no one answered. I had seen an old powder-blue Chevrolet pickup in his driveway during my earlier visit, and I saw it parked near some barns near the back of his home. I drove around to the barns, parked next to his pickup, and saw Sizemore and his wife in the barn.

"Oh, that's right," he said. "We were supposed to meet today."

His wife said nothing.

"Come on," he said. "Get in my pickup, and we'll ride over to where he was shot."

Turning onto a back road, he told me why he hadn't been home: His wife didn't want him to talk to me. He eased onto Highway 11 and pulled into the murder site, now thick with underbrush that had grown after the state removed the tree and tables.

"There used to be a big walnut tree here," he said. "It was huge. The state had picnic tables here."

He got out of his truck, walked to the side of the highway, and told me what he found.

"He was lying on his left side," Sizemore said. "That was a scary time. His sign was still on his back. My daughter was five or six years old, and we were watching Red Skelton on TV. We heard a knock on the door, and this young man and his wife had a seven-month-old baby. He said somebody had been hit by a car. She was scared to death."

It was Willis Elrod and his family on their way home to Birmingham.

"I got a flashlight, and we walked out to the driveway," Sizemore said.

"I shined the light on the sign, and I was reading the sign. I thought he'd been hit by a car. Then I shined the light on his face. It [a bullet hole] was in his right temple and right over his head. [Another] was over his ear. I didn't know a thing about him marching.

"A few cars gathered here. Next thing you know, everybody's stopped. You'd thought it was a bad accident. I called the sheriff. Then they went to having radio reports out here."

He mentioned the chopping of the tree to confuse the marchers and others who wanted to resume Moore's walk. His father, Ernest, gave the order.

"He said, 'I want that tree removed.' And the state removed it," he said.

Removed it with dynamite.

"Just obliterated it," Sizemore said. "All that was there was a stump."

Sizemore, like McDowell, seemed sure of how the murder unfolded: The plan had begun in Collbran and implemented as soon as Moore arrived in an isolated area, where there would be no witnesses.

"That was the conclusion," Sizemore said. "A man had been taunting him since he saw him walking at Collbran. He was waiting to pick the right place."

Harry Sizemore was known throughout Etowah and DeKalb Counties as a member of one of the area's leading farming families. The Sizemores owned 607 acres and raised 140 head of cattle in the valley between Lookout and Sand Mountains, their pastures rich with orchard grass, bluegrass, and white clover. Harry had dabbled in politics as the custodian of the county's voting machines, a position he had held since 1958, but the murder case increased his visibility in northeast Alabama. In 1970, he became the youngest chairman of the Etowah County Commission. The job had its perks when family troubles arose. Rayburn and Sizemore became so close that Rayburn refused to issue a warrant in July 1973 when Sizemore fired three shots at some men who had set a five-foot cross on fire in his driveway, one of whom was a twenty-year-old man who had been married to Sizemore's daughter for nine months.

"I cannot issue a warrant on the evidence which I have seen," Rayburn said at the time, even though Sizemore had wounded his former son-in-law in the head, hand, arm, and ear with birdshot.

Sizemore was elected to a second term as county commissioner in 1974, but his political career ended in scandal. In October 1977, he pleaded guilty to five counts of bank fraud involving the Alabama City Bank and was removed from office. Years later, he made an unsuccessful bid for the county commission and retired from politics.

He still had fond memories of politics. One of his favorites was how Bill Rayburn, the Etowah County district attorney, needled him.

"He used to tease me: 'Mr. Harry, why don't you just confess to shooting Mr. Moore?'" Sizemore said.

"Well, I might one of these days," he told Rayburn.

Sitting in his truck, looking at where the walnut tree once stood, Sizemore chuckled.

"Of course, he knew I didn't do it," Sizemore said.

So that's what the investigation became to Bill Rayburn and Harry Sizemore.

A joke.

CHAPTER 16

Noble Yocum, the Etowah County coroner, wore a suit and fedora as he directed the crime scene on the night of the murder, looking more like the insurance salesman and real estate businessman that he was in his spare time than a man who investigated deaths. After examining William Moore, he was apparently so horrified by what he saw that he told a *Gadsden Times* reporter, "Nobody with sensible logic would have committed such a dastardly crime." He found a bullet in Moore's shirt pocket, the diary, and the copies of his letters to President Kennedy and Ross Barnett. As coroner, he was responsible for calling Mary Moore and conducting the autopsy. More than any local official, the murder seemed to disturb him, but his conscience hadn't been too scarred. He still called Mary Moore collect.

I met him at a steakhouse in Rainbow City, a suburb of Gadsden. At eighty-three, he was still working part time at a funeral home in Attalla. His memories of the case were so vivid that he still recalled the identity of the first officers at the murder scene and how he found the cartridge cases.

"[Moore] stopped in that store for cheese and crackers, and he got into a discussion with some characters and something transpired," he said. "They immediately took issue with him. They [the investigators] uncovered evidence about him stopping at Collbran. I never met those people. I'm not a detective."

He was the coroner for four terms, famous for his radio reports about crimes and deaths in the area. He was so popular, in fact, that he was once reelected with 32,000 votes, more than any local candidate.

I noticed something unusual about him as he talked about the murder: The longer he spoke, the more agitated he became.

"I saw the spent cartridges at the scene, Tony Reynolds [the chief deputy] and I," he said. "They were in and around the body. The reaction was that of an outsider coming in here to interfere with the due process of law and the integration of the races. We didn't have problems at that point."

Yocum took Moore's body to Collier-Butler Funeral Home in Gadsden, about fifteen miles south of the murder site, and found Mary Moore's phone number in Moore's wallet. He dialed the number and charged the call to her. "I might have the wrong Mrs. William Moore," he said. "Her minister answered the phone in a mobile home park. He said, 'She's not here—she lives next door. Hold the phone. I will get her.' It was eight to ten minutes before she got to the phone. She accepted the charges, and I explained to her what happened. The next morning, she said on CBS, 'Noble Yocum called me collect from Gadsden, Alabama.' That was the extent of my contact with her.

"She accepted it as a matter of fact. Obviously, she appeared to have expected it or anticipated it."

No one in Gadsden, though, expected the area to be overwhelmed with national and international news coverage. A West German television crew came to Gadsden on the morning of May 9 to film a documentary on the murder. Murray Kempton, one of the nation's most distinguished journalists, filed an article from Fort Payne for the *New Republic*. The CBS documentary never aired, but at least three folk songs about the murder did. When the case finally went to the grand jury, the residents of Gadsden were so distressed by how their city had been depicted that they were ready for the case to end.

"The *New York Times* city desk called," Yocum said. "They asked, 'Tell me, is it true that people there carry rifles or guns in pickup trucks?' I said, 'No, we do enjoy a certain degree of civilization in these parts.' At that time, everybody was pointing fingers at Alabama."

He found the whole incident "quite bizarre," as he put it. Why come to Alabama on a one-man crusade with the self-appointed purpose to save the world with racial tensions so high? He often wondered if an organization had paid Moore to make his walk.

Gadsden, he said, breathed a collective "sigh of relief" when the grand jury refused to indict Simpson. The case was over at last, and the city was through with William Moore and the Northern newspapers.

"No one felt [the murderer] committed a crime against society," he said. "That was the general opinion in this area. He was a victim of his own plot and it backfired. They took it very personal. They took it in hand, and that was the result."

His account of the murder was like Sizemore's: It had been planned for several hours, with the picnic area likely chosen because the murderer could park near the highway and still have a clear shot at Moore. The killer was also hidden by the black walnut tree and the curve. No other spot on the highway provided such protection for the perpetrator.

"They [the murderers] picked the spot," Yocum said. "They could have waited longer and it would have been more isolated. It appeared to me somebody didn't like [Moore's walk]. Well, I could understand the reasoning. He was from outside this area, and he came in to interfere with our routine. We're not known for violence, certainly not in Keener."

The murderer, in his estimation, was about twenty miles up the highway in Collbran. He had angered the men at Simpson's store, he said, and at least one of them decided to kill him.

He unleashed the last of his frustrations as we were about to leave the steakhouse, the old sensitivities as raw as they were after the murder.

"We were innocent victims," he said. "He brought this on himself. We didn't do it."

Zev Aelony knew better. He was a Freedom Rider, a member of CORE, and an organizer of a civil rights group known as Students for Integration. As a longtime admirer of Mahatma Gandhi, he had been an activist since he was a teenager. He had been arrested during the Freedom Rides in Jackson, Mississippi, and jailed in Parchman Farm, the notorious Mississippi prison, where he went on a hunger strike. Using his spoon, he had written a message on a prison wall: "You Reap What You Sow," an inscription that earned him more wrath from the guards.

In the spring of 1963, he went south again to participate in the William Moore Memorial Walk. He was twenty-five, with horn-rimmed glasses and black hair, a native of California. At the Alabama-Georgia line, he observed the reenactment of the message he had written two years earlier on the Parchman wall.

"The people in CORE that I heard from viewed [Moore] with considerable courage," he said. "They had advised him against [the walk], but they viewed it as noble. Many of us recognized that we were in far less danger than he was because of the publicity that we had. We felt [society] could not reward somebody for killing somebody else. It was the law of the slayer rule: You can't kill your parent and claim your inheritance. We figured if killing Bill Moore would prevent people from trying to bring others together, we had to carry it on.

"We had copies of his letters. We were on a walk to do the same thing that he was going to do, to bring his letters [to Jackson]. We wanted to show young people—Black and white—that we could bring people together. We were not threatened. We wanted to show people we could live together."

His memories of Fort Payne included the trial in early June at the DeKalb County courthouse, the county's first look at a Black lawyer. Fred Gray of Tuskegee, the lawyer for Rosa Parks during the Montgomery bus boycott, defended the Freedom Walkers. Aelony recalled Al Lingo, sitting with the local prosecutors, removing his revolver from his holster during testimony and spinning it on the table in an attempt to intimidate the judge, Warren G. Hawkins, a protégé of Bill Beck. After a while, he picked up the gun and began spinning the chambers.

"Fred Gray [the defense attorney] got a description from the officers who had arrested two SNCC workers who were observers," Aelony said. "They said they had arrested them in Georgia, and the charge had to do with walking into Alabama. The judge on hearing this looked at the prosecution and looked back at Gray. Lingo was glaring at the judge and started spinning the chambers emphatically."

Bob Zellner, another Freedom Walker, was already familiar with the judicial system in Alabama. On January 9, 1963, only five days before George Wallace's inauguration, he was arrested by Lingo and state investigator Willie B. Painter on conspiracy charges. Neither officer had a warrant, and Lingo had not been inaugurated as the new director of public safety. Zellner was arrested, though, and sent to jail by Municipal Judge D. Eugene Loe. The city gave him no chance to post bail. Wallace's inauguration was only a few days away, and Zellner couldn't be on the streets, planning racial demonstrations.

"Wallace and Lingo did that," Zellner said. "We later found out he was a Klansman, Lingo was. The murderer of Bill Moore was active in the Klan, too. Bill Moore's legacy was that he was a strong believer in people. It was one of those contradictions: They said he was an atheist, but he acted morally—more moral than those who professed to be religious. He didn't seek martyrdom, but to anybody from the outside, what [he] was doing would lead to almost certain death."

Zellner, like Moore, was a white activist with Southern roots. His father, a Methodist minister, and grandfather had been members of the Klan. He lived in small towns in southern Alabama before moving to Mobile, where he graduated from high school in 1957. In the fall of 1961, a mob beat him with lead pipes and baseball bats in McComb. Mississippi, where he and some fellow SNCC members had gone to protest the expulsion of a Black high school student for her participation in a sit-in. During the beatings, a man tried to pull out his eyeballs.

"I have been in some situations where I thought there was a high possibility I would die," he said. "I would do everything I could to keep from getting killed. [Moore] had spent time in the South, and I think that was what he was [counting] on: 'I know Southerners. I know Mississippians. They're good people, but they had a really bad idea.'"

Zellner believed the afternoon of May 3, 1963, at the Alabama-Georgia line was among those situations where he had a chance to die. The crowd, as he recalled, appeared to direct most of their anger at the white Alabamians in the group—Zellner and Sam Shirah, whose seventh-grade Sunday school teacher at Clayton United Methodist Church was George Wallace.

"The crowd went absolutely crazy," Zellner said. "They were yelling, 'Shoot them. Kill them.' The troopers were shocking us with cattle prods. I have almost no memory of the pain. I have a vivid memory of the mob. They would have killed all of us if they could have."

Almost forty years later, Aelony had a regular reminder of his activism—a sore spot on his back from a brick someone in the crowd had thrown at him.

"It was people expressing the frustration in their lives in hateful ways," he said. Zellner and the other white men—Shirah and Eric Weinberger, a member of CORE from New York—endured some of the worst of the abuse. In Gadsden, Zellner was kicked in the head by one of the policemen. Weinberger, the son of an NAACP board member, fasted while he was in jail at Fort Payne and in Gadsden and continued to go without food while he was in Kilby Prison. In one month, he lost nearly thirty pounds. He ended his fast on June 3, when Aelony handed him a bottle of orange juice outside the DeKalb County courthouse.

In a letter to his parents on May 16, Shirah described the conditions in jail.

"Eric and Bob were treated brutely [sic] by the police because they were not cooperating. They were drug down the steps at the Fort Payne jail and when we got to Gaston [sic] I saw one of the offericiers [sic] kick Bob in the head."

The brutality continued at Kilby Prison in Montgomery after Virgil Pittman sent them there.

"Then yesterday they moved us here to Kilby Prison," he wrote. "It was the same thing all over for Bob and Eric. The prison gards [sic] would drag them up the stairs and every step I could feel the pain myself. When we got into the pen where they're keeping us the Ass. [sic] Warden ask [sic] "Why do they do it. Why don't they walk up the steps. Richard Haley [a Black member of CORE] said back, "Bacause [sic] that within them is grater [sic] than that outside them. and though they be brused [sic] and scratched and prehaps [sic] even killed, they have known something very few of us will ever know. Blessed are you when men shall persicute [sic] you for My sake." The Ass. [sic] Warden did not reply."*

* Samuel C. Shirah Jr. Papers, Historical Manuscripts, Special Collections, University of Southern Mississippi Libraries.

CHAPTER 17

To receive my first break, I had to go far from the fear in Gadsden and Little Wills Valley. David Stout, the former mayor of Fort Payne, was in Montgomery, two hundred miles from the valley. He was the spokesman for Paul Hubbert, the head of the Alabama Education Association (AEA) and the most powerful man in Alabama. I met Stout at AEA's headquarters near the Alabama Capitol, where Confederate flags still flew on the lawn. His job was to entertain me before my meeting with Hubbert, and he seemed eager to talk about anything except state politics or his boss. He told me about being a native of Fort Payne, the city's longtime mayor, and a 1965 graduate of Fort Payne High School. I asked him if he remembered the murder of William Moore, and he appeared to relax.

"Oh, yes," he said. "I remember it quite well. I always thought it would make for one of those made-for-TV movies."

He remembered several things about the case: Moore had spent the night in Fort Payne at Black's Motel. The state police had found the rifle above the fireplace in Floyd Simpson's store, and the Ku Klux Klan in Collbran had been active at the time. He also told me about the exalted cyclops of the DeKalb County Klan in the 1960s, Hoyt Kelly, whom he described as a rabid defender of white supremacy.

Stout told me about an incident at a Fort Payne gathering spot known as the Mouse Trap, a popular hangout for local youths. In the 1960s, he had been part of a local band known as the Ernie King Soul Band, which included a Black member, Ernie Davenport. The DeKalb County Klan disapproved of an integrated band playing at the Mouse Trap, so much so that it made a bomb threat. Many in Fort Payne suspected that Hoyt Kelly made the call. Stout told me, too, that Hoyt Kelly had started a junior Klan made up of local teenagers. Some of the junior Klan members had entered the club and confronted the band members to stop them from playing at the Mouse Trap.

Later, Stout and a cousin, Jim McGee, started a newspaper in Fort Payne, the *Northeast Alabamian*. Both were fascinated with the murder. Their classmates at Fort Payne High School had included the children of Gaddis Killian and Floyd Simpson. Their newspaper office was in downtown Fort Payne, near Bill Beck's office, and they often asked him about the case. Finally, Beck showed them the case file, which contained photos of William Moore's body at the murder scene—photos that looked as if Moore was asleep on the side of the highway, as the radio dispatcher had said when he informed Roy McDowell of the murder.

As we headed toward Hubbert's office, Stout gave me a tip: Contact McGee the next time I was in Fort Payne. He was now the Fort Payne city clerk.

"He can tell you a lot about it," he said. "He'll remember everything about meeting with Mr. Beck."

I discovered that people in Fort Payne were as nervous as the people in Etowah County. A former police chief, Bob "Skinny" Parker, had been talkative when I called him, telling me how Floyd Simpson and Gaddis Killian had been so active in local politics that candidates could count on them for delivering votes. Then, perhaps realizing he might be giving too much information, he said, "Now, who did you say you were again?"

McGee, though, enjoyed talking about the case. He told me that he had seen William Moore walking through Fort Payne on the morning of April 23, 1963, as he was driving to school with his mother, an elementary school teacher. He caught a glimpse of Moore's sign and wondered what it meant, sparking his lifelong fascination with the case.

His career at the *Northeast Alabamian* had given him a chance to satisfy his curiosity. Part of Beck's daily routine was to walk from his home to his office across from the courthouse. During one of his daily walks, he told McGee to come to his office to see the file.

"He said, 'My guys were innocent. They weren't doing anything wrong,' McGee said. 'He seemed proud of his role.'"

Beck was defiant, though, when Morris Dees, cofounder of the Southern Poverty Law Center in Montgomery, came to Fort Payne in the late 1970s to pursue a conviction in the William Moore case. By then, the Klan was dead in DeKalb County. Dees was on a crusade to kill the Klan in the rest of Alabama, and resurrecting the William Moore case was among the best ways to advance Dees's cause. Beck, though, was a longtime Klan sympathizer, and the men responsible for the murder were still alive.

"He always took their side in the community," McGee said. "Mr. Beck deeply resented Morris Dees coming here. He spoke with great disdain for that young Jewish lawyer. Mr. Beck acted like he didn't give him much time."

My meeting with David Stout had been beneficial in two ways: he was the first person to tell me about Hoyt Kelly, and he had led me to Jim McGee.

A few weeks later, though, I found someone who was even more valuable, the person who became my most trusted source.

The village of Valley Head, population 611, was ten miles north of Fort Payne. It was tucked between the mountains, a location that turned it into the coldest town in Alabama on winter mornings, when the cool air rushed off the ridges and settled between the mountains.

Kenneth Hammond, a barrel-chested and graying man in his early seventies, was Valley Head's mayor. He was fond of self-deprecation, referring to himself by a variety of nicknames—'the Rat" and "the Fat Rat," among them. He was also given to dark moods and depression, usually because of his failed political ambitions. In the 1970s, he had been mentioned as a leading candidate for governor or the U.S. Senate, but accusations of improprieties during his term as the Alabama Public Service Commissioner had ruined his career.

"I'm just a lonely old redneck sitting up here with no one to talk to," he said.

He was considered one of the state's most promising and combative politicians after his election to the Alabama senate in 1962, a former college football player who enjoyed a fight as much as a discussion about politics and history. In his early thirties, he had enough political foresight to cite integration as one of his priorities for his first term, the first elected official in Alabama to favor civil rights. After defeating Bull Connor in 1972 to become the public service commissioner, he was the second state official to appoint a Black member to his staff.

He had a brilliant mind for politics and history, his instincts so strong that he predicted the dominance of the Republican Party in Alabama from the senate floor in 1965, more than twenty years before it happened.

"It's hell to sit here and see the Democratic Party in the state of a dying jag," he said. "In five years from now, South Alabama, with the exception of possibly two counties, will turn completely Republican."

Many regarded him as the county's foremost authority on politics and history. But he was too much of a battler, too willing to challenge the state's most powerful people, to achieve his political goals.

"During my lifetime, I've left many a whupped one over this state," he told Marshall Frady, George Wallace's first biographer.

His most famous battles were against Wallace, the state's most powerful person. In October 1965, Hammond was the most outspoken opponent of a bill that would have allowed Wallace to succeed himself as governor, then against state law. During a filibuster, Hammond said Wallace used "Nazi tactics in a filibuster," and he was prepared "to destroy democracy at its best." Hammond said on the senate floor that Wallace's goal was "a dictatorship which would make Huey P. Long look like a piker." He said Wallace had made Alabama a "haven for hate-mongers" and was ready to do the same to the rest of the country.

"In order to pick up support, he is going to put the white race against the minorities of this country the same way Adolf Hitler pitted the master race against the Jews," Hammond said.

Jim Allen, the lieutenant governor from Gadsden, walked out in protest. Unfazed, Hammond reached for a paper bag that contained a small package. He plopped it on the table in front of him, and the noise produced such a thud that the senators and reporters were sure a gun was inside the bag. It was, instead, a tape recording "with every damn promise the administration made to me."

His final shots included a reference to Seymour Trammell, Wallace's top aide.

"I understand the finance director wants to play rough," Hammond said. "That suits me. . . . The hate-mongers may kill me before I leave the capitol."

The attempt to kill him, Hammond believed, came after he returned to Valley Head. In a scenario similar to the murder of William Moore, a black car with two men in the front seat waited for him in the parking lot of a Standard Oil station, this time in the daylight of a Sunday afternoon. Watching from a front window of Winston Place, the antebellum home where his parents lived, Hammond called the FBI office in Gadsden and informed the agent of the whereabouts of the black car. Hammond and his wife, Maureen, drove to the station and approached the driver of the black car.

Hammond recognized Hoyt Kelly, sitting in the driver's seat. He didn't know the man in the passenger's seat, also an officer in the DeKalb County Klan, but the man knew Hammond's wife.

"How are you, Maureen?" asked the man, Cecil "Cotton" King.

Cotton King, a cousin of Maureen Hammond's, was also an officer in the DeKalb County Klan, ranked behind Hoyt Kelly and Guyton Tutor in the organizational hierarchy. When I asked Hammond what would have happened if he hadn't confronted the men in the black car, he said, "They would have either burned down our house or killed me."

The men in the black car might have intimidated William Moore, he said, but they didn't frighten him. In the pocket of his sport coat, he carried a .25 Beretta pistol, his favorite gun, for protection.

"I'm not scared of nothing," he said.

Kenneth Hammond was careful, however, in our early discussions about the murder. In those meetings at the Valley Head town hall, he waved his arm through the cloud of smoke from his Phillies Blunt, his favorite cigar, and dismissed the investigation as "a fucking joke," as he put it.

"Ah, that thing was chloroformed thirty minutes after it hit the media," he said. "Everyone hit the cabbage patch after that. Everybody used everybody."

He was more interested in giving me history lessons and how he could break down the beat boxes in DeKalb County—filibustering me, he called it. He wanted to see if I was, in fact, a serious student of history and politics. His classroom was the council chamber, where a portrait of John F. Kennedy hung on one of the walls. He gave me books about Theodore Roosevelt and the Ku Klux Klan, and I gave him a biography of Wallace. He underlined important passages in the books he gave me, trying to help me understand the attitudes of William Moore's murderer and the people who handled the investigation. He gave me a copy of Wallace's inauguration speech on January 14, 1963—the infamous "segregation today, segregation tomorrow, segregation forever" speech. He still had his original copy, adorned with the Alabama state seal on the cover page. Now and then, he tried to impress his fellow citizens of Valley Head with such a memorable piece of state history. None of them, though, was interested in discussing politics with him.

Knowing he had my attention, he lectured me on the importance of Wallace's inauguration speech and its role in the William Moore murder.

"That gave them [the Klan] the semi–green light," he said. "The yellow light didn't go up until the Schoolhouse Door. It was obvious it [the murder] got chloroformed. The climate was the key. It was the key to everything."

His favorite subject, though, was an analysis of the county's vote totals from his victory in the 1970 state senate race—"my comeback," he called it. He had been beaten soundly in 1966, after he had opposed Wallace on the succession bill, losing by 3,500 votes to Dan Stone, a Pontiac dealer in neighboring Cherokee County. Four years later, after reconciling with Wallace, he defeated Stone decisively. With Wallace's blessing, he had managed to receive support from Klan leaders from Sand Mountain after he had bought steak dinners at a restaurant on the town square in Trenton, Georgia.

It had been thirty years since Hammond had campaigned outside of Valley Head, but he rattled off the voters in those county beat boxes as if he were running for state senate again. When he reached beat 3, box 1—the Collbran box—he informed me of the most prominent families in the area, including Hoyt Kelly's family.

I told him of my connections to that area: Many years earlier, one of my aunts and uncles had lived on Lookout Mountain in a community known as

Dogtown, and their surname was Jordan.* The Jordans were a large family, and I knew many of my uncle's siblings still lived in the area, including my uncle's youngest sister. As a teenager, I had spent the summer with them, and I heard my aunt and uncle talk about her during our nightly gin rummy games.

Hammond recoiled when I told him I was related to the Jordans, as if he had been sucker punched. He considered himself a master poker player, a veteran of all-night card games in Chattanooga. But my family connections to the Jordans had caused his poker face to disappear. With a smile forming at the corners of his mouth, he paused and said, "I see you know a lot about our county."

That was all he said, but he had said enough. His expression told me everything I needed to know. I had stepped into a mess.

Was this what my mother was trying to tell me before she died? I was about to find out.

The Genealogy Room in the DeKalb County Public Library was full of information about the area's prominent families. The families of Floyd Simpson and Hoyt Kelly were among the most deeply researched, with books and folders providing their history for generations. I found the former exalted cyclops's name in the index of a book about the Kelly family, and his biographical sketch gave me the information I feared: I was distantly related to him.

My uncle's youngest sister had married the former exalted cyclops. My uncle died long ago, but my favorite aunt, the matriarch of our family, was still alive. I called her the day after my discovery in the DeKalb County Public Library and asked her about Hoyt Kelly. She responded with a deep, hearty laugh.

"Yes, I know him," she said. "He's very outspoken."

She told me she knew several members of the Kelly family and many residents of Collbran, including Gaddis Killian. She said my grandfather had known Hoyt Kelly's father and had "great respect for him." They had worked together for the local highway department in the late 1950s

* Pseudonym. Family to be known from hereon as the Jordans.

and early '60s when the new interstate came through Little Wills Valley. My grandfather had also worked for the DeKalb County Co-Op on Sand Mountain, where Hoyt Kelly's father, one of the area's leading farmers, bought farming supplies.

"Do you think Hoyt Kelly would ever talk to me?" I asked.

"Well, sure he would," she said. "What would you want to talk to him about?"

I told her about the murder. She said nothing.

"I'm not saying he had anything to do with it," I told her. "I just might want to talk to him about it at some point."

She thought that was a bad idea.

"I think I'd go in a different direction," she said, her voice almost a whisper.

For a while, I considered ending my search. Marty Smith, the Valley Head town hall clerk, thought I should. Bozo told me her brother had been a member of the Fort Payne Ku Klux Klan during the civil rights era. I figured she likely knew who killed William Moore, like most people in the county who were familiar with the murder.

"When are you going to stop for the sake of your family?" she asked me.

I told her that I had invested too much time to stop. It had been three years since those peculiar conversations with Roy McDowell, Harry Sizemore, and Noble Yocum. I told her I wanted to unravel the rest of the case.

"Do you think that dead man is driving you?" Marty Smith asked, after I told her I was continuing.

No, I told her, I felt like my past was driving me.

Bozo and I developed a routine: I'd find him most mornings in the council chambers, where he was usually reading and smoking a cigar. He'd lecture me about Alabama politics, and then I'd ask my questions about the murder.

"I am a fiscal conservative and semi-liberal on human rights," he said. "Two things I fought for: Blacks needed equal voting rights and equal job opportunities. I'm interested in economics and politics—and history."

Much of the history of Bozo's county and the history of the Klan were connected. The Klan met on Saturday mornings in downtown Fort Payne at a building owned by a prominent lumberman and Wallace supporter.

Among the first items on the Klan's agenda was a discussion about political candidates. To many, the Klan was "a way of life," Bozo said, especially in the southern part of the county. Bozo launched into another filibuster about some of the county's best-known Klansmen.

"Gad Killian is an old-timer, in his eighties today," he said. "Hoyt is a young man, pulled a hitch in the navy. He's got one leg withered up on him. He was a [truck] driver and ran a nice grocery in Collbran. Gad Killian is very respected, was a mailman on Lookout Mountain. Lookout Mountain was heavy on the Klan. He was with the old group of the Klan."

So was Floyd Simpson. The Simpsons, he said, "lived in the ridges" of southern DeKalb County in an area known as Adamsburg and Dogtown. It was well known in that part of the county, he said, that the murderer had used Simpson's rifle to kill William Moore.

"They called Simpson 'the Rifleman' after that," he said. "It was a running joke in all these cafés around here."

After one of our discussions, I drove to Collbran on a morning in late summer, curious to see if Floyd Simpson's old general merchandise store was open. Several merchants along the highway were participating in the "World's Longest Yard Sale," an annual event on U.S. 11 that stretches for more than six hundred miles through the Midwest and Deep South. Gaddis Killian was chatting with a customer, a tourist from out of state, when I pulled next to the area where the Gulf gas pumps used to be.

In its early years, the building was divided into three areas: the general merchandise store, the Collbran post office, and the living quarters for the proprietor and his family. The fireplace was past the entrance, just where David Stout said it was. I saw where Floyd Simpon hung his rifle, and I saw the counter where he conducted business. Gaddis Killian greeted me after finishing with his out-of-state customer. I asked him about the store, and he gave me the history of the building, full of details. At eighty-four, his memory was strong, but his hearing seemed to be fading.

"We built this building in 1938, the store part," he said. "The post office came in in 1942. We started selling Gulf gasoline in 1938."

The store had wood floors and a furnace in the back. License plates from all fifty states were on the building, many of them lining the wooden awning over the entrance. On one of the walls was a campaign sign from

Kenneth Hammond's 1972 bid for the Alabama Public Service Commission president. Another sign read, "Love Your Enemy, It Will Drive Him Crazy."

He wore a plaid shirt and khakis, just as he had when he stood at the Alabama-Georgia border and watched the Alabama state troopers arrest and stick the marchers with cattle prods on the afternoon of May 3, 1963. The fedora, though, was gone, but the George Wallace campaign buttons ("Wallace for Governor, Our Kind of Man") were still around.

"I started this store with $125," he said. "When people pulled into the store, I'd jump off those front steps. Later on, I started having problems with my ankles from all the jumping."

He was twenty-one when he began operating the store, twenty-five when he became the postmaster in Collbran. Just before World War II, he married and built a white frame house next to the store. With his civic and political interests, along with the demands of raising a family, he left the store business, leasing it to a friend in 1952. Ten years later, he leased it to Floyd Simpson.

"I guess my only problem is that I talk too much," he said.

We did not talk about the murder, though. I made him mad anyway.

Seeing a stack of old magazines near the front door, I asked him, "You a big reader?"

"Was I a big leader?" he snapped.

He seemed sensitive.

"No, were you a big reader?" I asked.

"Oh, yes," he said.

At one time, though, he had been a leader of some sort, judging by the campaign buttons and license plates in his store. One of the plates indicated his position on Governor John Patterson's staff, one of only sixteen men in the county to receive the honorary title. Clearly, he had once been influential, a man with too much to lose to be in the black car when William Moore approached the park in Keener.

Driving away from the store, I saw some crates near the highway with Hoyt Kelly's name on them. To have a chance to solve the murder, I knew I needed to find a way to meet him.

CHAPTER 18

I spent the fortieth anniversary of the murder on U.S. 11 traveling the highway in search of people who remembered William Moore. I started with a meeting with Bozo Hammond at the Valley Head town hall. Bozo began with a more open and detailed discussion about his early years in state politics, especially his battles with Hoyt Kelly. Most of their disagreements were about George Wallace and the Klan's support of candidates from the southern part of the state, particularly the Black Belt counties, where integration was an even more explosive issue. The candidates from southern Alabama, he said, were more rabid segregationists than the ones in North Alabama.

"I used to tell them, 'I don't have to see who y'all are voting for—90 percent of them are from South Alabama,'" Bozo said. "And then he [Hoyt Kelly] jumped on the Communist thing: 'They're just a bunch of Communists'—meaning the North Alabama people. I just thought, 'You're a frontline infantryman for South Alabama politicians.'

"We fought the Civil War all over again under George Wallace under the guise of states' rights. That man, Moore, he was on a death walk. It was a Bataan Death March."

Their feuds became more intense after Hammond's confrontation with Hoyt Kelly in the fall of 1965 at the Standard Oil station in Valley Head. Believing his life was in danger, Hammond drove to the state convict camp in the southern part of the county, where his father, Harry, was the superintendent. His father allowed him to sift through the convicts' files, then Hammond picked out five men capable of handling a job for him: The men were to kill Hoyt Kelly and his Klan associates if he was killed.

"They [the Klan] weren't the only people with cutthroat artists," Hammond said. "I was an old maverick back then. I told my daddy, 'I don't care if there are sheets all over them damn trees in Collbran, just do it.' He said don't worry about it. All I told my daddy was, 'If anything happens to me, have that place taken care of. Go down that railroad track and blow the damn place up.' He picked out five people. The only thing I can tell you is they weren't no angels.

"The ol' Rat went through those files. I took care of the families. All I can tell you is, none of them went hungry. If their families needed help, I helped 'em."

Hammond did some more investigating at the convict camp. He spoke with convicts and others who had information about the murder of William Moore. They told him about two meetings in Gadsden and Attalla before Moore entered Etowah County on the afternoon of the murder. One meeting was at a diner on the downtown square in Attalla, the other at the Panorama in Gadsden, where Roy McDowell was having coffee when he was informed of the murder. Klan members and others gathered at the diner in downtown Attalla, Hammond said. Local officials—the "upper crust," as he called them—met at the Panorama.

"You got to remember when that poor SOB was in Tennessee, they knew he was heading south," Hammond said. "They knew about thirty-six hours ahead of time, about the time he hit the Dade County line. All I picked up on was through these convicts at the camp. There was a meeting of key officials at the Panorama, and them rednecks, they met at the hole-in-the-wall restaurant. All I knew was that it came up in conversation that two places were mentioned."

Then, for the first time, Bozo told me that he had seen William Moore as he entered Alabama on the afternoon of April 22.

"He was at the Georgia line," he said. "He was a young man. I saw him with his signs—'Eat at Joe's, Black and White.' It was a sandwich sign. He wasn't bothering a damn soul."

But the mood shifted the next morning when Moore entered the southern part of the county.

"He was at the wrong damn place when he was at Collbran," Bozo said. "If he'd gone over the top of Sand Mountain, he might have gotten some potatoes thrown at him, but he might have made it through Etowah County. It was that damn climate. That was the key to every bit of it."

The state's racial climate, he said, was reinforced each election day. Alabamians stepped into voting booths and were greeted by ballots with the logo of the Democratic Party, the state's dominant political party since the end of Reconstruction. A crowing rooster, the party's symbol, was accompanied by a slogan: "White supremacy—for the right." The slogan was still on the ballots in the 1960s.

Robert Shelton, the state's most powerful Klansman, was spotted frequently with members of the governor's cabinet. During the early days of the Patterson administration, he was seen with Charles Merriweather, the state finance director. With Merriweather's arm draped around his shoulder, he walked through the first floor of the capitol in the spring of 1959, heading to the office of the Alabama Purchasing Division before being summoned to a phone in a lobby.

In his first year as governor, John Patterson scheduled meetings with Klan members, including Shelton, in his office and appointed a Klansman, Glenn Stacy, to the jury commission in Monroe County in southwest Alabama.

"But the worst thing was that crazy Ed Eddins and those damn black and white rabbits," Bozo said.

E. O. "Big Ed" Eddins was a state senator from Demopolis, Alabama, a town of about seven thousand near the Mississippi line. On May 22, 1959, only weeks after Shelton was seen walking through the capitol with Merriweather, Eddins said *The Rabbits' Wedding*, a children's book depicting the marriage of a male rabbit with black fur to a female rabbit with white fur, should be "taken off the shelves and burned." "There are many other books of the same nature and others that are Communistic which should be burned as well," Eddins said.

Upon hearing Eddins's views, the author of *The Rabbits' Wedding*, Garth Williams, said the book was "only about a soft furry love and has no hidden message of hate." As the illustrator for such children's classics as *Stuart Little*, *Charlotte's Web*, and the *Little House* series by Laura Ingalls Wilder, Williams was only interested in artistry, not politics. He said he was "completely unaware" that animals with white fur had blood relations to white human beings.

"I was only aware that a white horse next to a black horse looks very picturesque," Williams said.

By the spring of 1962, with the Democratic gubernatorial primary only days away, the Klan was so bold that Shelton accompanied Wallace during campaign stops in the west Alabama towns of Holt and Gordo. Shelton followed the Wallace entourage from town to town in his four-door Cadillac with three citizen-band radio antennas.

During the stop in Holt, a reporter asked him if he was for Wallace.

"I'm not doing anything to hurt him," Shelton replied.

Did Shelton think Wallace would win?

"Well, whoever wins, you will know we were for him," he said.

Less than two months after the election, Shelton and Calvin Craig, the Georgia grand dragon, credited the Klan's support for the elections of Wallace and John Patterson. They said the Klan "elected two governors in Alabama" and would elect Georgia's next governor, although they declined to name whom the Klan would support.

Wallace's inauguration day vow of "segregation today, segregation tomorrow" reinforced the Klan's smugness, inflaming the state's racial hostilities even higher as William Moore prepared to march through Alabama.

"It was like letting the mustangs out of the corral," Bozo said.

From Valley Head, I headed north to Trenton, Georgia, about twenty-five miles from Bozo's office. I drove to the town square, where the Dade County courthouse, a brick-and-concrete structure built in 1926, stood on less than an acre at the split of U.S. 11. I entered the courthouse and found a roster of county officials near the front door. Only one name had a connection to the William Moore case—Rex Blevins, a probation officer. He was the son of Allison Blevins, the former Dade County sheriff.

Blevins was in his early sixties, friendly and talkative, a good storyteller with a strong memory of William Moore.

"Seemed like he had a sign or something," Blevins said. "People were jeering him and talking to him. Daddy told him there might be a problem. Daddy got him and took him toward the Alabama line. He knew there were problems here."

The Ku Klux Klan was among those problems. Blevins said there was "a pretty good group of Klan" in Dade County in 1963. Some of the Dade County Klan members came from the ridges of Sand Mountain, an area of Alabama called the "Big Woods," known for its production of moonshine whiskey. Some of those Klansmen from Sand Mountain had participated in the floggings of seven Black men on the night of April 2, 1949, as Dade County Sheriff John W. Lynch and three of his deputies watched.

Allison Blevins, remembering the unfavorable national publicity that came to Dade County after the floggings, ordered Moore and his cart into his patrol car and drove him to Rising Fawn, near the Alabama state line.

"He had asked Daddy for protection," Blevins said. "He had been threatened, and he took him on to Alabama. I remember he had a little wagon with spoke wheels that were made of wood."

The unfavorable national press came anyway when the marchers passed through Dade County a week after the murder. Some of the locals threw rocks. Others beat the marchers or shoved them after rushing from a crowd of onlookers.

"Dad hollered at people to shut up and leave 'em alone," Blevins said. "He told them they were just trying to get to Alabama. I had never been exposed to anything like that. Most people hadn't."

Moore hadn't referred to Allison Blevins or the drive to Rising Fawn in his diary. He didn't mention any threats in Trenton either.

With the mustangs out of the corral, I wondered if the driver of the black car had already started his taunting as William Moore began the second day of his walk.

The timeline that Bozo Hammond had given me—almost two days' notice before Moore's arrival in Collbran—seemed to fit.

Margaret Osborn was the former owner of Byron's Café, a block building that had once been among the most popular diners in Collinsville. Everyone in town knew her as "Mertie," her lifelong nickname. She had spent much of her life serving her hometown, first as a restaurant owner and then as the Collinsville city clerk. At eighty-two, she spent her afternoons on her front porch near downtown Collinsville making potpourri. Her memory of the afternoon of April 23, 1963, was clear: William Moore entered her restaurant around two o'clock looking for a late lunch, plopping on one of the stools at the front counter. The menu included barbecue and vegetables, usually turnip greens and sweet potatoes, the food he had known from his youth in Mississippi.

"Just good ol' country cooking," she said.

Byron Sells, her father, opened the café in 1938 in downtown Collinsville, next to the Cricket Theater, the town's only theater. She moved to a block building on Highway 11 in 1959 after the theater owner informed her that he was expanding and she needed to find a new location. She found a Shell gasoline station in the north part of town, next to the Jacoway Motel on Highway 11. As she moved in, she discovered some surprises in the garage: bootleg whiskey stashed under the hydraulic lifts.

On the afternoon of the murder, she was alone in the kitchen, her lunch crowd long since gone, when William Moore entered the restaurant.

"I knew he was up there on the highway pushing or pulling a cart," she said. "It didn't mean anything to me. I had no idea what he was doing except that he had a special motive. I was just interested in getting the kitchen cleaned up between meals. He was disheveled. He looked like he needed a shave to me. I wanted to feed him and be on his way."

There was little to no conversation between them.

"He didn't tell me any of his philosophy," she said.

The restaurant, like others in Collinsville, was segregated. She told me she served Blacks, one of the first in the area to do so, but she made no attempts to hide her disdain for William Moore.

"[I thought] he ought to get a life and be working to amount to something," she said.

Roy McDowell came to her restaurant the day after the murder. He was on his way to Collbran, she said, and he told her about one of his chief suspects, Gaddis Killian.

"I had known [McDowell]," she said. "He must have come in to eat. They already had an inkling about the men at Portersville—or north of Portersville. They called it Collbran. It was the Gad Killian outfit. That's who they suspected. They had three of them up there who were brothers. But that name, Gad, that name caught my attention."

She had known the Killians for years. Some in the family were house-painters, she said, and they painted many of the houses in Collinsville, including her next-door neighbor's. One afternoon, as the Killians painted her neighbor's home, she took a bath. With her infant son playing in the den, she soaked in the tub but soon discovered that her son had run outside. With no clothes or towel, she dashed into her yard, the painters watching from next door as she retrieved her son.

"I won't ever live that down," she said. "It tickled 'em."

She figured William Moore's walk likely angered them. In an area known for its strident attitudes on race, Collbran was a hotbed for white supremacists, especially the area around Gaddis Killian's store.

"Some people thought they were racist," she said. "When he [Moore] went by, he stopped there [the store]. That's the word that we got there, that it was Gad they were looking for. That's the impression I got from Roy."

The next morning, I called Cecil Reed, the longtime sheriff of DeKalb County, a pleasant man who had the folksy charm of a veteran rural politician. Reed told me to meet him for breakfast at McDonald's, and he was already there when I arrived, nibbling on a biscuit.

In the spring of 1963, he was a twenty-three-year-old deputy sheriff, spending most of his time arresting bootleggers and moonshiners. He was quick to point out that the murder wasn't in his county.

"It [the murder] wasn't local," he said. "It all happened in Etowah County. We were all concerned about him [Moore] making it through DeKalb County. He carried a sign that said, 'Mississippi or Bust.' Me and a state trooper, Bill Stone, went to the county line to make sure he got through DeKalb County. I got in the car with [Stone]. He asked me if I wanted to go with him."

Around 4:00 p.m., they parked at the county line and waited for Moore to enter Etowah County. About thirty minutes earlier, he had finished his meeting with Gaddis Killian and Floyd Simpson on the south end of Collinsville. Reed and Stone parked on the shoulder of U.S. 11 for about fifteen minutes, maybe twenty, and watched him lumber past Stone's highway patrol car.

"We were pleased to see him go on to Mississippi," he said. "Yeah, I thought he might make it, but I knew it was risky."

The Klan had been active in Fort Payne for years, he said. He recalled Klan rallies near downtown Fort Payne, many of them held in the parking lot of a hardware store owned by Guyton Tudor, an officer in the Klan for many years.

"They had a pretty good little crowd, about fifty or sixty, just about every Saturday in the '60s," he said. "He just let 'em use the parking lot. They didn't give us any trouble, and we didn't bother them."

And, as he recalled, he and Bill Stone didn't bother William Moore either.

On my way out of Fort Payne, I bought a copy of the *Gadsden Times*. The newspaper was publishing a five-part series on the murder that week, and the second installment was on the front page that morning. The story ended with Don Whisenant passing the roadside park moments before the murder. Quoting an Alabama state troopers' report, the *Times* had misspelled Whisenant's name, but the details were accurate.

> William Don Wessonate was headed home to Collinsville after leaving work at a service station at the intersection of Alabama 77 and U.S. 11 in Attalla.
>
> As he topped the hill about five miles from the county line, near a roadside park with picnic tables, Wessonate saw taillights. He hit his brakes, afraid it was the police. He had gotten some speeding tickets along that stretch of highway and did not want to take a chance on more.
>
> But as he passed the car, he couldn't see anybody inside. Yet he had just seen taillights. It was a big black Buick, maybe an early '50s model.
>
> That's when he noticed a man, trudging along, pushing a cart and wearing some odd signs. Wessonate was curious but he drove on, giving little thought to the man walking along the highway. But it would not be the last time he heard about the man and his one-man march.

My first stop in Gadsden was the library to find a phone book. The newspaper had mangled the spelling of William Don Wessonate, and I wanted to find someone—anyone—whose last name sounded like Wessonate. I found a W. D. Whisenant who lived in Southside.

"That wasn't me—that was my son," the man said. "He was in the newspaper this morning."

His name was Douglas Whisenant. His son was Don Whisenant, and he had driven a 1956 green-and-white Ford on the night of the murder.

"He saw the man pushing the cart," Douglas said. "He saw a black car. He thought it was a Buick. He was going home to Collinsville. He didn't think much about it. He didn't think nothing like that was going to happen."

CHAPTER 19

Don Whisenant smelled like a mixture of hand cleaner and gasoline as he sat in his 1956 Ford on the night of April 23, 1963. It was a repulsive aroma for his wife, Paulette, six weeks away from giving birth to their first child, a daughter named Teri Lynn. Don worked long hours pumping gas and washing trucks at Doc Cleveland's Gulf at the intersection of Alabama 77 and U.S. 11, managed by his uncle Cleo Nelson. The stench on his hands and clothes made Paulette nauseous.

Don used the money from working at the gas station to buy the car that sped through Little Wills Valley each night after the station closed. He installed a glasspack muffler for the hot-rod sound that was the envy of the service station crowd and former Etowah High School classmates. He had created one of the fastest and loudest cars in the valley, and he had three speeding tickets from Alabama state troopers to prove it.

On their way home each night, Don and Paulette headed north on U.S. 11. Past a viaduct was Norris High School, Attalla's all-Black high school. From there, they followed the railroad tracks that hugged the base of Lookout Mountain and on to Reese City, Crudup, and Keener. Most nights, they passed the roadside picnic area in Keener around 8:20 p.m. Less than five minutes later, they arrived at Pleas Anderson's farmhouse near the border of Etowah and DeKalb Counties, where they lived with Paulette's parents and her four sisters, occupying an upstairs apartment.

Paulette was supposed to be finishing her senior year at Collinsville High School, but her marriage to Don a year earlier and the pregnancy caused her to drop out of school before graduation. He was twenty-one, and she was eighteen; they celebrated their first wedding anniversary earlier that month. They had a nightly ritual on the lonely ride home: Where would they pass the Greyhound bus tonight? Most nights, they met the bus at the picnic area in Keener.

Around eight twenty on the night of the murder, the bus out of Collinsville was running late. It was at the top of the hill on the north end of Keener, near Hilltop Grocery, which had closed at around 8:00 p.m. The Whisenants, though, were more concerned about the car that was in the roadside picnic area, parked under the walnut tree. Moments earlier, it had pulled across Highway 11 and eased next to the concrete picnic table, parking just off the warning stripe of the highway.

The car appeared to be a black Buick, chrome trim, and a hubcap missing on the driver's side.

"I saw the taillights as I was coming up," Don said. "When I got there [to the picnic area], I didn't see anyone in the car. Forty or fifty yards later, I saw that man."

It was William Moore, pulling his postal cart and wearing his integration signs over a windbreaker. The Ford's headlights flashed off the chrome of the cart as it rounded the curve, the reflection piercing Don's and Paulette's eyes. Through the glare, the Whisenants managed to see many of Moore's features except for his face. They figured the black car in the picnic area had run out of gas. The man pushing the cart must be hauling a gas can from one of the service stations.

Why, though, did it look as if no one was in the car? The Whisenants had seen the black car pull across the highway, and the taillights had blinked on and off only moments earlier. Paulette speculated a woman was inside and had ducked in the seats until her husband arrived with the gas can.

"[Don] was a good car length in front of [the black car] when we passed him," Paulette said. "All I knew was the taillight went on and off. You could tell they let their foot off the brake. About that time, here [Moore] comes. He's pulling a wagon. He's got some gas. We thought that's what it was. We assumed he's got stuff to put in the vehicle. That was our discussion."

The black car was parked ten to fifteen feet off the highway, by Paulette's estimate. The Greyhound bus, the only other vehicle on the road, was barreling down the hill past Hilltop Grocery and the house next to the store, where Garvin Robinson's daughter, Jo, and three grandsons lived. With the bus approaching, the men in the black car could shoot now or wait for the bus to pass. Paulette was sure the men in the black car had shot William Moore as the bus was near the edge of Keener.

"If I'd turned around or looked in my rearview mirror, I'd have seen it," Paulette said.

Don and Paulette learned of the murder early the next day. Upstairs in their home in Collinsville, with Paulette's sisters off to school and her father off to work at the steel plant in Gadsden, the Whisenants listened to a radio broadcaster describe the murder. They figured they were the last people to see William Moore alive. Don called his father, wondering what he should do. Should he call the police to tell them what he saw?

"No," his father told him. "Don't get involved. Just keep your mouth shut."

Don and Paulette drove to Attalla, where Paulette usually spent the day with Don's mother, Inez, while Don was at work. At his parents' house, his mother informed him the FBI had already been by, ready to question him about what he had seen in Keener. Inez gave the agents Don's new address, and he and Paulette returned to Collinsville.

As they sped north on U.S. 11, Don and Paulette wondered how the agents knew what Don had seen. He had told only one person—his father. Don passed the FBI agents at the Etowah-DeKalb county line, and the agents followed them into the Andersons' driveway. They asked Don to show them the location of the black car in the picnic area and to accompany them to Floyd Simpson's grocery store to determine if his car had been at the murder scene.

"How did y'all know anything about me?" Don asked the agents.

"We have ways of finding out things," one of the agents said.

At the murder scene, Dewey Colvard, the Etowah County sheriff, asked him to park the car where he had seen the black car. He parked it about twelve to fifteen feet off the road, parallel to the highway.

"Well, he almost parked it in the same tracks," an officer said.

With Colvard and McDowell in the front seat, they drove Whisenant to Floyd Simpson's store. He recognized the car immediately because Simpson's car had a missing hubcap, like the car he had seen at the picnic area in Keener.

"There were three of us in the car," Whisenant said. "I was in the back. I was driven by the store in an unmarked car, and it had that marking."

Paulette was sure, too. For years after the murder, she saw the black car parked under those pine trees at Simpson's store when she went to Fort Payne.

"I had dreams about that car," she said.

The Whisenants encountered more unusual twists in the investigation. The state troopers set up a roadblock near the murder scene, searching for motorists who had information about the murder. One of the troopers identified the Whisenants' car quickly when it approached the roadblock.

"He looked at his watch and said, 'You were right on time,'" Don Whisenant said.

It was 8:20 p.m.—the time of the murder. The Whisenants didn't recognize any of the troopers. How did they know their car passed the picnic area at the same time each night?

"That was something I never knew," Paulette said. "I can't think of how they knew it was us coming there at that time by that guy. I mean, we were two people just going up the road, and our conversation was interrupted by the taillight incident and this man pulling the cart."

Later, Paulette heard Don and his father discuss the murder. They spoke in whispers because they didn't want to upset Paulette while she was pregnant, believing she was too fragile to hear such upsetting news. She listened anyway. The conversation was indeed shocking: Don and his father mentioned the families of Paulette's classmates at Collinsville High School. They believed those families had relatives who were involved in the murder. Two names stood out to her—Killian and Burt.

One of Paulette Whisenant's former classmates, Sara Killian, was among the most popular seniors in the Collinsville Class of 1963. She was the daughter of Gene Killian, one of the painters in Margaret Osborn's neighborhood when she dashed out of the bathtub to chase her son. Gene Killian was one of Gaddis Killian's older brothers, and he lived across the highway from Floyd Simpson's store. He was among the five men at the store on the morning that William Moore passed through Collbran.

Paulette also knew Agnes Killian Jacoway, the owner of Killian Wholesale Grocery in downtown Collinsville, the oldest and largest wholesale grocery in North Alabama. Killian Wholesale Grocery and the Oliver Hall Company ("The Largest Business of Its Kind in Alabama," read the sign on the side of the store) were the signature businesses in Collinsville, both at the end of Main Street, next to the railroad tracks.

The other name that Paulette recognized, Burt, was among the most prominent families in southern DeKalb County. Jerry Burt, another of Paulette Whisenant's classmates, was a member of the Collinsville High School football team. She knew him as "Ratchford," his longtime nickname.

"All the people I knew who were kin to that bunch were really good people—Sara Killian, Mrs. Agnes Killian," Paulette said. "They were nice, but they had some mean sons. I remember the store in Collbran. Those guys up there used to play checkers. I had no idea they'd kill people. They were good ol' people, sitting around like Mayberry. That's what Collbran reminded me of."

In early June, Paulette delivered her baby girl, Teri Lynn. Three months later, on the morning of September 9, Don Whisenant went to the Etowah County courthouse in Gadsden to testify at the grand jury hearing for Floyd Simpson. Arriving at the courthouse, he saw some men gathered near the entrance. He recognized them from his trips to Collinsville and through Little Wills Valley. One of them was Gaddis Killian.

"I was nervous," Don said. "I was around their family, waiting to go in, so I was uncomfortable. The Killian guy was there—Gad Killian. All the Killians. They were all there."

The Klan also sent messages to Virgil Pittman, the judge who had charged the grand jury that morning. Crosses were lit in his front yard and racial epithets were burned into his lawn. I told Pittman how nervous Don Whisenant had been when he had seen the Klan before his grand jury appearance.

"Well, I can understand why," he said.

Whisenant's appearance before the grand jury was brief.

"All I remember is asking me what I'd seen," he said. "[They asked] if I could positively identify the car belonging to Mr. Simpson."

After the grand jury hearing, Don Whisenant came home with a bottle warmer for Teri Lynn—a gift from an FBI official in Gadsden, as the Whisenants recalled. The bottle warmer was the agent's way of showing his appreciation for Don missing work to testify. Soon, there were other favors. Don began working for Agnes Killian Jacoway at Killian's Wholesale Grocery. His father and an uncle, Melvin, were employed there, too. There was no discussion of the murder.

Don did some investigating of his own about what he saw that night in Keener. An uncle, Bill Cook, had owned the barbershop in Collinsville since 1946, and his uncles and the regulars heard the tale of the murder. The Buick's taillights had blinked on and off because the men in the front seat had ducked toward the floorboard so that the Whisenants couldn't see them. The first shot had come from inside the car, and the second one was likely out of the car. Don Whisenant also believed the investigation and the grand jury trials were a hoax. After the grand jury hearing, he never heard from another state or local investigator.

"You wonder if people in high places wanted it solved," he said. "At the time it happened, it wasn't out of the question that that stuff would be covered up."

CHAPTER 20

The Etowah County courthouse seemed like a logical place to find out if a cover-up was still intact. Johnny Grant, then the chief investigator for the sheriff's department, knew plenty about the case. He had been hired by Felton Yates, among the first county investigators at the murder scene. Through the years, he heard some of the veteran deputies discuss the case, but none of them attempted to revive the investigation. As the fortieth anniversary of the murder neared and cold civil rights cases were opened and prosecuted, Grant pursued an investigation, thinking he might have the same success as the investigators in the Birmingham church bombing case.

"I tried to find the gun," he said. "It went from here to the state lab to the FBI lab. Nobody knows where the gun is at."

He couldn't find the case file either.

"We don't have a file," he said. "If we had a file, it's gone now. What I've learned, I got out [of] the newspaper. I pulled the newspapers at the time and looked at those."

He also contacted Cecil Reed, the DeKalb County sheriff, and discovered that Floyd Simpson, the chief suspect, was dead. His search was over.

"It got to be real interesting, who the man was and what happened," he said. "I think if it happened now, with the ballistics on the rifle and the whole advancement of forensics, I think we'd have stood a better chance of solving it."

But there was a file. It was in the Etowah County courthouse, in the office of District Attorney Jimmy Hedgepeth. Hedgepeth, though, refused to let me see it because he still considered it an open case.

"I don't let anyone look at my files," he said.

He suggested I go see former District Attorney Bill Rayburn, and he gave me instructions to the Rayburns' house across town. Rayburn was in his mid-seventies, retired after six terms as district attorney. Rayburn had returned from his morning walk when I met him in his front yard.

"The FBI sent an agent down here named Zimmers," he said. "He said it wasn't the weapon. It was one similar. That was his testimony. The other thing, [Moore] had a cart he was pulling.

"There were religious connotations [on the cart]. Some thought [the murder] was religious rather than racial. It's been so long."

It had been a long time, but it was not so long that he was unable to recall how local authorities tarnished Moore's character. I asked him if his case was weak.

"Well, the evidence we had was up to the grand jury," he said. "We presented it all. The FBI agent testified before the grand jury. The evidence was up to the grand jury. I always think that we tried our best to make a good case. We did then."

Most of his memories were about McDowell, Floyd Simpson, and Bill Beck. He remembered McDowell had monitored William Moore's walk through Etowah County and that McDowell was having a cup of coffee when he received the call about Moore's death. His main memories, though, were of Beck. He remembered Beck entering the courthouse the day after Simpson's arrest, his voice echoing through the jail. From the top floor of the courthouse, Rayburn heard Beck's voice booming through the dayroom, where Rayburn and W. R. Jones of the Alabama Department of Public Safety questioned Simpson.

"He was in the sheriff's office on the first floor, having a fit, demanding to see his client," Rayburn said. "When we went up there to question [Simpson], he was washing his hands—said he wanted to see his lawyer. [Jones] was seeking a confession. I realized [Simpson] was nervous."

Forty years later, Rayburn seemed nervous, too. Clearly, he was ready for me to leave—never inviting me into his house or asking me to sit on the front porch. Still standing in his front yard, he told me about his grandfather's ties to Beck. They had been friends through their professional and fraternal connections. They were Masons, lawyers, and politicians.

It was the most important case in his twenty-four years as district attorney, and he had been unable to receive an indictment. For the remainder of his career, he never tried to resurrect the case.

"Why didn't you pursue another investigation?" I asked.

"Because I never heard any more about it," he said.

He suggested I go back to Hedgepeth's office or head to Roy McDowell's home in Southside. He was through talking.

"Mr. McDowell needs to look at the file," he said.

I did as I was told and drove to Roy McDowell's house in Southside. His life had changed considerably since our first meeting. Mildred, his wife of more than sixty years, was ill, and some nurses were caring for her inside their home. I found McDowell outside, wandering behind his house. I told him Bill Rayburn had sent me with instructions to look at the case file. He told me again that he didn't have it.

He and Rayburn had been close in the final years of their law enforcement careers. Rayburn hired him in 1979, a week after McDowell resigned following a demotion at the sheriff's department.

Again, McDowell told me that Simpson's rifle was the murder weapon.

"I remember [the FBI] saying that was the gun that shot those bullets," McDowell said. "I remember when we found the gun. It was in the store, over the fireplace. He [Simpson] was in the store. I imagine he was shook up when he saw us. I never knew him prior to this. He appeared to be a quiet guy."

McDowell suggested I talk to Shaun Malone, who had written a tribute to Moore in April 1988, the twenty-fifth anniversary of the murder. Malone, then a student at the University of Alabama and a recent graduate of a local high school, had interviewed McDowell for his op-ed column in the *Gadsden Times*.

Before heading back inside, McDowell had a final message: The investigation was handled properly.

"Oh, yeah, we got the right guy," he said. "I thought, 'Well, we've done run the ballistics with the FBI.' I figured when they ran the ballistics, it was his gun. He had to have something to do with it."

❖

Shaun Malone had practiced law in Gadsden for eight years. In his early thirties, he was already part of city politics, serving as a substitute municipal judge, positioning himself for the circuit judge appointment that he would receive the following spring. His office was downtown, near the Coosa River, and I found him before he headed to a lunch appointment.

He had been fascinated for years with the William Moore case because his family was from Keener, where his great-grandfather had operated a general merchandise store. On the twenty-fifth anniversary of the murder, Malone, then a prelaw student, conducted his own search to solve the murder.

"The significance of his death goes far beyond a senseless murder on the highway," he wrote.

"Moore's killing represented the first death of a civil-rights activist in the movement for social equality. Those two shots that cut down his stand against segregation magnified the problem that was at hand throughout the country. Moore was a peaceful man who considered himself a Southerner and was white. Yet throughout the irrational minds of many Americans he was considered a threat, a threat to the demise and abolishment of a segregated South."

The column was headlined, "The Forgotten Civil Rights Hero."

"What I was trying to do then was to get a marker put up, a state historical marker," Malone said. "It went nowhere."

Through the years, he had heard tales about the murder from relatives in Keener and others, satisfying much of his curiosity.

"It was a Klan killing," he said. "It was understood that that's what it was."

He pieced together the clues and made the same conclusion that many in Etowah County had: Floyd Simpson was the murderer.

"From what I heard," he said, "they had the guy [and] they didn't do anything about it."

With that, his search ended. My discussions with Bill Rayburn and Jimmy Hedgepeth, though, told me that Don Whisenant's instincts about the case were right.

People in high places didn't want the case to be solved, and little had changed since 1963.

I planned to stay in the area until at least 8:20 p.m., the time of the murder. I wondered, too, if some former activists or others might be at the murder site to observe the anniversary.

With almost eight hours to kill, I drove to an area of the county known as Wharton's Bend, where George Geer, the only sheriff's investigator still alive, had a home in a heavily wooded subdivision near the Coosa River. A thunderstorm had passed through the area the night before, and tree limbs had fallen in Wharton's Bend. George Geer was in his yard, gathering debris, as I approached his home.

His strongest memories were of arresting Simpson on April 25, two days after the murder. The black car and Simpson's rifle were the most important parts of the investigation, as he recalled.

I remember it was before we got into Fort Payne," Geer said. "Felton drove. [Simpson] didn't say anything that I recall. When we get up there to get him, the .22 [rifle] was there, and the black Buick was there."

He and Yates were sure they had the right man. Geer said the black car was the most important clue. From the start, investigators knew the murder weapon was a .22 rifle because of the shells found at the murder scene. Finding the black car was more difficult, even though they were sure that the murderer had been in an old Buick. Don and Paulette Whisenant had provided the information when the FBI had found them on the morning after the murder.

"We put out a search for a black Buick, which that guy had," Geer said. "That led us to Mr. Simpson."

George Geer was different from the other investigators and officers. He was unemotional about the case, discussing the murder as if it had the importance of a speeding ticket.

"I don't know of anybody in Etowah County who gave it much thought," he said. "We had no problems here. I didn't have no feelings either way, same as now. It was his right [to walk]. You'd see people out hitchhiking. But as far as giving any thought to racism, that wasn't discussed."

He was so unemotional, almost aloof, that I asked him if he thought the county should have prosecuted the murderer.

"When somebody kills somebody, somebody should pay," he said.

He didn't sound convincing.

❖

Bill Beck's old law office was across from the DeKalb County courthouse. His sons, Danny and William Morris Jr., known as "Moose," became lawyers, too, and they joined their father's law firm, Beck and Beck. Later, Moose Beck entered the banking business, leaving Danny as the only heir to Bill Beck's law practice. The office was undergoing renovations when I went to Fort Payne on the afternoon of April 23, so Danny Beck moved temporarily to a small building in downtown Fort Payne, across from the store where the Klan met on Saturday afternoons in the early 1960s.

Danny Beck was eating a late lunch when he invited me into his office to give me his father's version of the murder. He started with the murder weapon.

"[It] was a semiautomatic, real lightweight," he said. "You'd load it from the stock and held fifteen rounds."

More important for Bill Beck, the Remington .22 rifle with a nylon stock had one feature that assured Floyd Simpson's acquittal: It was impossible to determine if it had fired a bullet.

"That was the one rifle you could not prove ballistics on at that time," Danny Beck said. "That's all I knew. There was a prominent forensics expert in Montgomery with the AB [Alabama Bureau of Investigation]. He did the analysis on it and compared rounds and whatnot with another one—the same type of rifle. He could not prove the ballistics. That was an unusual weapon for that time."

Danny Beck was seventeen in the spring of 1963, a junior at Fort Payne High School, where he was a classmate of Floyd Simpson's and Gaddis Killian's children. He told me he wasn't interested in politics or social issues at the time. All he cared about then, he said, was playing football for the Fort Payne Wildcats and what his mother, Vera, cooked for supper. But one aspect of politics intrigued him: his father's relationship with George Wallace, a friendship so close Bill Beck could walk into the governor's office and introduce his youngest son to the most powerful man in Alabama.

"I had on green tennis shoes the day I met him," he said. "Years later at Marion, they were having Governor's Day, and Governor Wallace came. There was a reception line, and I was going to introduce myself. He said, 'Why, hello, Danny. Where are your green shoes, boy?' All these officials were waiting for him at Marion, and he passed the time for me."

Bill Beck had been dead for thirteen years, but his story was still the pride of the Beck family. Danny Beck was quick to recite his father's credentials: raised on a farm in northeast Alabama, dropped out of school in the fourth grade to help with the family farm, entered the army at sixteen but withdrew because he enlisted without his parents' permission. He played baseball at Newberry College in South Carolina and football at Jacksonville State College in Alabama. After marrying, he began receiving nightly law lessons from his father-in-law, John Isbell, the U.S. attorney for the Northern District of Alabama who had founded the law firm. He passed the bar exam easily—the highest grade in his group, according to Danny Beck.

But Danny Beck lacked his father's gift of wit and aggression. He was slow to respond when I asked him how his father had known Floyd Simpson for so long.

"Maybe he played football for him at Collinsville," he said.

But that was impossible. Floyd Simpson was no football player, and he had never attended Collinsville High School—certainly not in the 1920s and early '30s, when Bill Beck was still coaching. Floyd Simpson, born in 1922, was in elementary school when Bill Beck stopped teaching and coaching and joined his father-in-law's law practice in 1932.

Finally, I asked Danny Beck if I could see the case file. He refused.

"I am honoring my father's wishes," he said. "That's the client's file. That's the client's case. He never felt like he should allow the file to be shown. That's their business, no one else's."

I reminded him of the story that Jim McGee and David Stout had told me: Bill Beck had allowed them to see the file because of their fascination with the murder. But he was firm. I could not see the file out of respect for Floyd Simpson's privacy. He was adamant, too, that Simpson was innocent.

"That case was won on briefs," he said. "If I remember, there was no trial. After the forensic evidence came forward, there was no case—no evidence whatsoever to link the defendant to the crime."

❖

I returned to Keener just before 7:00 p.m., about the time William Moore arrived at Hilltop Grocery on the night of the murder. There was no indication that anyone had planned a formal observance of the murder. Instead, an old hound dog ran across the highway toward the former site of E. D. Amos General Merchandise. By 7:00 p.m., dusk had fallen. It was a Wednesday night—church night in the Deep South—and some cars were parked at the Keener Baptist Church, the only sign of activity in town. Three people were inside. One of them, a woman named Joanne, remembered the murder.

"We couldn't believe it happened either," she said. "Nothing like that had ever happened in our part of the country. I think his [Moore's] heart was right."

Another woman wanted to know if Moore was Black or white. White, said Joanne.

"Did they hang him?" a man asked.

"No, they shot him," Joanne said. "Harry [Sizemore] had them move the picnic tables after that."

Then the old sensitivities returned.

"Why bring up old wounds?" Joanne asked.

I told her of my interest in the case and the historical significance of the murder. Neither warranted any attempts to resurrect a forty-year-old murder, even if it was unsolved, as far as she was concerned.

Out on the highway, a family played baseball in their yard. By 8:00 p.m., it was dark, except for the lights at Harry Sizemore's house and a patch of blue over the ridge of Sand Mountain. I waited at the murder scene until 8:20 p.m., and then the last moments of William Moore's life became obvious to me: He had no idea what awaited him as he rounded the curve and approached the picnic area. He saw nothing except darkness.

A black walnut tree. A black car. The black of night.

That was all.

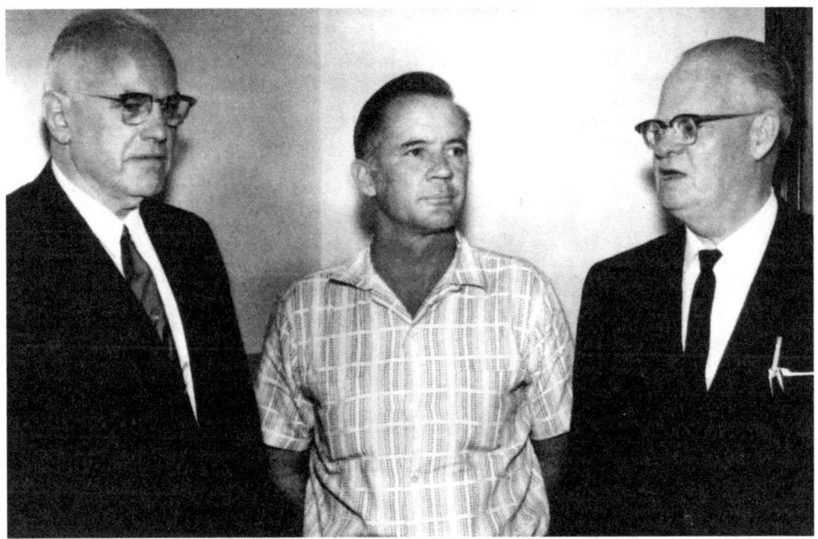

Floyd Simpson (center) is flanked by his two high-powered attorneys, William M. Beck of Fort Payne and Roy D. McCord of Gadsden, after his release on bond on April 29, 1963.

Albert J. Lingo (hand raised), the head of the Alabama State Troopers, came to Gadsden often during the city's racial demonstrations in the summer of 1963. Lingo and his troopers created such tension that one federal official, a former military officer, said later that conditions in Gadsden reminded him of the battles at the Punchbowl, site of pivotal conflicts during the Korean War.

The Hilltop Café and Service Station was a Keener landmark after it opened in 1937. William Moore ate his last meal—a can of corn and a pecan pie—at Hilltop. A state of Alabama investigator believed Moore's killer was at Hilltop as the investigator interviewed Moore less than one hour before his death.

Roy D. McCord, shown here at a Democratic National Convention, holds his hand over his heart in a show of loyalty to the Democratic Party. Like virtually all of the principal players in the William Moore investigation, McCord was known for his devotion to the Democratic Party.

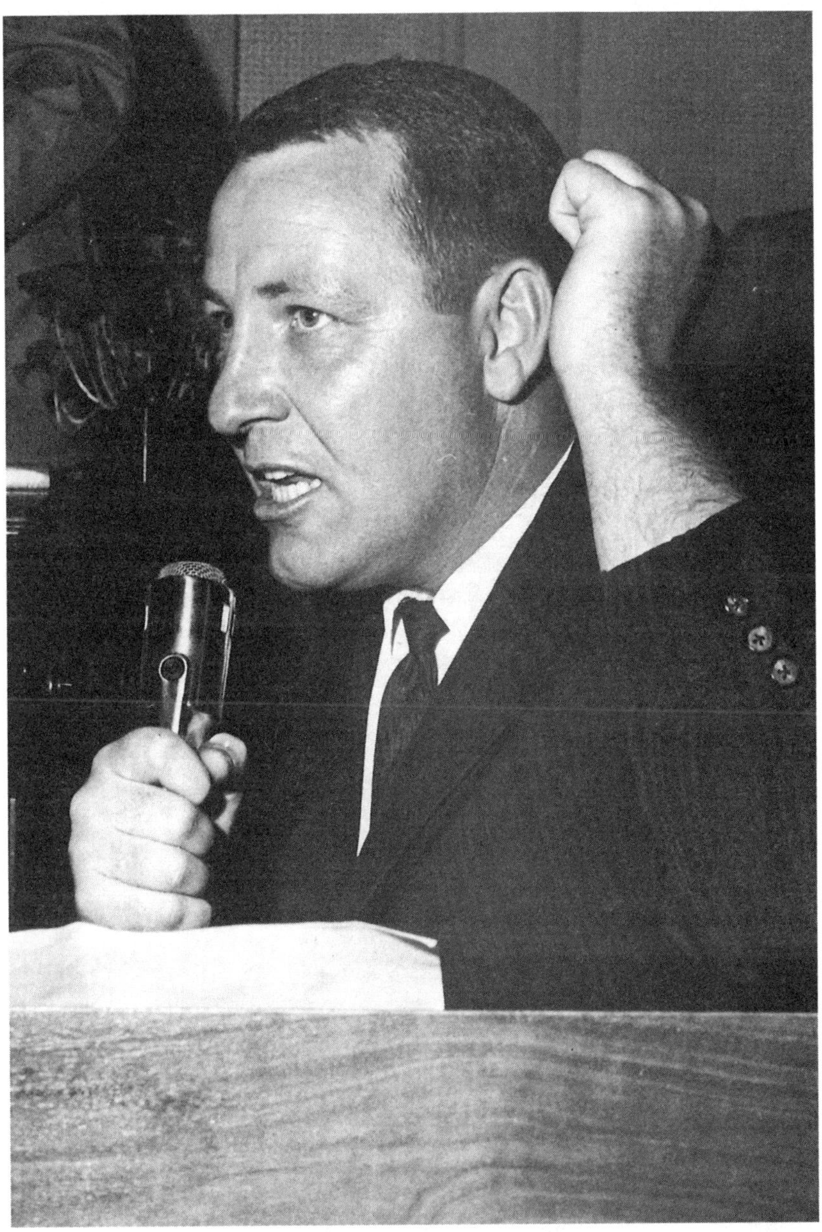

Alabama Senator Kenneth Hammond of Valley Head gives a fiery speech on the floor of the Alabama senate during his first term, from 1963 to 1967. Hammond was Governor George Wallace's chief antagonist, earning him the enmity of the Ku Klux Klan.

William M. Beck, shown here in the mid-1960s, became the interim president of Judson College in Marion, Alabama. The appointment was another sign of his growing political influence during George Wallace's first term as Alabama governor.

Hubert Jackson Jr., alias Jerry Hunt, threw firebombs at the Temple Beth Israel in downtown Gadsden on March 25, 1960. Jackson, sixteen, also shot two Beth Israel members in the most violent attack on a Jewish temple in American history until a 2018 shooting at a synagogue in Pittsburgh.

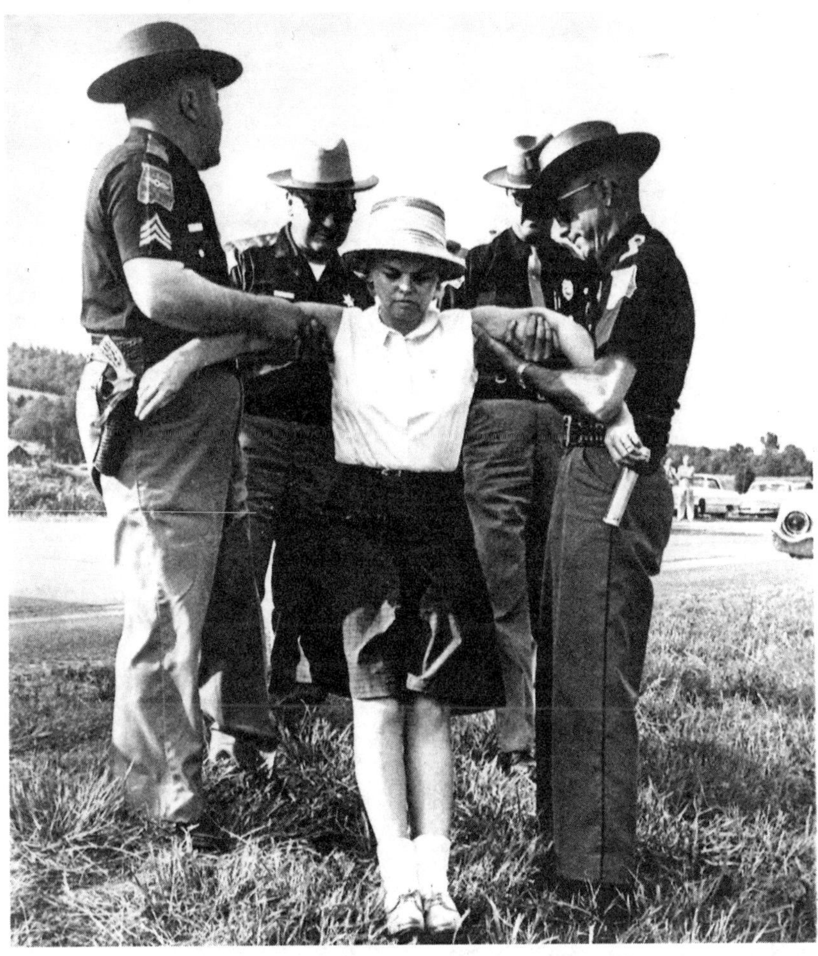

Two Alabama highway patrolmen carry Madeleine Sherwood to a patrol car after officers broke up a memorial service in Keener for William Moore. Miss Sherwood, a Broadway actress, was part of an integrated group holding the service along U.S. Highway 11, where Moore was killed.

William Moore announced his presence to many in Fort Payne when he ate breakfast at Lefty Cooper's restaurant on Gault Avenue on the morning of April 23, 1963.

Alabama Governor George Wallace appears on NBC-TV's *Meet the Press* on June 2, 1963, as Alabama prepares for Wallace's "Stand in the Schoolhouse Door" at the University of Alabama and Gadsden braces for the long summer of demonstrations. As another sign of the nation's growing anger over race, Wallace's television appearance was moved from Washington, D.C., to New York City, where he received full police security, the same protection given to President John F. Kennedy and Cuban Premier Fidel Castro, and Russia's Nikita Khrushchev, the first secretary of the Communist Party of the Soviet Union.

A 1964 aerial photo taken near the intersection of Alabama Highway 35 and the construction of Interstate 59 shows the seclusion of the route William Moore took through southern DeKalb County. At the top of the photo, U.S. Highway 11 stretches through Collbran and Portersville and the edge of Collinsville.

Bill Beck, shown here during his political resurgence in the mid-1960s, became the chairman of the board of trustees at Judson College, a private woman's college in Marion, Alabama. Here, he represented Judson at a presentation that honored Judson's outstanding alumnae.

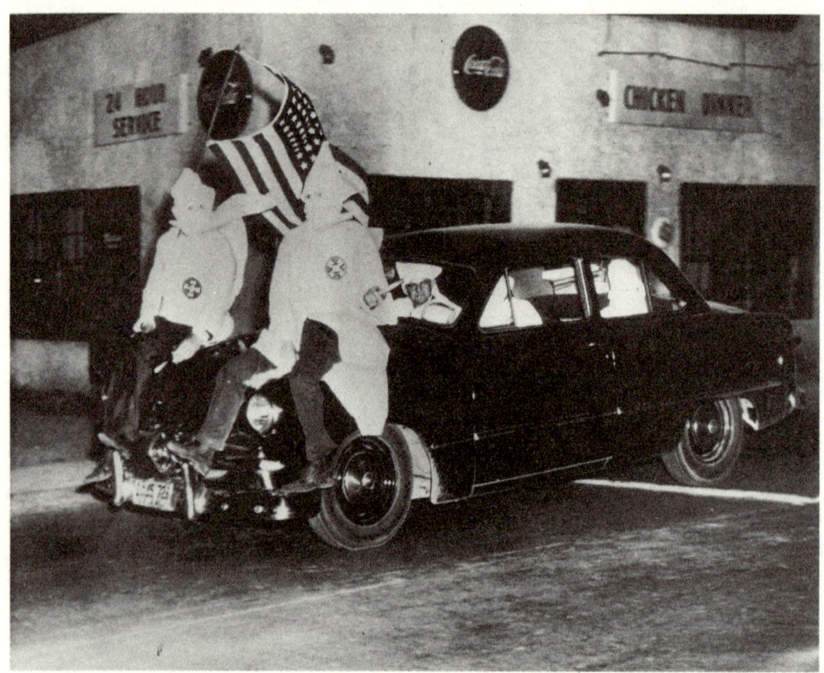

A group of Ku Klux Klansmen parade through downtown Gadsden on the night of March 5, 1949. Klan parades through downtown were considered an almost-regular Saturday night occurrence in the late 1940s and 1950s. This one was considered noteworthy. A longtime Gadsden resident told the author that the man in the Klan robe in the passenger seat, his mask removed, was Gadsden Police Chief Fay Boman. The *Gadsden Times* published the photo in its Sunday editions, noting in the caption that the man in the passenger seat was familiar with the city. Later, a city resident who was a candidate for the state legislature said in a letter to the *Times* that he was "firmly convinced that one of the individuals [in the photo] is employed by the police department."

Integration leaders march toward the Gadsden city hall on June 16, 1963. An estimated 250 protesters participated in the march, which began at a downtown meeting hall. The weekend protests caused Etowah County Sheriff Dewey Colvard to ask Alabama officials in Montgomery to send state troopers to the area. (Alabama Department of Archives and History, donated by Alabama Media Group. Photo by Anthony Falletta, *Birmingham News*.)

Dr. Martin Luther King Jr. speaks at the Galilee Baptist Church in Gadsden on the night of June 21, 1963, while more than forty Alabama troopers patrolled the area. Responding to reports that police used cattle prods on fifty demonstrators earlier that day, King said, "They can get all the cattle sticks to prod us they want, but we are not cattle. We are American citizens and our rights must be protected." (Alabama Department of Archives and History, donated by Alabama Media Group. Photo by Ed Jones, *Birmingham News*.)

A Ku Klux Klan sympathizer holds a sign in support of Gadsden police on March 11, 1978, when Klansmen and Black leaders held demonstrations in downtown Gadsden on the same day. The shooting death of Collis Madden, twenty-seven, by Gadsden police and sheriff deputies sparked the protests. Madden was unarmed when he was killed after a high-speed chase. An Etowah County grand jury returned no indictments after a special session was called. (Alabama Department of Archives and History, donated by Alabama Media Group.)

A view of Little Wills Valley and the Collbran community, the heart of the area that Time magazine described as “no place for pilgrims” in its May 10, 1963, issue. (Special / Robin Conn.)

Author Mike Marshall stands at the former roadside park in Keener, where William Moore was murdered on the night of April 23, 1963. (Special / Robin Conn.)

Author Mike Marshall stands next to the state historical marker near the site where William Moore was murdered. The marker, dedicated in the spring of 2019, was the area's first formal recognition of the murder. (Special / Robin Conn.)

The Etowah County Commission donated $3,000 to cover the cost of this memorial marker, which was dedicated on the afternoon of April 13, 2019, almost fifty-six years after the murder of William Moore. (Special / Robin Conn.)

Floyd Simpson's store still stands on U.S. Highway 11 in Collbran. It remains next door to the house where Gaddis Killian, the longtime owner, lived until his death in 2008. Gaddis Killian and his wife, Lorene, operated an antique business in the store's final years in business. (Special / Robin Conn.)

PART IV
UNDERSTANDING

CHAPTER 21

Charlie Hicks was now back in the radio business in the foothills of the Great Smoky Mountains, where he began his career as a late-night disc jockey. He had covered a plane crash and civil rights demonstrations after leaving Gadsden, but he considered the murder of William Moore to be the most important news event of his career.

He could still envision his first trip to Keener. He imagined the fields where he interviewed William Moore about one hour before the murder and the picnic area where he saw the black car waiting under the black walnut tree on his way out of town, and he remembered his wife, Gail, assuring him that Roy McDowell wouldn't let the man in the front seat harm William Moore. He considered himself perhaps Moore's last chance to save himself on the night of April 23, 1963, with his pleas to let him take him to D & J Truck Stop Cabins. After only a few months in Gadsden, he already knew it was no place for a white civil rights sympathizer like William Moore. Neither was Keener, an isolated farming community tucked between the mountains.

"It was desolate," he said. "There were some houses and a store building, but they were scattered where he was walking. When I saw him, he was at the loneliest stretch of road—woods on one side. There was a field—or a meadow—where I was talking to him. We talked on the side of the road."

He was twenty-four at the time, a native of Robbinsville, North Carolina, a small, all-white town near the Tennessee border. After marrying in 1958, he and his wife, Gail, moved to Sevierville, Tennessee, where he worked for a radio station that invited Dolly Parton, a then-unknown singer, to perform in the studio. In 1962, he and Gail moved to Gadsden, along with their infant son, Charles Jr. The Hickses saw racism in Gadsden that they had never observed in Tennessee—the "white" and "colored" water fountains and Ku Klux Klan rallies in Little Wills Valley, among other things.

Most days, Charlie Hicks was the midmorning disc jockey at WGAD-AM, known on the air as "Charlie B." On April 23, 1963, however, he was also the station's substitute news reporter, a duty that fell to him because the station's news director was called to National Guard duty. Around 6:00 p.m., he received a phone call at his home in Alabama City from the radio station. An anonymous caller had given the station a tip about a man walking on Highway 11. He was walking south, the caller said, and the station needed to send someone to Keener to interview him.

"I told them I'd take a look," Charlie Hicks said. "I went on up the road, and I saw him walking."

Moore's cart and poster were the first things Hicks noticed.

"Where are you going?" he asked Moore.

"To Mississippi to see Ross Barnett in regard to segregation," Moore replied.

Hicks was no civil rights sympathizer, but he knew when a man was an obvious target for murder.

"This is not your cause," Hicks told Moore. "This is a Black and white issue and you're white. Why are you doing this?"

Hicks opposed Northerners who came to the Deep South in support of civil rights, but he was concerned for Moore's safety as the sun dipped behind the ridge of Sand Mountain. With his wife and infant son sitting in his Ford Falcon, he stood in the fields near Hilltop Grocery for twenty minutes, almost pleading with Moore to end his walk. Moore responded with his usual stubbornness.

"I'm going to walk right up to the governor's mansion in Mississippi and ring the doorbell," Moore said as he began his interview with Hicks. "Then I'll hand him my letter."

But Charlie Hicks, even after only a few months in northeast Alabama, had deciphered the area's tolerance for civil rights sympathizers: Moore had little chance of making it through Etowah County, much less through Alabama and Mississippi.

"This is a lonely stretch of highway, and you're in the state of Alabama," Hicks told him. "I'm sure you're aware of how people feel about this."

Hicks informed him of Gadsden's reputation: This is a dangerous town, he told him.

"I understand," Moore replied. "But this is something I have to do."

"Why do you have to do it?"

"It's something I feel I have to do."

"Don't you feel you need to do it in the daylight? There aren't a lot of houses or cars out here at night."

In the twilight, Moore appeared composed after a long day of walking despite the disturbances farther north on Highway 11. Only Moore's feet, bloodied and blistered, were damaged. His shoes were off, and bandages covered his feet.

"There's a motel down the road," Hicks told him. "Why don't I take you to the nearest motel? It's dangerous for you to be doing what you're doing at this time of night."

"No," Moore said. "If I did that, I'll have to come back to this spot and start from here."

"I don't understand."

"I've got to walk it all."

At 7:30 p.m., McDowell pulled into the store parking lot as the conversation was ending. Climbing out of his car, he instructed Moore to sit in the passenger seat while he talked to Hicks.

"What do you think?" McDowell asked Hicks.

"I think it's dangerous," Hicks said. "I got a call to come up here, and I came to interview him about what he was doing. I volunteered to take him to a motel to get him off the road and start [walking] the next day."

"That makes sense to me," McDowell said. "I'm going to see if I can get him to a motel."

Believing Moore was safe, Charlie Hicks drove his family back to Alabama City. He was about a mile down the road when his headlights flashed onto a black car parked in the roadside picnic area. Through the darkness, the headlights gave him a glimpse of two men sitting in the front seat.

Turning to his wife, Charlie Hicks said, "I hope they're not waiting on [Moore]."

But they knew what the men in the black car had planned.

"I'm sure the highway patrol will take care of him," his wife said.

After nine, someone from the radio station called again to inform Hicks of the murder. He drove to the murder scene, then to the radio station, where he stayed for the rest of the night and into the early morning hours of April 24. When the morning was over, he had spoken to more than one hundred newspapers and radio and television stations.

Soon, he grasped the enormity of what he'd experienced: He had been among the last people to talk to William Moore, and he had also seen the killers as they waited in the black Buick. He was part of the biggest story in Alabama and perhaps the biggest in the country. Now he was worried about his family's safety.

On the morning of September 8, he testified before the grand jury. Bill Rayburn asked him some questions—three or four questions, by his estimate—and then some grand jury members had more questions. None were about the murder or the investigation. He answered questions for about twenty minutes, and he left the courthouse. Driving home, he realized no one on the grand jury was interested in the truth about the murder. He knew the outcome four days before the grand jury announced its decision.

"They were more interested in what he said and why he was doing it," Hicks said. "I had a family. I didn't want to jeopardize my family. In that day, people did things."

The Hickses stayed in Gadsden for two more years. There was occasional talk of the murder until they moved to North Carolina, but no one seemed upset that the murderer had not been prosecuted. Most of Charlie Hicks's friends and acquaintances believed as Bill Beck did: Gadsden had suffered needlessly, the victim of the Northern newspapers.

"It was all blown up," as he put it.

When Chuck Hicks was old enough to understand, he listened to his father's tales about the murder and the demonstrations in Gadsden that summer. Hicks Senior told Hicks Junior about the officers using cattle prods, and the policeman who handed him a gun during the protests.

"What I heard was they were able to trace the bullets to a gun," Chuck

Hicks said. "They knew who owned it. It's always given me chills to know I was inadvertently in the middle of it all."

Family members noticed a change in Charlie after the incident. They believed he became more tolerant, finally grasping the meaning of William Moore and his walk to Mississippi. His son referred to it as Charlie's "fifteen minutes of fame, and that was it." But it was more than that. It was also the moment that Charlie Hicks understood the outcome of the civil rights movement: If white men were willing to die for the cause, then Black people would receive their rights one day.

"The big thing in that incident was, it was a white guy," Charlie said. "I've often thought about it. I don't think they would have killed him if he was Black. But a white man, it was a more serious situation. I think what it was saying was that it was a betrayal of white people. It must have been that he was prepared to die, but it was hard for me to comprehend at the time. Now, I can understand it. I could have understood if [he] was Black. But the fact that he was white, I couldn't understand it. I wouldn't have done it."

There was no such introspection among those who had been at the store. Bill and Louise Robinson had been away from Keener since Garvin committed suicide in the county jail in 1965 and Conola sold the store. Bill and Louise returned to Sand Mountain, divorced, and settled in communities about the size of Keener. They had married when Bill was seventeen and Louise was an aspiring beautician. She ran the beauty shop at the back of the store, and Bill helped his parents run the store. They lived on the top floor, across from Garvin and Conola. All of them were home on the night of April 23, when William Moore entered the store at around 7:00 p.m.

Garvin Robinson was at the front counter. He was known for his fondness of liquor and his quick and vulgar comments, usually about his female customers. Conola was usually at the back of the store, sitting in an easy chair and dipping snuff. The store had concrete floors and stone walls, stocked with groceries from a wholesaler in Gadsden. William Moore wandered through the aisles, looking for supper. After picking up a can of corn, a pecan pie, and a copy of the *Gadsden Times*, he handed $0.30 to Garvin Robinson, leaving him with $50.15—the equivalent of $272 today.

At the back of the store, Conola Robinson told her son, "He's a tramp."

"That was the talk for weeks," Bill Robinson said. "Mom talked about that tramp that came through. That's what everyone was saying."

For weeks, they also spoke about his conversation with some of Hilltop's regular patrons. Sitting on the bench in front of the store, eating his can of corn and pecan pie, William Moore spoke of how Blacks in America were still enslaved one hundred years after the signing of the Emancipation Proclamation. There was speculation that the conversation had turned into a confrontation, just as it had at Collbran.

"I guess they got a kick out of the story that he was telling," Bill Robinson said. "He was talking about a lot of things. He was talking about where he had been—all the miles he had been. I knew he was dirty. And he had long hair."

Louise remembered her ex-husband being so curious about the murder that she and Bill drove north on U.S. 11 the day after the murder. They stopped at the store in Collbran, where Bill questioned the occupants of Floyd Simpson's store as she sat in the parking lot. Bill did not remember driving to the store the day after the murder, but his memory of the black car speeding through Keener remained strong.

"I was upstairs," he said. "There was a black car that was coming down the highway at a high rate of speed. I didn't see it, but I heard it. That was the shooter. But we didn't know what was going on at the time. That [car] was the talk for a long time. Not many things happened in Keener."

Bill Robinson, though, had no sympathy for William Moore. He was a troublemaker from the North, in his view, seeking confrontation and attention.

"He did ask for it, yes," he said. "He appeared to be pretty mean. That was the impression. Nobody had had any experience like that. Wow, it was scary."

It was more frightening for Willis Elrod and his family, the first to discover William Moore's body. Elrod, then a twenty-four-year-old salesman for Gulf Oil in Birmingham, and his young family were driving home in his 1956 Pontiac after visiting relatives in Gaylesville, near the Alabama-Georgia line. Just after 8:30 p.m., the Elrods—Willis, his wife, Martha, and infant daughter, Sherri—left Collinsville and headed south on U.S. 11. For the next few miles, until they reached Keener, they met only two or three cars, none of them driving at a high rate of speed. Passing the roadside park in Keener, Elrod caught a glimpse of what appeared to be a body lying on the side of the highway. As his headlights flashed onto the body, Elrod turned to his wife and said, "Look over there." About a quarter mile past the picnic area, he veered to his left and, with no traffic approaching, made a U-turn.

Entering the picnic area, he pulled his car by the table, easing past Moore's body and back onto the highway. He saw blood coming out of Moore's left temple, his feet tangled on the cart.

"The first thing I saw was the two-wheeled cart, then the body," Elrod recalled years later. "The cart was behind the body. My first thought was, 'Yeah, he has been hit by a car.' When I saw the blood on his head, I thought it was from a hit-and-run. I pulled by the roadside table and around his body, then went back onto the road and over to Mr. Sizemore's."

Across the highway, Harry Sizemore was watching the end of the *Red Skelton Show* with his wife, Betty, and his six-year-old daughter, Cindy.

"Call the sheriff," Elrod told Harry Sizemore.

Standing on the front porch as Sizemore phoned the sheriff's department, Elrod watched a Greyhound bus swerve to miss Moore's body in the road. Sizemore grabbed a flashlight, and he and Elrod went across the yard and onto the highway. Shining his flashlight on the left side of Moore's face, Sizemore exclaimed, "My God, this man's been shot!"

For a moment, they wondered if the killer was still in the area, perhaps hiding along the embankment beside the railroad tracks. The killer, though, was long gone. William Moore had been dead for about forty minutes. Word of the murder passed through Keener after Sizemore's call to the sheriff's office; the town's party line telephone system spread the news. A crowd began to gather under the walnut tree, many of them members of Garvin Robinson's family and regulars at his store.

Robinson gathered his grandsons and drove them a mile down U.S. 11 in his Studebaker pickup truck. Tommy Baird, one of Garvin's grandsons, was twelve years old, confused by what he witnessed at the murder scene. A dead man was on the side of the highway, a white man killed for sympathizing with Blacks.

"It was a weird feeling for a kid, not fully understanding," he recalled. "I was too young. We didn't have any Blacks close by. I think [he was killed] because of the sign. It was a bad time, him supporting Blacks and wanting to free Blacks. Somebody just took his ass out. The local police were part of the groups who were opposing the Blacks. It was rough back then. They knew [who did it], but they didn't want to press it, or they didn't care."

Tommy Baird and his grandfather returned to the store after the state police and the sheriff's deputies arrived at the murder scene. For days, the town talked about the murder while the Baird boys played with William Moore's dog.

"It was a big old bird dog," Baird said. "He might have given it to one of my other brothers."

Later that year, the dog died.

"He ran out in the middle of Highway 11 and got killed," Baird said.

CHAPTER 22

I had to drive up the western slope of Lookout Mountain, navigate a maze of narrow, twisting roads, and locate a campground in the woods to find someone who had pursued the murder with the tenacity I had. Mickey Strickland, in fact, had invested more than I had. She lived in a cabin in Mentone, where she and her husband operated Strickland Campground. She also wrote for the mountain newspaper, the *Groundhog*, and aspired to attend creative writing school at Boston University when I contacted her. She had researched the murder for more than twenty years and planned to write a book before ending the project recently, a decision based on her inability to find a publisher and the time to complete the manuscript. Her interest in the murder was personal, like mine. She had been a student at Fort Payne High School in the spring of 1963, and she knew many of the families who were involved in the murder.

Her research and her connections to the case had led her to some firm conclusions: Floyd Simpson was no murderer, in her estimation. She considered him "a kind and gentle man," as she described him, who had been convinced by the murderer or someone associated with the murder to say nothing about how Moore was killed.

"He was a hero to people around here, but no one believed he did it," she said. "He wasn't the kind of man who'd do it."

She regarded him as a strong family man—good to his children and a staunch advocate of education. His daughter, Carolyn, popular with students and teachers, was among her classmates. Floyd Simpson's emphasis on education had such an effect on Carolyn that she became one of the top students at Fort Payne High.

The *Fort Payne Times-Journal*'s front-page article about the fundraiser for Simpson was an indication of the family's support in the community. The most visible indications, though, were the jars stuffed with coins and cash at virtually every cash register in the county.

"I tell you, the sympathy, it was all on Simpson's side," she said.

She likened the William Moore story to *To Kill a Mockingbird*, the coming-of-age tale about racial justice in small-town Alabama, later adapted into an Oscar-winning movie starring Gregory Peck as Atticus Finch, the courageous Southern lawyer.

"The problem was," she said, "all of the Gregory Pecks were on the other side."

Politicians and preachers of the biggest churches in the county were members of the DeKalb County Klan in the 1960s, she said, enticed by the political power that accompanied membership or sympathy. William Moore's miscalculation of the Klan's strength—"the stupidity," as she put it—was among his biggest mistakes, she said. The preacher of the Fourteenth Street Baptist Church, the Reverend Willis Griffin, admitted to the *Fort Payne Times-Journal* that he was a member of the Klan. The *Times-Journal*'s lead story on October 15, 1964, was an account of an incident at the Veterans of Foreign Wars County Fair. Two men believed to be members of the Klan cut the ropes holding the tent of "a Negro Minstrel Show," as the newspaper called it.

"When asked if [the two men arrested] represented the Klan, Griffin said, 'I can't speak for them, but I am a member of the Klan and we are going to see that the entire county remains segregated,'" the newspaper reported.

A few days later, the *Times-Journal* published a front-page editorial about the Klan, citing the incident at the county fair as an example of how a "disease was gripping Fort Payne that if not given the proper attention it could become fatal." The disease, said the newspaper, was hate. That hate had transformed Fort Payne from "a wonderful community of love thy neighbor and Do Unto Others as You Would Have Them Do Unto You to a community [of] distrust, anxiety and fear." The newspaper's editorial prompted the Reverend Griffin to write a rebuttal in which he cited the Golden Rule, as the *Times-Journal* had. Griffin, however, contended the

Golden Rule applied to his DeKalb County neighbors "but not our invaders, traitors and agitators."

Even police officers were unsafe. The night after the incident at the county fair, the Klan burned a cross on the lawn of the policeman who had arrested the two Klansmen. A group of the state's top Klansmen came to Fort Payne a month later, including Gary Thomas Rowe, the FBI's top Klan informant. Rowe described the Reverend Griffin as "a particularly rabid Klansman." He was a candidate that fall for DeKalb County City Council, running on the slogan "Have Broom Will Sweep." Griffin bragged to the Klansmen from Birmingham about his newspaper column in the *Fort Payne Times-Journal*, informing them that it was the latest of several opinion pieces that had appeared in the local newspaper.

As the former pastor of the Second Baptist Church, one of Fort Payne's largest churches, Griffin had preached about salvation and sin on the front page of the *Fort Payne Times-Journal*.

"I have stood against sin in this town, and I have hated sin, but at the same time I have loved the people," Griffin said.

On the radio, Griffin condemned the evils of alcohol. In church and at summer revivals, he portrayed himself as "soul winner." At the Klan's regular Saturday morning meetings, though, he supported violence.

"Oh, he's not just a Klan chaplain," Hoyt Kelly told Rowe. "He has a church in town with a large congregation. We couldn't operate without him. He helped us find land for a rifle and pistol range so the men could practice shooting every Saturday."

Mickey Strickland interviewed William Moore's wife, Mary, in 1989, before the commemoration of the civil rights memorial, the Southern Poverty Law Center's shrine to the forty-one victims of civil rights–era murders. Before heading to Montgomery, Strickland drove Mary Moore from Mentone to Keener, the first time she had seen the murder site. She was still emotional twenty-six years after the murder.

"Oh, Bill," she recalled Mary Moore saying, her voice almost as a sob.

Mary Moore allowed Strickland to see Bill's scrapbooks, filled with newspaper articles about his activism and letter after letter that he wrote to the editors of newspapers in Baltimore and Binghamton. At the bottom of each clipping, he scribbled the names of the publications and the date of publication. He had also saved the Father's Day card that his stepson had given him. The inscription read, "May I live to be, as good to my dear daddy as he is to me."

"His wife told me that everything he did, he did it 100 percent," Strickland said. "He tried everything he could to make a difference."

Mickey Strickland said she knew the murderers and the participants in the plot to kill William Moore. She believed one of them was Cotton King, a former Klansman who had died ten years earlier at a hospital in Gadsden. I recognized him from Kenneth Hammond's story about the former exalted cyclops stalking him in the fall of 1965, after Hammond's speech on the senate floor opposing George Wallace's attempts to succeed himself. Cotton King had also been one of Floyd Simpson's neighbors in the final years of his life, both living in Fort Payne at the foot of Lookout Mountain.

Two of the men she mentioned were still alive. I was unfamiliar with one of them—Jasper Fike, a lifelong resident of Collbran who worked for the state as an engineer. His name, though, was in the state investigative file that Strickland gave me. A portion of Colonel Al Lingo's notes included this passage:

> An anonymous phone call was made to radio station WGAD to Charlie Hicks, and also to the *Gadsden Times* reporters Thom Wilkerson and Bill Basenberg. They were told to go north on Highway 11 and they would find something newsworthy. All they saw was a 1950 black Buick with a big heavy-set man at the wheel with his arm hanging out the window. Someone later identified the man as Jasper Fike . . . who lived near the Floyd Simpson store.

Fike was, in fact, a large man. He was a tackle on DeKalb County High School's 1946 county championship team and a former mess sergeant in his National Guard unit. At thirty-five, he had remarried earlier that year to a woman who worked in one of Fort Payne's hosiery mills. He was a regular patron of Simpson's store and accustomed to confrontation. In addition to his service in World War II and the Korean War, he had fought in a dark parking lot in downtown Chattanooga with a Chattanooga resident, whom he accused of taking his wallet on a spring night in 1957.

A few days after the murder, one of the witnesses, likely Wilkerson or Basenberg, accompanied state investigator Ben Allen on a trip to Simpson's store. Fike was in front of the store with the other regulars, and Allen drove him to Gadsden. Two witnesses identified him in a lineup, and police gave him a lie detector test. He passed and Dewey Colvard released him.

The notes indicated officers were aware of the killers' plan.

"Floyd Simpson would never talk about where he was at the time of Moore's death. His acquittal led some to speculate that he did not actually committ [sic] the crime, but loaned his gun and auto to those who did."

James Hedgepeth, the Etowah County district attorney, also denied Strickland access to the file. But she was more successful than I had been. Hedgepeth was out of the office when she arrived, and she convinced his secretary to allow her to see the file. When he returned, he ordered her to give him the file. Through the years, though, she had pieced together enough information to understand what Moore encountered in the final moments of his life. She believed the men in the black car had summoned Moore to the driver's side and shot him as he leaned toward them.

Bored by life on the mountain, she decided to go to Boston to enroll in a creative writing school. She informed me of her plans to leave and said she would give me her notes and papers.

"I can't do anything with them, but maybe you can," she told me.

I drove up the mountain two days later and knocked on her front door. A box stuffed with her research was on a table on the front porch. Her husband answered the door, and he instructed me to take the box. He said she had already left.

Among the items was a letter from Mary Moore. The final paragraph read, "Bill's death has cost me many times financially & mentaly [sic]—I hope I can eventually publish my book on then & now & [since] still to be written—Hate! It never stops."

Before she left for Boston, Mickey Strickland told me about James Aderholt,* one of the top attorneys in Fort Payne. She said she had spoken to Aderholt while she was researching her book, and he had identified the murderer to her. She believed he would tell me, too.

---

* Pseudonym. To be known from here as James Aderholt.

Aderholt was known for his quick wit and confrontations in the courtroom, a combination that had made him one of the area's most famous lawyers. To commemorate the recent anniversary of the murder, he and a friend had gone to the murder scene, remembering how Moore was killed. He was evasive, though, when I asked him who had been with him on his ride to Keener.

"I can't remember," he said.

"You mean you're one of the top lawyers in North Alabama and you can't even remember who was with you the other day?" I said.

After that, he was more open, telling me he had been with a doctor who had a fondness for history. Then he told me how I could solve the murder.

"[The former exalted cyclops] knows who did it," he told me.

In the years after the murder, Aderholt said Hoyt Kelly, Floyd Simpson, and Cotton King were almost inseparable. In late 1965 or early 1966, Aderholt, then a young attorney with an already formidable reputation, was hired by the Klan. During a meeting, someone mentioned the murder—Aderholt was unsure who—and they began to talk about it.

"The four of us were in some place, and the shooting [of William Moore] came up," Aderholt said. "There was a conversation about it, and it was rather startling."

The Klansmen told Aderholt who did it and how it happened. Aderholt said he never told state or federal authorities about the conversation because the information was part of the attorney-client privilege. His notes and the files from the case, he said, were destroyed years ago.

"Go see Hoyt Kelly," he said. "He can tell you everything you need to know."

After Mickey Strickland returned from Boston, she wrote letters to newspapers, trying to reopen the prosecution of the murder. Months earlier, a grand jury in Philadelphia, Mississippi, had indicted Edgar Ray Killen, a former sawmill operator and preacher, for the murders of three civil rights workers in the Freedom Summer of 1964. Killen, a member of the Ku Klux Klan, had long been considered the organizer of the mob that killed Mickey Schwerner, James Cheney, and Andrew Goodman, but he had gone free for forty-one years. Mickey Strickland believed Alabama needed to follow Mississippi's example and find the killer of William Moore.

"I am heartened by the efforts of other states to take the cold case files of murdered civil rights workers into this time with renewed efforts to find their killers," she wrote. "I can only hope Alabama follows suit as soon as possible. While the case of William Moore in 1963 resulted in no indictment being returned for his killing, the facts are still there—and Moore is still very much dead. And the killers are old men now and some of them are deceased, but justice is immortal, or should be. . . . If Alabama wants to come into the new century with pride instead of humiliation, the legal system should petition Etowah County for the sealed records of the crime scene and events leading up to his horror—and do something about it. I have seen these records, although they were later denied to me by James Hedgepeth, former district attorney of Etowah County. There is a lot of evidence in those papers, and while I do not believe the man arrested and taken before the grand jury was guilty of the act, I wonder how much coercion it took for him to keep his mouth shut."

Fear, though, still surrounded the murder. Late one afternoon, before a town council meeting, Bozo introduced me to the Valley Head city attorney, whose father had been the circuit clerk in Fort Payne during the civil rights movement.

"Watch this," Bozo said to me.

"Hey, do you remember Cotton King?" he said to the attorney.

The city attorney was stunned, mumbling an acknowledgment of the old Klansman, and turned to go into the town hall.

"See him freeze up?" Bozo said. "Like getting a hold card in poker."

A few weeks later, when he was having problems with a gas line at the town hall, Bozo called a gas company in Anniston, home of Kenneth Adams, the Ku Klux Klan leader who orchestrated the firebombing of the Freedom Riders' bus in 1961. When Bozo saw the gas company worker wearing a belt buckle with a Confederate battle flag emblem, he winked at me and asked the man if he knew Adams. The gas company worker said he had attended high school with Kenneth Adams's daughter, born without arms. She had taught herself to type with her legs, refusing attempts to give her prosthetic arms, and she became so prolific that she could type forty-five words a minute and take eighty words of dictation a minute.

Bozo seemed startled.

"That tells me the man upstairs is taking notes," he said.

Many of the Klansmen and the men involved in the murder had encountered great hardships. Mickey Strickland said Jasper Fike's first wife committed suicide in 1956. Gaddis Killian overcame mental exhaustion that required hospitalization. Willis Griffin's church, the Fourteenth Street Baptist Church, was destroyed by a tornado in the spring of 1973. Floyd Simpson faced perhaps the greatest tragedies of all. In addition to the deaths of his twin babies, he experienced the murder of his mother in 1977, another unsolved crime.

There were also examples of their children finding better lives and rejecting white supremacy. Gaddis Killian's son, Roger, was elected class president at Fort Payne High School before embarking on a law career. After his high school graduation in 1965, he wrote a letter to the editor of the *Fort Payne Times-Journal*, denouncing the recent rise in Klan activity. He planned to return to Fort Payne after his college graduation, he said, and he wanted his hometown to rid itself of elements such as the Klan when he returned to Fort Payne to make a living.

"I see no point in the existence of secretive organizations such as the Ku Klux Klan," he wrote. "The Klan can be credited with creating an uneasiness in the racial situation. If it continues with clandestine acts of disloyalty to law and order, then we can expect a full scale attack from the other extreme."

His letter caused Hoyt Kelly to reply.

"I have noticed in your paper recently articles written by persons who claim to be Southerners yet they call for the Klan to be put out of business," he wrote. "They accuse us of violence. I challenge any one of these so-called do gooders to prove there is a member of the United Klans of America Inc., Knights of the Ku Klux Klan serving time for any crime. These people who would destroy our organization must have forgot their history; following the War between the States, during re-construction, no white man could hold public office or vote if he served for the Confederacy. The Klan was the very organization under ex-General Nathan Bedford

Forest, who rode forward and restored state and local government back to the hands of the Southern white people. We have forgot our forefathers who spilled their blood for our rights; If we don't wake up and start speaking up for our rights and voting these liberals out of office we won't have any left. I believe if a known Communist were to run on the Democrat ticket, there are people right here in DeKalb County who would vote for him rather than desert the party."

Hoyt Kelly, like William Moore, wrote letters to newspapers. Bozo said he liked attention. I still wondered, though, if he'd be willing to talk to me. A preacher in Valley Head, the Reverend Richard Ellis, thought I should call him. The Reverend Ellis pastored Lea's Chapel, the first white church in DeKalb County to integrate its congregation. He told me Hoyt Kelly had undergone a dramatic personal transformation that included his acceptance of Christ. For confirmation, he called Charles Burt, a former Fort Payne city councilman who knew Kelly.

Burt said Hoyt Kelly was, indeed, a changed man. The Reverend Ellis handed the phone to me, and I told Burt that I had a family connection to Hoyt Kelly.

"Well, if you know him," he said, "you know he's a little bit different."

CHAPTER 23

I spoke to Hoyt Kelly for the first time on a night in January as he watched a Democratic presidential debate on television at his home in Collbran. Almost immediately, he was suspicious of my call, wondering who suggested I phone him.

The Reverend Ellis from Lea's Chapel in Hammondville, I told him.

"I don't know him," he said.

Sensing his apprehension, I informed him about our family connections. My mother was from Sand Mountain, I told him, and my favorite uncle was his wife's older brother. He seemed to relax, but he had more questions.

"Where was your father from?" he asked.

"Gadsden," I told him.

I knew then that he would talk to me.

"How far back do you want to go?" he asked.

"All the way back," I told him.

He agreed to meet a week or so later, after consulting some friends and a former preacher. On the drive over, I tried to imagine what he looked like and how he would receive me. Did he enjoy attention as much as Bozo said he did? Would he try to intimidate me, applying the "fear factor" that Bozo said he liked to use? Or would he try to dominate the conversation, being so outspoken, as my aunt described him?

He was waiting on me in the parking lot of the gas station and convenience store he had once owned, helping a friend with a truck as I pulled into the driveway of his small and tidy home at the base of Lookout Mountain. He ran toward me, limping slightly because of an ankle injury he had suffered when he was an ironworker. Entering his house, I recognized some furniture that my uncle had made. My uncle's hobbies included woodworking, and he liked to make tables and flower stands for his relatives, including my mother.

Hoyt Kelly was chatty and friendly, nothing like I expected. He was short—about five feet nine, by his estimate—and thin with silver hair and eyes that blazed. He spoke with a twang that sounded more southwestern than Deep Southern, and he enjoyed discussing firearms, politics, the military, and religion. His chief priority, he said, was "serving the Lord."

Trying to put him at ease, I told him some stories about my uncle, recalling the strength of his handshake, the strongest of any man I'd known. I told him that my uncle had shaken my hand so hard when I was child that I vowed to make him grab his hand in pain when I was older.

"He didn't want you shaking hands with no dead fish," Hoyt Kelly said.

He spoke freely about his years in the Klan and his recent religious conversion. He told me a close friend had come to his home during some difficult times, and they began to pray, starting him on the life of spirituality that now consumed him.

"I wasn't living like I should have been living—like a father and a husband," he said.

We had talked for about an hour when he mentioned the murder. I interrupted him as he began discussing the investigation of Gaddis Killian. I held up my hand and informed him of my interest in the murder.

"I don't want you to ever tell me anything about the murder that you don't want me to know," I said.

He talked about the case anyway, telling me that he was in the area on the night of the murder.

"I had a job that night on Highway 11," he said.

"Which direction?" I asked him. "North or south on Highway 11?"

He wouldn't say. He was more interested in talking about the meeting at the store.

"Let's cover that a little," he said. "Everybody was courteous to [Moore]. I have read articles that claim he was talked down to. That's not true."

He told me that he was among the five people at the store on the morning of April 23. The others were members of Collbran's leading families, all founders of the community in the mid-1800s. Claude Burt was an employee of Alabama Great Southern Railroad. Gene Killian was a painter and another of Gaddis Killian's older brothers. Jack Killian was perhaps the community's most prominent farmer. He was also Collbran's representative in the county's 4-H Foundation and the returning officer for beat 3, box 1, transporting ballots to the courthouse after each election. Floyd Simpson was the new proprietor of the store.

"He [Moore] came in the morning, around noon," Hoyt Kelly said. "I know for a fact nobody talked down to him. Everybody was concerned about why he was doing it and [him] being from New York. I know several people remember this: There was a black Buick or Pontiac that followed him toward Gadsden and turned around and come back. Floyd Simpson was not—and I don't believe that he could be—the shooter. I saw him when I left. He was sitting in the window of his store, doing his books. He did it every night before [closing], on his ice-cream box up against the window."

He considered Simpson a strong family man. Simpson's commitment to his children was so deep, he said, that he never missed one of his son's baseball games. Simpson's brother, Alton Ray, was one of Hoyt Kelly's closest friends—a mentor, he called him. Kelly considered Bill Beck another of his role models.

"I always liked Judge Beck," he said. "When I was in school, we used to go over to the courthouse and watch the trials."

Power came almost immediately for Hoyt Kelly after the murder. In 1964, two years after becoming the head of the DeKalb County Klan, he entered the governor's office in Montgomery and asked George Wallace to help him acquire a new driver's license. His old license, he said, had been suspended because of the speeding tickets he had received during his truck-driving deliveries. Within days, he received a new license, courtesy of Wallace.

He wanted to be a lawyer and enrolled in night-school classes at the junior college on Sand Mountain. He planned to attend law school in Birmingham after graduating, but he never made it past junior college. He was important there, too. The dean of the night school at the junior college, aware of his position in the Klan and his ties to the state's most powerful politicians, asked for his help. The dean needed a commencement speaker for graduation, and he asked for Hoyt Kelly's assistance. He found Jim Allen, a U.S. senator who had been the Alabama lieutenant governor in his early years as the exalted cyclops.

"He met me at the Holiday Inn in Fort Payne and followed me up the mountain," Kelly said.

Kelly was so powerful, in fact, that he became the titan (organizer) for the Klan in North Alabama and the grand dragon (state leader) for the Klan in Alabama. One former Klan associate considered him the most influential Klan leader in the history of North Alabama.

"I thought [Hoyt] was ten feet tall," he said. "He stood out that much from the crowd."

Two months later, I attended church with Hoyt Kelly and soon met many of his longtime friends. One was a woman who flew a Confederate battle flag from a flagpole in her front yard and had a portrait of Robert E. Lee over her mantel. In her barn were letters from Kenneth Adams. She lived near the former exalted cyclops's church, in a lush valley near the Little River Canyon, a wildlife preserve on Lookout Mountain.

The preacher of Kelly's church, the Reverend Ricky Clanton, was the son of a former Klan member who had known the former exalted cyclops during his peak years of power.

"[The former exalted cyclops] was like a CIA agent or somebody in the mob," Clanton said. "He could make one phone call and get fifty or hundred men together with guns to do whatever."

When the preacher was a boy, maybe nine or ten, he overheard a conversation that scared him. The former exalted cyclops came to his house to return one of his father's high-powered guns. A discussion ensued, and the preacher was frightened by the talk. The story was important: it verified that the members of the Fort Payne Klan borrowed guns from fellow members. I already knew Klansmen in northeast Alabama loaned cars to one another. A Klansman had allowed another Klansman to borrow his car before the 1950 murder of Charlie Hurst, a rolling store operator in Pell City.

In one of our first meetings, Hoyt Kelly confirmed that Klansmen loaned cars to one another. He also told me that he was so close to law enforcement officers that some of them were Klan members.

"I don't mind you saying we had law enforcement people who were secret members," he told me.

He knew the sheriff, a U.S. senator, and the governor. Those connections allowed him to do big things. Around 1969, as the anti–Vietnam War movement divided, he arranged for a monument to be placed in front of the DeKalb County courthouse, a marble slab honoring the county's residents who died in the war. A reference to the Ku Klux Klan was at the bottom of the monument.

"It's the first lasting [Vietnam] memorial put up by anyone in the U.S.," he said.

The Klan's demise, though, had already begun. Viola Liuzzo, a housewife from Detroit, was murdered near Selma on the night of March 25, 1965, hours after the end of the Selma-to-Montgomery march as she and an African American man transported marchers between Montgomery and Selma. President Lyndon Johnson appeared on national television after the murder to announce the arrests of four Klansmen and to warn Klansmen to "get out of the Ku Klux Klan now and return to a decent society before it is too late."

"Things like that were the beginning of the end of the Klan," Hoyt Kelly said. "A lot of people in the Klan didn't uphold that type of behavior. I was questioned several times by the FBI."

He was a young man then, just starting a family, searching for power. The response to William Moore's walk through Fort Payne and Collbran—shock, he called it—helped him seize it. Moore was an easy target. Sizing him up at the store, Hoyt Kelly saw his gentle expression and his awkward and uneasy ways.

"This man," he said, "I doubt if he ever harmed anybody in his life."

Yet there were plenty of reasons for people in Little Wills Valley to hate him: his Northern accent, his signs, his intention to deliver the letter to Ross Barnett, his meddling in the South's affairs.

"Nobody in the South [or] in this community shared the views that he had at the time," he said. "I guess you could say he was part of the era in our history of making change. At that time, there were truck stops up and down Highway 11. They had dining rooms for Blacks and whites. I guess the sign, it stuck out."

So did his race.

"That stood out, a white man," he said. "You would have to say one thing: He was dedicated."

Again, he told me that Floyd Simpson was not the murderer.

"I believe with all my heart that he was innocent," he said.

He considered the black car to be the key to the arrest. A black car, he said, had followed Moore almost the entire way since he began his walk through Chattanooga. Several motorists near the murder scene had seen a black car, leading to Simpson's arrest.

"Floyd owned a black Buick," the former exalted cyclops said. "When I left to go on a trip, his car was there and so was he."

I asked him again about his trip that night. He still seemed evasive. This time, the former exalted cyclops said he went to "pick up a load going out."

Collbran and Fort Payne, meanwhile, rallied around Simpson and his family, convinced he had not been the murderer, even though his car and gun were the most important parts of the investigation. Jack Killian led Simpson's legal defense fund and collected enough money to pay for his legal fees.

With the best lawyers available, Simpson's legal fees were high. But Simpson had something even stronger than his high-powered defense team—a lack of enthusiasm by the prosecution.

"I think they had to have somebody to charge," Hoyt Kelly said. "People were strongly supportive of Floyd and his family. It could have been because it was so different in this area. It was something very, very different. There hadn't been nothing in the civil rights movement here. It was like he was here today, gone tomorrow. That's the long and the short of it."

He was an exalted cyclops for fifteen years until 1977. In his final months, he was leading meetings in an abandoned gas station on Highway 11, on a lonely stretch between Fort Payne and Collbran.

"That's a part of my life that I preferred never happened," he said. "I can't change it. I hope with the help of God that it never happens—my association with the Klan."

Now that he had found religion, he was sure he had been forgiven.

"I can say God wouldn't approve of it—of mistreating any individual or any race of people," he said. "That's not to say I ever mistreated any individual, but I have in that time used words that He wouldn't approve [of]. I got forgiveness. All of my sins were washed away when I was saved. He forgave me for all of my sins when I accepted Jesus Christ as my savior, and His dying on the cross and His blood cleansed me."

He spent many days telling people on the mountain the story of how he found Christ in 1991, when news of his religious conversion was big news among the sock mill employees in Fort Payne.

On at least one Saturday each month, he met with the sick and the troubled residents of the county. First, he gave his testimony to the nonbelievers—"the lost," as he called them. Then, as a way of introducing himself, he passed out small crosses and a card.

The card read:

The Cross in My Pocket
I carry a cross in my pocket
A simple reminder to me
Of the fact that I am a Christian
No matter where I may be

This little cross is not magic
Nor is it a good luck charm
It isn't meant to protect me
From every physical harm

It's not for identification
For all the world to see
It's simply an understanding
Between my Savior and me

When I put my hand in my pocket
To bring out a coin or key
The Cross is there to remind me
Of the price He paid for me

It reminds me too to be thankful
For my blessings day by day
And to strive to serve Him better
In all that I do and say
It's also a daily reminder

Of the peace and comfort I share
With all who know my Master
And give themselves to His care.

So, I carry a cross in my pocket
Reminding no one but me
That Jesus Christ is Lord of my life
If only I'll let Him be

In his testimonies, the former exalted cyclops recalled how he had almost died in high school, when he and a carload of friends were in Scottsboro for a Future Farmers of America function. They went to see *Quebec*, a 1951 adventure movie starring John Barrymore, at the drive-in theater. Sitting in the middle of the front seat, he leaned to his left to get a better view of the screen, ducking past the metal strip in the middle of the windshield. A friend sitting behind him was handling a sawed-off shotgun, and the gun accidentally fired as the former exalted cyclops moved, blowing a hole in the front seat and shattering the windshield.

"I'd have busted hell wide open," he told his friends.

He believed that he had been saved to tell his life story to the people on the mountain and in the valley.

"What I've got, people need to know," he said. "If you follow the teaching of Christ, you know you're supposed to get out among the people."

The transformation appeared so complete that he was almost ashamed when I mentioned his Klan robe. In a previous meeting, I had asked him if I could see it, and he said that it was in a barn that belonged to a relative in Collinsville. He told me that he needed to ask his relative if the robe was available. Driving to church on a Sunday morning, he informed me during the ride up Lookout Mountain that the robe was unfit for me to see. Some rats had eaten away at the robe, he said. I suspected he might be lying, so I tried to push him to change his mind.

"I'd just like to see it," I said.

"I hope you never do," he said.

CHAPTER 24

After attending church with Hoyt Kelly one Sunday afternoon in the early spring, I decided to go to the Black section of Fort Payne, known as Douglas during segregation. I parked near the base of the mountain, in the shade of the tall pines and hickories, and heard a man singing as he mowed his yard. I walked to his front lawn and introduced myself. His name was Kenneth Underwood, and he said he knew Hoyt Kelly well. In 1963, Hoyt Kelly patrolled Douglas before dark, as he was allowed to do during the civil rights movement. Seeing Kenneth Underwood's younger brother at the ballpark, Kelly shouted, "Boy, you better get your black ass home."

"He rode his bike home all tore up," Underwood said.

In those days, said Underwood, Kelly's hatred was so strong that he wouldn't touch a Black person. He distanced himself from Black people, he said, refusing to shake their hands. In those days, there was a lot of fear among African Americans. Clara Underwood, Kenneth's sister-in-law, said Blacks feared the store in Collbran because she heard there was a hanging there. A legend in the Black community was that the blood of a dead man, the victim of another racial killing, washed up on the highway during rainstorms. Was Clara Underwood referring to the murder of William Moore? She insisted the man was killed long before Moore's death.

Clara's husband, Roscoe, was the first Black student to attend Fort Payne High School. Roscoe remembered an incident involving one of his cousins, who was part of an integrated group of musicians that included future members of Alabama, the famous country and Southern rock band. The Klan's opposition to the group was so fierce, he said, that one Klansman told his cousin, "I've got a .12 gauge waiting on you."

It sounded similar to the story of the Ernie King Soul Band at the Mouse Trap—a story that ended with a confrontation between the band and the Fort Payne Junior Klan. After the bomb threat was phoned in to the Mouse Trap, the band was approached by members of the Junior Klan, one of whom was believed to have been the teenage son of a Klansman who was at the store when William Moore passed through Collbran.

Most Blacks in DeKalb County lived at the foot of Lookout Mountain in Fort Payne and in the hills of Collinsville. Herman Kerley lived most of his life in a brick house off U.S. 11 in Collinsville, at the foot of a hill lined with small frame houses and vegetable gardens. As a preacher, Kerley knew about the power of salvation. He had witnessed it again in the transformation of Hoyt Kelly.

In his years as the Douglas High School principal, Kerley watched Hoyt Kelly park his car near the school, as if to intimidate students, faculty, and administrators.

"What was his reputation in those days?" Kerley asked. "It wasn't good."

Herman Kerley believed Hoyt Kelly had seen Jesus in the form of William Moore, trudging down Highway 11 with hecklers and assassins following him, waiting until dark to kill him as he walked on his sore, blistered feet.

"Maybe that pricked him and caused him to come to Christ, and he can get forgiveness for it," he said. "That's what they did to Christ. They just didn't shoot Him. I figure that's why [he] got religion. He started seeing God in the man he killed. It gnawed at him. He started feeling guilty."

Like Bozo Hammond, Kerley was sure that the murder was premeditated, so much so that he believed local officials were aware of the plan.

"I'd say it was orchestrated to a tee," he said. "I'd say it was well planned. We all knew he was coming. We wanted to see what this man was like."

The regulars at the bridge over Little Wills Creek, at the intersection of U.S. 11 and Alabama 68 in downtown Collinsville, gathered on the concrete rails, waiting for Moore to finish his lunch at Margaret Osborn's café and his conversation with Lavone Williams, the owner of Collinsville Dry Cleaners. Moore walked across the bridge and spoke to some of the regulars, many of them older Black men.

Even then, said Kerley, a black car was following him.

"[Moore] was killed in Etowah County for a reason," Kerley said. "It was easier to cover up there. Where they shot him, you could see in both directions for about a mile. You can see what was coming either way. They could see him coming as soon as he left the store. They met at that store as soon as he left—right there where the fire department is today. They called that the bus stop back then."

From there, the phone calls to the radio station and the *Gadsden Times* were likely made, Kerley said. Roy McDowell's instincts were correct: The killer and his accomplice had been watching.

"The man who did it, he wasn't going to go alone," Kerley said. "He was going to pull the rest of them with him. I figure that's why he was never arrested. There were four or five of 'em, I'd say—law enforcement, lawyers, others. You don't want any more than that. You get too many and people will start talking."

He wondered if the story would ever be told, with the cover-up intact after all these years. But he believed something so sensational needed to be revealed, especially now that most of the people involved were dead. He likened the murder to "one of these movies"—a plot that was audacious in its planning, outrageous in its execution, and historic in its consequences.

"It'd be better than O.J.," he said. "They figured they'd kill the movement, but they didn't. That's why the state cut down the tree. They were tired of people gathering there and protesting, so they just cut it down. People got so upset that some of the whites threatened to go to this cemetery where Blacks and whites were buried, and they talked about digging up the Blacks. That's how threatened they felt. Finally, they just had to guard the cemetery 24/7."

He was emphatic: The murder was a setup, and Bill Beck was the mastermind.

"Beck, he was a mover and a shaker," he said. "He might not move it the right way, but he'd move it. You could have three people in a [legal] matter, and they'd all be on opposite sides, and he'd represent all of 'em. He'd do things that weren't ethical. I knew of that happening."

He also knew that another person had been chosen to be the killer, but he declined. Money, Kerley said, was involved.

"People would contribute to the cause—powerful people," he said. "They wanted him [Moore] dead, but not in this county. There was some chickening out in the deal. [Then] they upped the ante. I think it was a show of power. People with money were tied up in the Klan. They picked out somebody to do the dirty work."

CHAPTER 25

The recent publicity about the murder troubled Hoyt Kelly. Mostly, he seemed upset about the accusations that Floyd Simpson was the murderer. In addition to the *Gadsden Times*' series, the *Los Angeles Times* sent a reporter to Fort Payne in 2002 to write a story about the murder. The story ended with the reporter meeting Simpson's wife, Lucille, at her home at the base of Lookout Mountain and refusing his request to interview her or her children. As the reporter drove away, he sensed the stares of Lucille Simpson and Floyd's youngest child, Todd.

A book about the murder, *Freedom Walker*, was published in 2003. Its conclusion was that Simpson "learned to live with a local reputation of being 'the man who'd gotten away with murder,' a dubious distinction which caused him to be admired by some of his neighbors and avoided by others."

"[The articles] opened a lot of wounds," the former exalted cyclops said. "There are a lot of people still living that that story would have an effect on."

I asked him who would be upset.

"[Simpson's] wife and children," he said. "You're talking about when an innocent person is wrote about, if they don't know the true facts, then [they] leave open an open-ended question. That story, there's been several written on it. A lot of facts were inaccurate."

The mistakes included the discussion at Simpson's store.

"He [Moore] was there twenty to twenty-five minutes," he said. "I know he had mental problems. He had been under the care of psychologists. It was on the radio—all over the radio—that he was coming down Highway 11."

A student of the history of Indians, Hoyt Kelly asked Moore, "Why don't you do something for the Indians? They're the most oppressed people who ever lived."

"They're not as bad off as Black folks," Moore told him.

He considered the outcome of the investigation to be the biggest mistake.

"A railroad job—that's my opinion," Hoyt Kelly said. "[With] the pressure, [they] had to arrest someone."

Only one topic seemed off-limits with Hoyt Kelly: his association with some of Alabama's most notorious white supremacists. I asked him about Kenneth Adams ("that was the wing of the Klan that was closest to Hoyt," Bozo said) and the bombers of the Sixteenth Street Baptist Church in Birmingham. By then, three of the bombers had been convicted—Robert Chambliss, in 1977, and Bobby Frank Cherry and Thomas Blanton, in 2001. Two other suspects had died long ago. Kelly said he had never met them.

A few weeks later, he called me at home one night. He wanted to tell me about something that happened at work earlier that day. He had driven a dump truck to a chert pit in Hammondville, hauling rocks and dirt, and headed over to a service station near the interstate, a gathering spot in the northern part of the county. He had seen a car with several religious stickers, and he approached the driver. The former exalted cyclops introduced himself, then handed a small cross and one of his cards to the driver. The driver identified himself as the Reverend Richard Ellis, the pastor of Lea's Chapel. The former exalted cyclops recognized the name immediately. He asked Ellis if he had suggested I call him, and Ellis confirmed that he had.

From then on, the former exalted cyclops seemed to trust me more.

"You know you asked me if I knew those guys who bombed that church in Birmingham?" he asked me. "I told you I didn't know them. That was a lie. I guess the Lord was working on me."

He told me that he had met Blanton and Cherry at Eastview 13, the Klavern in Birmingham. Cherry, like the former exalted cyclops, had been a truck driver in those days.

"I was shocked when I found out those guys were involved," he said. "They seemed so clean cut."

And what about Robert Chambliss? Did he know him?

"No," he said.

On an early April morning, Hoyt Kelly and I walked across Highway 11 and headed toward Floyd Simpson's old store. We were supposed to meet Gaddis Killian, who had recently celebrated his eighty-seventh birthday and still lived next to the old store.

"Don't ask him about that mailman," said the former exalted cyclops. "That still makes him mad."

I assured him I wouldn't mention it.

"If that store could talk," Kelly said as we crossed U.S. 11, "there would be some history told."

Was he toying with me again, making a veiled reference to the murder? Was this the fear "factor" that Bozo had mentioned? I let it pass. He seemed to be enjoying the attention, rehashing the best time of his life. He told me that he wished his years in the Klan had never happened, but I thought he was pulling a George Wallace ploy on me, trying to revise history. I thought he liked the power too much, like Wallace had.

Walking through the front door, I saw the same poster I had seen two years earlier—"Love your enemy, it will drive him crazy." Gaddis Killian stood in the middle of the store, near the register and a collection of old car tags. The former exalted cyclops informed him of my connections to Gaddis Killian's family, mentioning my aunt and my grandfather.

"His grandfather worked with [Jack Killian] on the state highway crew," the former exalted cyclops told him, a reference to the work on the new interstate in the late 1950s and early '60s.

Gaddis Killian was a gracious host, giving me a tour of the store and telling me of how it was built. The final stretch of U.S. 11, from Collinsville to Fort Payne, was completed after his family allowed construction through Collbran in 1935, he said. The following year, an older brother, Willard, built the store from timber harvested from land near the mountain that belonged to his family. He said his older brother operated the store for a year or two until he lost his business because of an arrest for bootlegging.

"I bought him out for $200," he said. "It was a lot to me. If a car drove up, I got out there before it stopped. I wiped the windshield, checked the tires. If it stopped long enough, I washed it. Pretty soon, [the other station owners] said, 'That kid down the road took my business.' I made twenty-nine cents my first day."

We left the store and walked to his home next door. As we headed to his basement, we passed under a shrine to his former political activism—a wall covered with political buttons, most of them George Wallace buttons. He talked about his years in the military, when he served as a marine postmaster in San Francisco, and we headed back to the store parking lot with the former exalted cyclops.

Hoyt Kelly had something he wanted to show me—something deeply personal.

"I'm going to show you where I lived a big part of my life," he said.

We went to the edge of Collbran, where a tall pecan tree stood near the edge of the road. The area had been a roadside picnic area, like the murder scene in Keener. The pecan tree hovered over the picnic table where guards on an armored truck frequently ate lunch. Hidden by the leaves, the former exalted cyclops and a cousin sat in the tree, holding their rifles before the guards arrived for lunch.

"In the summer, the leaves would be all covered up," he said. "We climbed up with our rifles, and we were going to rob that Brinks armored truck."

They were a couple of country boys, making plans and dreaming big, feeling bigger and more powerful than they were. They clutched their guns and wondered if they should fire, but they never did.

A few years after Hoyt Kelly remembered his failed heist, the pecan tree was chopped down, just like the black walnut tree in Keener, two fallen shrines to the former exalted cyclops's youth.

Out on the rifle range, a field near his childhood home, Hoyt Kelly was at ease. He shot his rifle at targets from long distances, pondering the state of America as he fired, how it was living too fast for his liking.

"Thomas Jefferson, that was his main sport, shooting," he said. "He said you can get out and think."

Out here, he prayed or reflected on some scripture he was studying. He said his skills had declined with age ("I can't see"), but he was still good enough to put a shot through the center of the target.

"That's the one that counted," he said, hitting the bull's-eye.

He used an 8-mm rifle with a scope, but he told me he had always been more comfortable with a .22 rifle. A .22 was his first gun, and it was also the weapon he had used when he was on a navy marksmanship team.

"I guess you could say I shot competitively in the navy," he said. "I don't aim. I point."

As he prepared to leave the rifle range, he gave me a shooting tip: The closer you are, the better you are. He put his gun in his truck and drove across the field to the barn where he and his younger brothers worked as boys. Sitting in front of the barn, he mentioned a photograph that was taken in front of the store a few days earlier, a snapshot of him and me. He said Gaddis Killian's wife, Lorene, asked that it not be used, worried that it might stir memories of the William Moore murder and revive an investigation.

He seemed to be toying with me all afternoon, talking about his preference for .22 rifles and shooting from close range. Now that he had moved around to the murder, he wanted to know if I wanted to go to the murder site. The same questions kept running through my mind.

Was he trying to scare me again? Did he want to see how I'd react once we arrived in Keener? Was this the criminal returning to the scene of the crime?

I turned away from him, trying to hide my surprise.

"Sure," I told him, "let's go."

I was more confused than frightened, trying to understand why he was driving to Keener. On the way, he gave me more history of the road, how busy it had been when it was the main highway between Chattanooga and Birmingham. Driving toward Collinsville, we talked about his roles in the Klan.

"In 1977, I was the state head of the National Knights of the Ku Klux Klan," he said. "I had state offices in the late '60s and early '70s for the United Klans of America. I was the titan, which would be the organizer, for the Seventh Congressional District—all the counties of the Seventh Congressional District, to the Mississippi line."

Later, I found FBI documents that explained Hoyt Kelly's departure from the United Klans of America. He had an "intense desire to become the Grand Dragon of Alabama," according to a memo, and his quest for more power had caused him to persuade Robert Shelton to make him the new leader of the Alabama Klan. Shelton, though, eventually supported the current grand dragon, John Adams of Decatur. On May 16, 1975, he and a Klan leader from Chattanooga announced they were joining the National Knights of the Ku Klux Klan. Both had convinced James Venable, the imperial wizard of the National Knights of the Ku Klux Klan, to make them grand dragons. The split had been led by Hoyt Kelly, according to the FBI.

The new grand dragons and members of their klaverns held a naturalization ceremony on September 7, 1975, at Monteagle, Tennessee, to recruit new Chattanooga klavern members and organize a klavern in Tracy City, Tennessee. After the meeting, four members of the Chattanooga klavern, including the new grand dragon of Tennessee, went to the home of a white family in Tracy City and ordered them to leave the county because they had adopted two Black babies.

On our way to the murder site, though, he wanted to be clear about his views on Blacks.

"I grew up with 'em," he said. "We had Blacks on our farm. I ate in their home. They were fine folks. Race was never a question. They had their place, and I had my place."

We were through Collinsville and into Etowah County, only five miles or so from the murder site when I mentioned the murder. We talked about the black car that had followed Moore, and I told him what I had heard about the murder.

"I heard there were two or three men in that black car," I said.

"Yeah," he said, "that's what I heard, too."

Finally, I asked him, "So who did it?"

What appeared to be the makings of a smile formed at the corner of his mouth.

"It was the man in the black car," he said.

He veered his truck across the highway, toward the edge of the road, and where the black Buick had been parked.

"This is where he was shot," he said.

Parked by the side of the highway, he recalled the murderer's strategy.

"Nobody would have thought about anybody parking there at the picnic tables," he said. "He [Moore] was braver than I would have been walking down here at that time."

He said he was convinced—deep in his heart, as he put it—what was about to happen to William Moore.

"He was the first Freedom Walker through here, and he was the last," he said.

He turned around and told me more about his leadership in the Klan. As a titan, he accompanied Shelton on out-of-state trips, sometimes as far away as Indiana, flying in his plane or traveling in his motor home. Driving through Keener, he surveyed the utility poles along the highway, remembering how he and the other Klansmen spent long hours tacking Wallace posters high enough so volunteers for rival candidates were unable to destroy them.

Those were times of power for him, working with the state's most famous politicians long before he turned thirty. With the marches in Birmingham and William Moore's walk through Little Wills Valley, Hoyt Kelly's Klavern grew quickly, its membership rising so fast that some of the state's most influential Klansmen came to Fort Payne.

"It was really a sign of the times," he said. "The whole civil rights movement—bang—it happened overnight."

On the edge of Collinsville, approaching the entrance to Trade Day, he passed the site where Simpson and Gaddis Killian spoke to Moore about five hours before the murder.

"Their curiosity is what got 'em [Gad Killian and Floyd Simpson]," he said. "They went down here to talk to him, and that's why they [the state policemen] picked them [Gad Killian and Simpson] up."

Pulling into Collbran, he told me how the FBI questioned him about the murder for seven years—from 1963 to 1970, by his estimate. I figured it was part of the FBI's Cointelpro program, designed to disrupt and discredit organizations that were considered subversive to political stability in America.

"It got so old that when they came to see me, I'd say, 'My name is Hoyt Kelly. Here's my social security number and my address,'" he said. "And then I'd say, 'That's all I have to say.' They'd say, 'Well, you know who did it.'"

CHAPTER 26

I didn't believe Bozo Hammond when he said he was through with politics. He had been saying for months he was retiring as mayor of Valley Head, and I kept telling him that he wasn't fooling anyone, least of all me. I thought he was more addicted to politics than his Phillies Blunt cigars and history lessons. As the deadline for filing neared, Bozo stopped coming to the Valley Head town hall. No one there had seen him in town, and I wondered if he was reverting to his days in the senate, trying to build the suspense before making his grand return. True to his word, though, he did not run for reelection.

With no political duties, he seemed more willing to discuss the murder, especially after learning of my meeting with the former exalted cyclops. Every now and then, though, he became irritable, as if he was having withdrawals now that he was unable to feed his political addictions. Bozo and Hoyt Kelly had been intense political rivals, so much so that Bozo still begrudged Hoyt Kelly for his support of politicians in South Alabama. Most of all, Bozo was still angry over Hoyt Kelly "coming into my territory," as the former exalted cyclops had done in the fall of 1965.

In the summer of 1965, as Bozo continued his attacks on Wallace on the senate floor, one of Hammond's fellow senators told a Montgomery newspaperman, "Little had changed since then."

"If you want me to, hell, I'll walk down Highway 11 at high noon," he said. "But if you kill me, you won't get away with it like you did before. After that, he didn't set no bear traps for me. He was dealing with someone who didn't show no fear. It wouldn't have done no damn good. It would have been warfare."

Bozo began to use two nicknames for Hoyt Kelly— "Jerry Lee Lewis" and "Billy the Kid." I didn't have to ask what he meant. Jerry Lee Lewis was nicknamed "the Killer." His reference to Billy the Kid was Bozo's way of saying the former exalted cyclops was "looking to put a notch in his gun."

Moore enraged the old-timers at the store, he said, but none of them was prepared to kill him. They had large families and jobs—too much to lose. The former exalted cyclops "and a few others took it on their own," Bozo said.

"He turned and hopped on that thing Jerry Lee Lewis–style," Bozo said. "It was ego and helping humanity. It's what drives a politician. Hell, he wasn't bashful. He wasn't trying to hide anything. [He] was like a young Turk in the mafia.

"They picked the time and the place. Everybody had a game to play. That was the key to every bit of it, that and the dark clouds that were coming out of Little Rock and Oxford. He [Moore] got in that hornet's nest that was waiting for him down there. You could almost break it down to modern-day politics of today. He was in the wrong place, wrong time, wrong territory."

Two men were in the black car as it eased into the roadside picnic area, he said, and both were out of the car when the murderer fired the first shot. The second shot, through the neck, was execution style, he said.

"They wanted to make damn sure he was dead," he said.

The cover-up, he said, began when the first radio reports of the murder were broadcast. The plan was easy because it was "fixed from the inside," as he put it. The most powerful lawyers and politicians in Etowah and DeKalb Counties were Baptists, Masons, and Democrats. Bill Rayburn, Virgil Pittman, and Representative Albert Rains were members of First Baptist Church of Gadsden, and Bill Beck belonged to First Baptist Church of Fort Payne. Beck, Wallace, Dewey Colvard, and Ace Williams were Masons. Their primary loyalty, though, was to the Alabama Democratic Party. McCord had been a regular at the Democratic National Convention for almost thirty years. He had been a delegate at the conventions in 1944 and 1948, and he was a longtime member of the Alabama Democratic Executive Committee. Rains had chosen Pittman to be the Democratic campaign chairman of the Fifth Congressional District in 1960. Pittman had responded with the largest voter turnout in the county's history, a decisive victory for the Democrats. In 1962, he was named cochairman of the state Democratic campaign, trying to repel unprecedented Republican advances in a surprisingly close U.S. Senate race between Gadsden businessman James Martin and Democratic incumbent Lister Hill, seeking his fifth term.

Pittman's connections to Beck began in 1947, after Pittman came to Gadsden and joined the law firm of Ed Miller, a member of the Alabama House of Representatives and the head of the Etowah County Democratic Executive Committee. When Beck needed a lawyer after a crash involving a bus that belonged to Northeast Alabama Bus Lines, his newly incorporated bus company, he hired Virgil Pittman.

"There were seven key players—two lawyers, some law enforcement people, Beck, all the way down, including your DA in Gadsden," Bozo said.

He considered Bill Beck and Bill Rayburn to be the chief participants, and the rewards were substantial. Every official associated with the murder case had a remarkable record of longevity in public office. Harold Richards and Dewey Colvard were the longest-serving sheriffs in the history of their counties. Richards was elected seven times and Colvard five until his death in the summer of 1974. Colvard was the first sheriff in Etowah County history to be elected without opposition. Noble Yocum was Colvard's successor after he died of a heart attack only weeks after being elected to a fifth term. Harry Sizemore became the youngest person to be the head of the Etowah County Commission, and Roy McDowell became sheriff. Bill Beck remained active in state politics as George Wallace's power increased. In 1965, Wallace appointed him interim president of Judson College, a school for women in South Alabama, and a special assistant in the attorney general's office. Rayburn never tried to run for state or national office again after losing his bid for Congress in 1964. He remained the Etowah County district attorney for six more terms until he retired as he approached his sixtieth birthday.

Floyd Simpson left the Klan and moved to a small frame house across from a Baptist church in Fort Payne. He was employed as a maintenance worker at the DeKalb County Hospital, where a coworker regarded him as "a very serious man—someone not to be messed with." Cotton King was among his neighbors. For a while, King ran a shoe store before joining Simpson as a hospital employee.

"Everybody had something to gain out of the hustle," Bozo said.

After years of trying to climb to the top, Hoyt Kelly reached the pinnacle of his powers in the Klan in 1975, becoming the grand dragon of Alabama. On August 30, 1975, he addressed a Klan convention in Stone Mountain, Georgia.

"The Jewish conspiracy and the Communist conspiracy interwoven with the so-called civil rights laws have broken the spirit of America today," he said. "And when I say the spirit of America, I meant the Ku Klux spirit. This is the master race. This is the ruling race of America today."

Bozo said the murder was more about power and intimidation. Race and civil rights made it easier to cover up.

"Hoyt, he uses the fear factor," Bozo said. "He likes it. In the end, he's looking at ego. It all gets back to two things: fear and Communism. Me? He don't bother me. He knows that. I got nothing against him."

Bozo did, however, have problems with the handling of the murder investigation.

"Nobody paid any attention to it in the drinking and benny-popping days," he said. "I'm sure there were a few who rejoiced. They got bolder and meaner, that hidden fear. They stayed in the boondocks and let it play out. As a whole, they got bolder and meaner.

"[Hoyt] wanted the publicity, I guarantee you. I'm sure within two weeks those people in Georgia and Mississippi knew 80 percent of the story. He wanted his name out there without going to jail. They meant to kill him [Moore]. They waited till he got out of DeKalb County and killed him. It was that confrontation at the store. [Hoyt] said he'd take care of it, and he did. I think he took it on his own to take care of it."

Hoyt Kelly and I corresponded long after our trip to the murder scene. Sometimes, we talked on the phone. Occasionally, he sent letters. Usually, we communicated by email.

His emails came more frequently when he became involved in a bitter county sheriff's race. One of the candidates, a longtime deputy sheriff, made references to the Klan's final years in DeKalb County. The candidate, Jimmy Harris, admitted to participating in Klan activities in the 1970s, but his involvement, he said in campaign literature, was more about fighting the Klan as an informant for Harold Richards.

"Young Jimmy Harris Infiltrates Klan," read a headline on Harris's website.

Hoyt Kelly was furious with Harris's story. There was no Klan in Fort Payne in 1978, for one thing—and no Klan in northeast Alabama, as far as he knew. Perhaps the Klan existed in Etowah County, but he was sure there was no Klan in DeKalb County. On August 3, 2006, he sent me an email that read, in part, "There are a lot of big mules, with big money on Harris' side. . . . If this county was ever investigated by the FBI, I think some people would end up in prison."

On December 4, 2006, after Harris was elected, the former exalted cyclops sent another email.

"I found out last week from the sheriffs [sic] office that Harris is trying to get a pardon for a guy on Lookout Mt. who was arrested several times for dealing drugs," it read. "Harris wants him for a deputy sheriff. There is much more. I went to visit Jimmy Phillips at the sheriff dept a month ago five minutes after I left his office Harris called him and wanted to know if I was confessing to killing the freedom walker in Etowah co."

CHAPTER 27

The FBI announced in 2007 that it was reopening the 108 unsolved crimes from the civil rights era, including the William Moore case. The Emmett Till Unsolved Civil Rights Crime Act was proposed by Congress that year, taking its name from the fourteen-year-old boy whose body was thrown into the Tallahatchie River by a Mississippi grocer, Roy Bryant, and his brother-in-law, J. W. Milam. The law was enacted in October 2008, after President George W. Bush signed the bill, and some of the nation's most notorious race crimes became news again in the Deep South.

On November 23, 2009, the FBI reopened the William Moore murder case and two other unsolved killings. The William Moore investigation lasted until 2012, when a report was sent to a relative of Moore's in Clarksdale, Mississippi. Cecil Reed told an investigator that the FBI interview was the first time he had discussed the case. He had been interviewed at least twice—by me as he ate breakfast in Fort Payne in 2003 and by the *Gadsden Times* reporter who had written the fortieth anniversary series on the murder. He told the *Gadsden Times* reporter that he never spoke to Moore as he entered Etowah County on the afternoon of the murder.

"We never spoke to him, and he never spoke to us," he said.

Reed had given me a similar account when I interviewed him later that week.

"Nothing was ever said," he said.

But Reed told the FBI that he and Bill Stone had a brief conversation with Moore at the county line. It had lasted only long enough for Moore to tell them that no one had threatened him, and he intended to sleep that night on the side of the highway, as he had in Wildwood, Georgia, on the first night of his walk. They watched him pass into Etowah County, he said, and they returned to Fort Payne.

The rest of Fort Payne was also banding together. Danny Beck said he was unable to help because the case file was destroyed in 2003. Hoyt Kelly was contacted, too, and his answer was the same as it was almost fifty years earlier: He wasn't talking.

Louise Nail Robinson, Garvin Robinson's former daughter-in-law, and her brother, Travis, invited me to the Keener reunion, held each summer at the old Keener School. Travis Nail drove from his home in Florida, and Louise came from Sand Mountain to meet me at the old school building. Travis wondered if I was aware of Harry Sizemore's recent death.

"I heard he committed suicide," Nail said.

Sizemore had, in fact, committed suicide, killing himself near a silo by his dairy barn.* Nail wondered if I had talked with him recently and interpreted my questions as a sign that "the authorities were closing in," as he put it. I told him that it had been nine years since I talked with Sizemore and that I had no need to speak with him again. Later, one of Sizemore's relatives told me that his family believed the suicide was caused by some medication that led to his depression.

"I'm sure he told you everything he knew," Nail said. "I'm sure that was it."

Travis Nail's family lived on Keener Lane, in the closest thing to a neighborhood in town—a dozen or so frame houses clustered at the foot of Lookout Mountain. Travis was seventeen on the night of the murder, a junior at Etowah High School in Attalla. Many years earlier, when he was in elementary school, he had ridden in the back of a truck on a rainy night to attend a Klan rally in Fort Payne. A preacher spoke to the crowd at a downtown park, he recalled, and the preacher seemed angry about the absence of blood in a recent version of the Bible.

"Fort Payne was the headquarters of the Ku Klux Klan, and he [Moore]

* Author's interview with Rick Correll, a cousin of Sizemore's.

came through the bad part of Alabama," Nail said. "When he came through Fort Payne, he didn't know what he was in for."

Nail and his father drove to the crime scene on the night of the murder. About twenty people were there, including Harry Sizemore, who directed traffic around Moore's body. For the next few days, as the murder became big news, Travis listened to the regulars at Hilltop Grocery and pieced together the narrative of the murder. He said Moore made one more stop after leaving Hilltop Grocery—at E. D. Amos General Merchandise to buy a soft drink and snacks. From there, he walked past the San-Ann gas station, where Carl Alverson watched him walk toward the picnic area. Travis believed Alverson saw the murder unfold as he stood in front of the gas station, watching the black car pass up and down the highway. Hilltop Grocery closed at around eight each night, leaving Alverson's station as the only business open on Highway 11 between Collinsville and Attalla, a stretch of almost twenty-five miles. From the front of his tiny office, Alverson saw the main characters take their places, waiting for Moore to arrive at the picnic area.

"I'm going to solve your crime," Nail said. "It would have been too dark. They were sitting there waiting on him. [The killer] altered his gun barrel. He put a cleaning rod or a pin [in the barrel]. All it's got to do is put a scratch in the barrel. It'll leave a different pattern on the bullet. It'll be an added pattern on it. The second [bullet], they won't exactly match. If you don't do anything to it, there will be an identical match. It was well-planned."

He also believed the murder was sanctioned by policemen and state and local governments.

"They felt like it was a Yankee white marching for Blacks," he said. "They wanted to get rid of him [Moore] and not get the Blacks in an uproar. They didn't want the publicity or the notoriety from the news media."

And so the black walnut tree was killed, too.

"For years, no one could tell where the spot was," he said. "It wouldn't have been good for the community to have what they have in Selma, where the Blacks come back every year to the bridge. They tore everything down, so there was no recognition of what happened. They even took the tree up by the roots and pulled it out of the ground. It was gone—everything was landscaped or cut down, and everything grew back up naturally.

"I didn't see it, but I remember hearing the dynamite go out of the ground. That's how they got the stumps up back then. They blew it out of the ground. Sometimes it took one, two, or three sticks. I figured that one took two or three sticks of dynamite. That was a big tree."

With the renewed threat of outsiders, Collbran's uneasiness returned. Investigators wanted to interview the former exalted cyclops, and a documentary filmmaker from Brooklyn requested an interview with Gaddis Killian's widow, Lorene.

Hoyt Kelly called me on February 4, 2012, after the documentary aired. At first, he talked about the death of the woman who lived across from his church and flew the Confederate battle flag from the flagpole in her front yard. A few minutes later, he told me about the documentary and the investigators who called him.

"A year ago, Channel 162 or 168 come out of New York and asked me about the Freedom Walker in Etowah County," he said. "I told them no, I've said everything I'm going to say to that. You can look at the interview. The only reason I did it was to get them off my eighty-something-year-old aunt. Everybody who was at that store that day—my dad, Floyd Simpson, Uncle Gene, Uncle Gad, Claude Burt—they're all gone except for me. No one knows. No one knows. I'm the only one who's still alive. I don't know who [did it]. I will never know and don't want to know. That is the way it is.

"Two weeks later, an investigator in Etowah County called me and said I'd like to interview you with another man about William Moore. I said, 'I've said everything I'm going to say. That was a black mark on this community. I wouldn't have had anything to do with that even when I was on my wild side.'"

The documentary ended with the filmmaker's attempts to interview Hoyt Kelly. At first, he agreed to meet with the filmmaker. Then, when the filmmaker came to his home, no one answered the door. Finally, he consented to an interview.

Kelly told the filmmaker no one in the area was the murderer.

"I'd put my life on the line on them words," he said.

I was convinced Bozo was right about the killer's motives. Above all, he had wanted power and recognition. I was also convinced that an event or someone in power had also motivated the killer.

Bozo told me that James Aderholt knew more about the murder than anyone except the killer, so I went to see him for the final time on a winter morning more than ten years after our first meeting. He was surprised to see me.

"Are you still interested in the murder of that crazy postman?" he asked.

I told him I was. He seemed flabbergasted, but he was willing to talk.

"They intended to kill him from the time he was in the county," he said. "They intended to kill him from the time they heard he was coming here."

He told me that as many as four people were involved. He said Floyd Simpson was in the car and that Simpson had called Moore over to the car and pulled the trigger. I didn't believe him. I thought he was lying or confused.

"Hoyt Kelly knows what happened chapter and verse," he said. "It was payback for when the Freedom Riders bus came through here a few weeks earlier. It was payback for that."

"The Freedom Riders bus in Anniston?" I asked him.

No, he said. The Klan had burned another bus.

"The bus was burned at the state line—the Georgia-DeKalb County line [on Lookout Mountain]," he said. "I've been hearing that ever since I've been here. People met that bus holding shotguns and pitchforks."

I told him that it sounded as if he had combined his stories—the burning of the Freedom Riders bus in Anniston and the meeting at the Georgia state line between the Alabama state troopers and the Moore memorial Freedom Walkers. He didn't waver. He was certain the story was true. He was also adamant about how to solve the murder.

"You know the secret to solving that case about the postman, don't you?" he said. "I've told you, right?"

Yes. Go see Hoyt Kelly.

CHAPTER 28

Alabama and Etowah County decided to honor William Moore in the spring of 2019, their first formal recognition of the murder since the grand jury trial. Jerry Smith, a retired dean at Jacksonville State University with a doctorate in education, convinced the members of the Etowah County Commission to place a state historical marker at the murder site. It had been the third attempt and the second in six years to erect a memorial across from the Sizemore dairy farm, but Smith was the first to propose a solution. He asked the six members of the county commission to spend $500 out of their discretionary funds, giving them the $3,000 that the Alabama Historical Commission needed to create a marker.

Six years earlier, Robert Avery, a Black Gadsden city councilman, said on the fiftieth anniversary of the murder that the city should honor Moore with a marker. But Avery found little support. He had been a participant in the demonstrations in downtown Gadsden in the summer of 1963. Smith, however, had the necessary credentials: friendships with influential local politicians and former law enforcement officials, including Johnny Grant, the former sheriff's investigator who was now a county commissioner. Grant arranged for Smith to appear before the commission, and Smith convinced the commissioners to spend the money for the marker.

As Smith completed his project, he found his longtime friends and acquaintances in Collinsville, his hometown, behaved oddly when he mentioned the murder. An old friend had created a model of how the town appeared in the 1960s, and Smith asked if I could see it. His friend refused.

"I'm telling you—and I'm surprised—that people are afraid this will come out negatively against Collinsville," he said.

A personal connection to the murder had caused him to pursue the marker. On the afternoon of the murder, he drove his 1961 Corvair toward downtown Collinsville. As he approached the intersection of Alabama 68 and Highway 11, the center of town, he saw Moore and the sign across his chest. Perhaps he said something to Moore—he is unsure what—and continued driving toward his father's hardware store near the intersection of U.S. 11 and Main Street.

"Did I see him?" Smith said. "Yes. Did I yell at him? I don't know. But I remember there were some people who might have done it."

At fifteen, Jerry Smith was already driving his lime-green Corvair to school and dating Sara Killian, the daughter of Gene Killian, one of the men at Floyd Simpson's store when Moore came through Collbran. Smith's family was part of the establishment in southern DeKalb County. His father, Doran, was a partial owner of W. C. Graves Hardware in downtown Collinsville, where some of the area's leading citizens, including Sheriff Harold Richards, gathered in a back room around a gas stove to discuss the latest news. The family business connections had their perks: Richards gave Smith a card that indicated he was an honorary member of the DeKalb County Sheriff's Department, a privilege that allowed him to own a gun without having to pay for a pistol permit and to avoid speeding tickets whenever police officers stopped him. He was also free to drive before receiving his license, but his mother drove him occasionally to Collbran to see Sara, who lived across from Floyd Simpson's store, near the Great Southern Railroad tracks at the foot of Lookout Mountain. Arriving at Sara's house, he noticed immediately the prominence of Floyd Simpson's store in the community: The daily procession of walkers had created a well-trod path from Gene Killian's house to the edge of U.S. Highway 11 in front of Simpson's store.

In Collbran, Jerry Smith attended church youth gatherings with the children of Gaddis Killian, Floyd Simpson, and Jasper Fike, even accompanying Sara to a dinner meeting of the Gravel Hill Baptist Church Training Union at Lefty Cooper's restaurant in Fort Payne. Sara and her thirty-two classmates were only three weeks away from graduation when she stepped off the school bus and into the parking lot on a morning after the murder. Jerry Smith thought she was crying.

"She was upset that her sweet Uncle Gad had been questioned about this murder," he said. "I had met Gad Killian several times, and he always seemed like a nice guy. He was like Gene Killian, nice and quiet."

Phillip Kimbrell* thought so, too. He grew up near the site where Floyd Simpson and Gaddis Killian met Moore on the afternoon of the murder. Like Jerry Smith, he had driven to Collbran to date one of the Killian girls, a granddaughter of Gaddis. His grandfather gave him a warning before a date.

"Be careful when you're in Collbran," his grandfather told him, "because those people aren't as friendly as they seem."

Phillip Kimbrell's grandfather told him about meeting Gaddis Killian and Floyd Simpson on the afternoon of the murder. Gaddis Killian and Simpson drove to his grandfather's business after their meeting with Moore. They asked him to help them "take care" of Moore—kill or "beat the hell out of him," as his grandfather's story went. His grandfather was considered one of the toughest men in town, a quick-tempered man who enjoyed fighting, but he declined Simpson and Killian's request.

"My granddaddy told me, 'You better believe there's more to that bunch than you think,'" he said. "He told me the story about what happened. He said Simpson wasn't the one who shot him."

Like others in Collinsville, though, Kimbrell still feared the murderer and the family of the murderer. He told the story under the condition that his grandfather and grandfather's business wasn't named.

"My granddaddy was as rough as a cob, but he wasn't a racist," he said. "I never knew him to be racist. They wanted him to get in the car, but he didn't. He said he told them, 'I ain't getting in there with no such stuff as that.' Later on, he said a Black guy from around here went walking with [Moore] and he come up gone."

Later that afternoon, Kimbrell introduced me to his father, who watched Moore pass through Collinsville. He saw Moore's signs and his exchange with Lavonne Williams, the owner of the dry cleaners. Kimbrell's father considered it a bad time, much worse than anyone in Collinsville realized. He believed only a despicable man—a man seeking power and recognition—was capable of being the killer.

* Pseudonym. To be known from here as Phillip Kimbrell.

He was convinced it wasn't Gaddis Killian.

"I just don't see a man like that risking everything," he said.

Gaddis Killian was forty-six in the spring of 1963, the father of four children and perhaps the most admired man in Collbran. He was too old and too respected. The murderer was likely younger, Kimbrell's father said, far removed from the county's establishment, almost an outcast.

"It was somebody mean, somebody who wanted to do something mean," Phillip Kimbrell's father said. "There was nothing to gain except reputation."

On the afternoon of April 14, 2019, the William Moore marker dedication ceremony was held at the Keener Baptist Church on U.S. 11, less than a mile from the murder site. Jerry Smith and Tafeni English, director of the Civil Rights Memorial Center at the Southern Poverty Law Center in Montgomery, were among the first to arrive. It was a cool, sunny day, but the ceremony at the murder site was canceled because heavy rains the day before had turned the area into a quagmire. Some wondered if Harry Sizemore's widow, Betty, would attend. The speculation ended quickly when word filtered through the fellowship hall that she was so opposed to the marker that she asked the county to keep it off her land.

The church had expanded since my last visit, with the addition of the fellowship hall. A board in the corner of the church said fifty-two people had attended services earlier that morning. About that many were there for the marker dedication ceremony, mostly old-timers from Keener and a few from Gadsden. Johnny Grant was also there to relay word that Betty Sizemore wouldn't attend.

Smith was the first to speak. He told the story about seeing Moore on the day of the murder and the impact Moore had made on him. English spoke about the contributions of the millions who participated in the movement, Black and white, many of whom frequently risked their lives.

"As ugly as that was, we must remember all of it, not some of it," she said.

After the ceremony, I met Johnny Grant in the church parking lot. He was now a county commissioner from the district that included Keener, so he was Betty Sizemore's contact in Gadsden when she needed to discuss her opposition to the marker. The original site had been on the Sizemores' property, but it was moved after her phone call to Grant.

"She said, 'Johnny, that monument is on my property. I don't want it there,'" he said. "It was six feet on her property. We moved it six feet. The marker is now relocated off Mrs. Sizemore's property."

For more than an hour, long after most of the crowd was gone, we talked about the murder investigation. Grant told me Mary Moore, Bill Moore's wife, often called the Etowah County Sheriff's Office, trying to convince James Hayes, the longtime sheriff, to reopen the case. But Hayes told her no new information was available.

Grant defended the investigation. He said that Bill Rayburn had decided initially to rely on the ballistics from the Alabama Bureau of Investigation and that state officials had told him that the ballistics from Simpson's gun were inconclusive. But the case files told a different story. He told me, too, that he had talked to George Geer, the former sheriff's deputy, and that Geer "hated what had happened," he said. But the George Geer that I met was unemotional, almost apathetic.

He offered one bit of important information: He went to Roy McDowell's house after his death in 2005 and found some notes about the murder. I suspected there was something in those notes that McDowell didn't want me to see.

"Everyone is dead," Grant said. "I tried to find the gun and the bullets to reexamine it. I knew the FBI had returned it. McDowell stayed and brought it back."

Finally, he got around to asking me the question he had wanted to ask.

"Do you think he [Simpson] did it?" he said

"Do *you* think he did it?" I asked him.

"Yes," he said. "They had the gun and the car."

Dewey Colvard didn't think so. After the grand jury trial, he told the former chief investigator for the San Luis Obispo County, California, district attorney's office that Floyd Simpson didn't kill Moore. In his letter to J. Edgar Hoover, dated December 10, 1963, the former investigator wrote,

> I am Caucasian, born in Alabama, educated in a California college. . . . We have just moved back to Alabama, and are a little puzzled over some things here, therefore, this letter. Why was not, and is not, a large cry made over the brutal murder of this postman who was shot in this county before we came back here? The sheriff here is a good man, and he asked your department to assist him. That postman was murdered as callously as anyone ever was, and regardless of his opinions, he was entitled to those opinions. The sheriff told me he was certain he had the rifle and the car, but the wrong person went before the Grand Jury.

Hoover responded on December 17. He wrote, in part,

> From the statements you have made, one of the cases you have referred to is apparently the brutal murder of Wiliam L. Moore, a Baltimore, Maryland, postman who was walking to Mississippi to protest segregation, on April 23, 1963. You may be interested in knowing that this crime fell within the purview of local statutes; however, the FBI made all of its facilities available to local authorities to assist them. These included the FBI Laboratory examinations of the evidence submitted, the handling of out-of-state investigative leads, and the testimony of an expert witness before Grand Jury proceedings. It is a matter of public record the Grand Jury of Etowah County, Alabama, announced a no bill had been returned on September 13, 1963, against the suspect charged with this murder by local authorities. Further, this crime received nation-wide publicity and was the object of concern for all conscientious Americans.

CHAPTER 29

Mary Moore's prophecy that "God keeps the books" came true in the summer of 2020. Long years of frustrations over police practices in Gadsden erupted after the deaths of George Floyd in Minneapolis and Breonna Taylor in Louisville. On August 6, Black Lives Matter protesters gathered by the Emma Sansom monument in downtown Gadsden, and some angry whites responded with taunts to Black Lives Matter advocates. Protesters carried signs that read, "We Can Do Better Gadsden." Counterprotesters responded with "Support Our Police" signs. Other Black leaders spoke of removing or renaming many of the city's Confederate symbols. Their primary target was the twenty-one-foot monument of General Nathan Bedford Forrest and Emma Sansom in Marange Park, where the Klan once gathered.

The monument had been a downtown landmark since July 4, 1907, when the Gadsden chapter of the United Daughters of the Confederacy unveiled it to a crowd of ten thousand. Forrest's name was also on the city's cemetery and one of Gadsden's downtown streets. General Forrest Middle School had educated students in Alabama City for decades before dwindling enrollment led to school consolidation and a new name for the building in 2006. Forrest's portrait hung in the school.

"He [Forrest] had a right to be in the organization as much as these [Black] folks have a right to be in the NAACP," said the longtime city school superintendent, Fred Taylor, during a controversy over the school's name in 1998. "That doesn't mean he wasn't a hero in the war. . . . Blacks will get on anything. It helps to create membership in their organizations and such."

With its sluggish economy and declining population, the city appeared ready for change. Believing the opportunity had arrived, Emma Sansom's descendants wrote an open letter calling for the statue's removal.

"The monument was erected to enforce white supremacy in Gadsden, which we abhor and lament," the letter read. "The only defensible action today is to remove the statue. Our community may have forgotten why this statue and others like it were erected. We must remember why in order to take wise action."

But the city council, in a 4–3 vote on July 7, 2020, decided to keep the statue and retain the cemetery's name.

"It's not very often that I'm disappointed, but I'm disappointed in the council because we had a chance to move forward and stop looking in the past," said Thomas Worthy, one of the councilmen who voted against the monument resolution.

More disappointment came earlier in the year when Goodyear, the city's largest employer since 1929, announced it was closing. The city's other trademark industry, the steel mill, shut down in 2000, ending one hundred years of manufacturing in Gadsden. Desperate for industrial growth, Gadsden turned to Pilgrim's Pride, a poultry rendering plant. Outrage was immediate, most of it about the prospect of the foul smells that poultry rendering plants were known to produce. Some of the angrier residents made protest signs that read, "Stop the Stink." Others printed T-shirts that said, "More Stinks Than This Plant."

The stink had been around much longer than any of them realized.

The monuments to white supremacy had also been preserved in DeKalb County. The Vietnam War memorial remained in the front of the courthouse in Fort Payne, but a marble block now covered the reference to the Klan. In Collbran, Floyd Simpson's old store still stood between Gravel Hill Baptist Church and Gaddis Killian's house, its doors closed since Killian and his wife shut down their collectibles business long before their deaths. With its tin roof and tin signs nailed to the pine walls, it was a novelty to amateur photographers and others who stopped to admire it. Down the highway, Hoyt Kelly was left to deal with the inquiries about the murder of William Moore that were revived by the dedication of the marker in Keener.

I decided to see him one last time. I pulled into his driveway on an afternoon in the late summer, his marine flag waving over the side of his house. The rear window of his truck, the only car in the driveway, was covered with stickers: "Blue Lives Matter" and "God Bless Our Troops, Especially Our Snipers," among them. I knocked twice on the front door, but no one answered. I walked to a side entrance, opened the screen door, and knocked twice. There was no answer there either.

I drove south, toward the murder site. On the way, I called Phillip Kimbrell to talk about the murder.

"Now you've got me nervous," he said.

Even he was scared. He had been so confident before, but now he was like everyone else.

I asked him if his grandfather had told him who the murderer was. He wouldn't say.

"But neither the man who did it nor his accomplice was named by the authorities, right?" I asked.

"That's right," he said.

"And no one has ever identified them?"

"That's right."

When I arrived at the murder site, I parked about fifteen feet off the highway, the same distance as the murderer. Across the road, a new family had moved into Harry Sizemore's farmhouse. His widow now lived on Sand Mountain. I turned around and headed back to Collbran. When I returned to Hoyt Kelly's house, I saw his wife's car in its usual spot, at the side of the house. It was late afternoon on a Friday evening, almost suppertime. Again, I knocked twice on the front door and twice on the side entrance. Hoyt Kelly or his wife had always answered before, but no one opened the door this time.

CHAPTER 30

The murder's most astonishing trait was its power to scare almost sixty years later. Todd Simpson, the youngest of Floyd Simpson's five children, sounded anxious, even afraid, when I told him that I didn't believe his father was the murderer.

Like most of his siblings, he still lived in the area. An older brother, Larry Wayne, had died recently, but another older brother and two sisters were alive. Only an older sister, Carolyn, now living in Georgia, had moved from DeKalb County. Todd described them as "a close-knit family" that continued to honor their mother's wishes that the Simpson children not discuss the murder of William Moore.

"I'll tell you what," he said, "I was born without my fingers on my right hand. Daddy made me a baseball bat and a baseball glove. He made me a pick for my guitar. He was an intelligent man. He went past what a dad should do to help me. I made all-county in high school baseball and had an opportunity to play baseball in college. He tried to help me every way he could."

He wondered if his father felt guilty because he was born with no fingers on his right hand. Todd never knew. His father wasn't much of a talker. Todd never heard his father or anyone in his family discuss the murder while his father was alive. He was almost forty when he learned about it.

A reporter from the *Los Angeles Times* knocked on his mother's front door one afternoon. Todd was out in the yard playing catch with his son, and he watched his mother and the reporter talk on the front porch.

"No, no comment," Lucille Simpson told the reporter. "I don't want to."

She told the reporter that the children wouldn't talk either. She wouldn't let them. The reporter left, and Todd asked his mother why she was upset. She told him that the reporter was asking questions about his father, but he didn't find out about the murder until later.

"My brother and sisters, they want to let it die," Todd said. "Mama's dead and Daddy's dead. They may know, but they ain't going to say nothing. I have no idea. I don't want to know. Daddy was acquitted. That was it."

I told Todd Simpson about history's misconceptions of his father: Everything written about the murder led historians and others to believe that his father was the killer. The FBI's reopening of the case concluded that Floyd Simpson was "the most probable subject involved in the murder."

He agreed that his father had been treated poorly, even by some in his hometown.

"An editor from the *Times-Journal*, he didn't put in there that he was acquitted," Todd said. "Me and my sister went to see him and said if he didn't correct that, we'd own the paper. He went back and put in a [retraction] and apologized."

I told him what I had concluded: His father was not the killer.

"All us kids know the truth and that's all that matters," he said. "You have gossipers all over the world, and all that stuff don't mean a hill of beans."

He said he was not interested in discovering what happened on the night of the murder. He believed starting another investigation was useless. Everyone who was involved in the murder was dead, he said.

I mentioned Hoyt Kelly.

"I mean, there you go," he said. "I don't know. I have no idea. I can't say nothing. All I do is have conjecture. What I'm trying to tell you is, he [Floyd Simpson] wasn't indicted. That's where it ended. I have no concern. I have no comment. Only fact is, he was in that grand jury and not indicted. That's it. It's plain and simple."

I asked him about Bill Beck, the lawyer who defended his father, and he told me that he had gone to school with Beck's sons and neither of them mentioned the murder. But both of Bill Beck's sons had been out of high school for more than a decade when Todd Simpson enrolled at Fort Payne

High School in the mid-1970s. He had gone to school with Hoyt Kelly's two children, though.

"Daddy is dead, and he's the only one who'd know or protect himself," Todd Simpson said. "I just want him to rest in peace."

Rest and peace, though, seemed impossible as long as people were unwilling to confront the truth. I knew how they felt. A few days after I talked to Todd Simpson, I found a newspaper story about two hangings in Gadsden that had been postponed in the spring of 1922.

"Should the verdict of the jury be upheld by the [state] supreme court there is a possibility that Uncle Bill Chandler will hang his fifth man while sheriff of Etowah county," the story said. "Uncle Bill has the distinction of being the first sheriff of Etowah county to execute the sentence of capital punishment on a condemned man in the county."*

The first was in the 1890s, when Charlie Holmes, an African American, was hanged for the murder of a policeman during Chandler's first term as sheriff. Two more African Americans, Vance Gardner and Jack Hunter, were hanged on December 29, 1905, for the murder of a white woman, Sarah Jane Smith. A third African American, Will Johnson, was scheduled to be hanged for the murder, but Governor William D. Jelks intervened, commuting his sentence to life in prison. Angered by the governor's actions, a mob of twenty-five masked and heavily armed men entered the county jail at around 1:00 a.m. on February 11, 1906, and demanded Bunk Richardson, who was also arrested for Smith's murder. The mob overpowered Chandler and the jailer, W. M. Dixon, and marched him to the Louisville and Nashville Railroad bridge across the Coosa River, three blocks from the jail. The rope was tied to the center section of the bridge, and Richardson was dropped twenty feet, his body dangling forty feet or so above the river. Four years later, when a new Louisville and Nashville bridge was built, the wooden railing that was used to hang Richardson, the marks of the incident still visible, was part of the new railing, its original location on the north end preserved.†

* *Gadsden Times*, May 2, 1922, 1.

† *Gadsden Times*, February 19, 1910, 1.

But there was one more hanging. Sheriff John Lister, Chandler's successor, hanged Walter Proyer, an African American, in the fall of 1914 for murdering a foreman at the Alabama Power Company station in East Gadsden. John Lister was also an Etowah County deputy when Bunk Richardson was lynched. Four months before the hanging, John Lister and Sheriff Chandler drove Richardson from the Jefferson County jail in Birmingham, where he had been held for safekeeping, to Gadsden on October 9, 1905, the night before Richardson's appearance before a grand jury.

John Lister was my great-granduncle.

The Bunk Richardson case—an incident that ranked among the "most sensational in the history of the State," in the view of the *Montgomery Advertiser*—was perhaps the first indication of the area's handling of a racial atrocity with regional and national awareness. Circuit Judge John H. Disque told the grand jury to conduct an exhaustive investigation ("leave no stone unturned in an endeavor to trace the lynchers and indict them," in the words of the *Birmingham News*). There was ample reason to believe the grand jury was capable of returning indictments. The sheriff had faced the mob on the night Richardson was taken from the jail, and the governor believed that people in Gadsden knew the identity of the lynchers. But the grand jury failed to find a member of the mob.

"We have used every means in our power and have earnestly and sincerely endeavored to trace the identity of those who lynched the negro Bunk Richardson, and regret to report that we are unable to return any indictments in this case," the grand jury said in its report. "Not a scintilla of evidence has been brought out by which the members of this mob could be apprehended. We have in many instances endeavored to trace those remarks made in a random, irresponsible and indifferent manner and have secured no evidence whatever that might lead to the truth of this deplorable and unfortunate affair."

Governor Jelks, though, was undaunted, sending a detective to Gadsden for additional investigation. Another grand jury met in October 1906, but it was unable to "obtain evidence to connect anyone with said crime," according to its report. Had the Bunk Richardson investigation been the legal precedent for the William Moore case?'

"Daddy's in the ground," Todd Simpson said. "Nowadays, people can say what they want and it doesn't matter. It just drops off me like raindrops on a windshield."

❖

A few months later, I attended a family funeral. A relative approached me and told me that Hoyt Kelly was ill. His memory was fading.

"I hope you got everything from him about that killing near the store," she said.

I had, I told her. She told me that she had once been frightened of him, too.

"I was always scared to death of him," she said. "Everybody always talked about him hush-hush. Mama and Daddy always sheltered me from that stuff."

I thought Hoyt Kelly had likely wanted it that way, always relishing the fear, even after he had found religion and passed out tiny crosses and cards to strangers. He told me that he was not afraid of death. He believed God had forgiven him for his sins when he was saved, so he was never going to confess. Everything was between him and God.

The story now seemed to fit together, the final pieces provided by Bozo Hammond and Phillip Kimbrell. I could see how the final hours had unfolded. The murder plans became more urgent after Gaddis Killian and Floyd Simpson met Moore in Collinsville. They needed a new killer after the businessman in Collinsville turned them down, and so the murderer was found after 4:00 p.m., when Killian and Simpson returned to Collbran. A final meeting was held in Keener minutes before the murder, at the new school or the store. Everyone had seen the large man with a beefy arm hanging out of the window driving the black car, but a new driver, a smaller man, slid behind the wheel of the black Buick at that final meeting. He was the better shot.

Deep within him, Hoyt Kelly was scared like everyone else. I had seen the fear when he had appeared in the documentary, and I had heard it when he called to tell me about the interview and the investigators who inquired about the murder.

The last time I saw him, he was in the shed in his backyard. He invited me in to show me his latest project. He lifted the top of a container, revealing a chest full of bullets. He was worried about talk of tougher gun laws, wondering if the government might do something to limit his supply, so he began making his own ammunition.

At last, I saw how he handled the fear. At close range, in an area where no one could see him, he took charge, seeking to claim the power and control that had always comforted him.

CHAPTER 31

I sensed the fear had begun to fade as Hoyt Kelly appeared to show signs of decline. He no longer drove his truck, and he stopped posting on social media, where his Facebook connections included Floyd Simpson's sons and Cecil Reed, the former DeKalb County sheriff who had met William Moore at the border of DeKalb and Etowah Counties.

Perhaps he was now considered too harmless to use his former Klan ties for revenge. But something else happened, something almost remarkable in Little Wills Valley and in the northeast Alabama hills. In the rising calls for justice in America, some of the more socially conscious residents believed it was time for a confession. Teri Loiselle, Don and Paulette Whisenant's daughter, was among those who thought the killer should be found. As the former wife of a Coast Guard officer who had traveled the country, she had been sensitive to Alabama's reputation for racial oppressions, sensing the slights when she informed other families where she had been raised.

"When you tell people you are from Alabama, you have to prove that you have love for all people," she said. "God made all of us. We are not to judge."

Now living in her father's brick house deep in the woods, she was the head of a multiracial family. Her daughter's partner was an African American man, and they had a multiracial grandson. Don, in her words, was "over the moon" in his affection for his great-grandson.

For many years, her father had neglected to tell her about the night of the murder. His only acknowledgment was a newspaper clipping about the murder that he kept in his safe. At the bottom of the article, he had written a note to his children:

I was the last person to see this man alive.

Instead, Paulette had been forced to tell Teri about what she and Don had seen after one of my first calls. When Teri finally asked her father about the murder, she heard him recall his fear for his young family.

"He believed his life was in danger," she said. "He was afraid for his life and my mother's life and mine. Who wouldn't be? The person who did this was prominent and had connections and you didn't mess with him or he would retaliate."

Her father had never told her about the murder because he was still astonished that he'd seen a murder victim only seconds before the killer lifted himself out of the floorboard of the black car and pulled the trigger. As he told the story of William Moore, he neglected to tell his daughter one of the most important details: The murderer was never arrested or identified. Instead, he gave her only a description of the murderer's reputation.

"The killer was somebody powerful and had connections," she said. "There was a level of fear. You didn't mess with him or he would retaliate."

Paulette was now dead. Don Whisenant, almost eighty-two and retired after forty-six years at Goodyear, was no longer scared. He, too, wanted justice. I met him at his daughter's home on the afternoon before Easter as he washed the sweat and dust from his hands and arms after completing his Saturday ritual of cutting his daughter's lawn. We sat in the shade of his daughter's garage and returned to the night of the murder.

Again, he recalled the fear of walking into the courthouse on his way to the grand jury hearing, as he had when we talked for the first time more than twenty years earlier. He saw and sensed the stares of the members of the DeKalb County Klan, including the glare of a man whom he believed to be Gaddis Killian.

"Well, I think they were trying to tell me not to tell the truth," he said. "I don't remember anybody saying anything threatening to me. They looked at you all the time. I was dreading going in. In those times, you could be retaliated against if you didn't do what certain people wanted you to do."

When he walked into the courtroom, he knew that the case that William Rayburn was presenting to the grand jury was not the true account of the murder. His uncles were barbers and operated the leading barbershop in Collinsville, Bill Cook's Barber Shop, and he had shined shoes there as a child in Little Wills Valley. The talk at the barbershop and information from law enforcement had given him the story of who had ducked in the floorboard of the black Buick as he and Paulette passed the murder scene. Hoyt Kelly was the killer.

Now that he was no longer scared of the Klan or Hoyt Kelly's family, he gave me details that he seemed hesitant to discuss in our first conversation more than twenty years earlier.

"After [law enforcement] talked to me at the scene, I showed them where [Moore] was," he said. "It seems like he was forty-two yards away [from the car] when I saw him. They assured me I was the last to see him. I learned they had harassed him coming down [highway] eleven and several people could verify that. They had seen the car."

His memories of the car were clear: The front hubcap on the driver's side was missing, and the right taillight was burned out. One of the investigators—Roy McDowell or the head of the FBI in Gadsden—told him that two people were in the car. Klan members spread the rest of the story. The killer was the driver of the black Buick. He began following Moore after he had stopped at Floyd Simpson's store, pursuing him for about twenty miles—through Portersville, Collinsville, and Keener. The first shot came from inside the car. The second was fired by the driver after he stepped from the car. He believed that the killer could have moved the body in his haste to escape.

Don Whisenant contradicted Bill Robinson's account of the black car speeding past Hilltop Grocery on its way out of Keener. Instead, he was sure that the car had turned left onto Highway 11 and made its escape out of Keener on Stephens Gap Road, only a few feet south of the roadside picnic area. From there, the black car turned right onto a back road that took the killer and his accomplice past the Sizemores' dairy barns and on to Collinsville and Fort Payne. The killer did not want him and Paulette to see him as they passed the black Buick, and he was convinced that the killer did not want anyone else to see him as he came through Keener after the murder.

I told him that I thought the killer was still alive, and he agreed. I told him what so many had said about the murder: Hoyt Kelly was the killer.

"I think so," he said. "Best I remembered, he had that reputation."

He agreed that Hoyt Kelly had used the murder of William Moore to strengthen his standing as the most feared man in Little Wills Valley.

"I think that was a big plus on his side," he said. "I felt like the guy who did it, he didn't want to get convicted, but he wanted people to know he did it. He liked the attention. It was his personality. He was the toughest dude."

Some of those who once feared him, people like a young Don Whisenant, were now brave enough to say that he should confess.

"He ought to do the right thing and admit it before he dies," he said. "He just flat got away with it. Didn't even send him to trial. Let him go from the get-go."

The fear had faded in Fort Payne, too. Less than a week after my meeting with Don Whisenant, I returned to Douglas, the city's African American community at the base of Lookout Mountain, and found Kenneth Underwood and his wife, Veronica, sitting in the shade of their front porch on a Sunday afternoon. Now in his late sixties, Kenneth Underwood spoke about Hoyt Kelly with the ease of a man who was recalling his pastor's Sunday sermon. He was, in fact, about to deliver a message of his own: It was time for Hoyt Kelly to repent.

Veronica, his wife of forty-six years, was more animated, still angered by acts of the man whom her neighbors in Douglas once knew as "the hooded man."

"He burned crosses on people's lawns," she said. "I knew about him burning crosses by the front porch of the church. Uncle Johnny Ray, the only telephone man in Douglas, had a cross burned in his yard."

And those crosses, she said, were made hastily.

"Let me tell you about his crosses," she said. "They weren't wood. It was a stick that he cut. You could see where it was burned. It was like a limb cut out of a tree. You could tell where he tied it together. It was about as tall as Kenneth was. The ground, it was burned. It had gas on it."

Kenneth and Veronica rattled off one story after another about Hoyt

Kelly's terrorism of their neighborhood. The acts usually came around sundown, about the time that the killer escalated his plan to kill William Moore. They remembered how crosses were burned at the home of Manual Lee, who ran a successful barbecue business in Douglas, and at First Baptist Church, the Klan's response to one of its members becoming the most trusted employee of Minnie Reeves, the owner of Reeves Motel on Highway 11.

Floyd Jackson drove Minnie Reeves's Cadillac all over town. He was a handyman who could repair almost anything. He was so dependable that she allowed him to run errands for her in one of the nicest cars in Fort Payne. An African American man in his early twenties driving a white woman's car was more than the Fort Payne Klan could stand, though, and so the cross was burned by the front steps of the First Baptist Church on a Saturday night, still smoldering when worshippers began arriving the next morning.

"I'll never forget it," Veronica said. "We were scared. We knew what it meant. Everybody was looking at it, [saying,] 'Wow, can you believe he did this?'"

Kenneth Underwood expounded on the story he had told me years earlier—the tale of how he and his younger brother, both of them elementary school students at the time, sped home on their bicycles from the neighborhood baseball field, trying to outrun Hoyt Kelly at dusk.

"He had a truck with lights across the top and a bar down the side," he said. "These high-beam lights would be wound around the bar, and he'd flash the lights at you. He'd take the lights and shine 'em on you. He'd say, 'Y'all ain't got no business out here. N——, go home.'

"He ran us from the ball field on our bikes, me and my little brother. We pedaled our bikes as fast as we could, and we loved to go to the ball field and play ball."

Almost ten years later, he chased Kenneth Underwood and his African American teammates back to Douglas after baseball and softball games against all-white teams from Sand Mountain.

"He watched us come off the mountain," he said. "The Black kids had beat the white kids."

"He was waiting for them," Veronica said. "He was laying in wait and said, 'Don't go back to the mountain. Don't do that again.'"

"They were afraid of him," Kenneth said.

They were afraid of him because they had heard his taunts as he rode through Douglas.

"If he caught us in a place we weren't supposed to be, he'd come by and swear obscenities, just for playing in our yards, which is our right," Veronica said.

They were afraid, too, because he always reminded them of his reputation.

"He'd say, 'Don't you know who I am? I'm Hoyt Kelly,'" Veronica said. "And people's eyes got real big."

They were also afraid of his power and his connections to law enforcement and some of Alabama's most famous politicians.

"He loved himself some Tom Bevill," said Kenneth, referring to the legendary U.S. congressman. "He had a truck covered with Wallace stickers."

They recalled how he drove through Douglas on election day, looking for the reputed alcoholics. He used liquor as enticements, they said, telling the alcoholics who to vote for and issuing a warning in case they were considering crossing him.

"He'd come around with bottles of liquor in Black neighborhoods," Veronica said. "He'd say, 'You got to vote for this man right here. I better not find out you didn't vote for him.' I remember him passing out liquor on every corner."

Alcohol sales were still illegal in Fort Payne in those years when George Wallace's power was greatest, but Hoyt Kelly was undaunted.

"He had [the liquor] in boxes," Kenneth said. "They knew these people were alcoholics. They knew they couldn't turn [the liquor] down. He'd pick 'em up and carry them down to the voting place."

The Underwoods believed he was fearless because many of the Fort Payne policemen and the DeKalb County sheriff's deputies were Hoyt Kelly's friends. Kenneth figured the liquor came from Gaddis Killian, whom he identified as a well-known bootlegger. In those years, the protection from law enforcement, they said, was as much a part of local life as making socks at the hosiery mills.

"He could get us arrested, but he never got arrested," Veronica said. "He could get away with anything."

❖

I returned to Fort Payne a few days after the first meeting on the Underwoods' front porch and asked Kenneth Underwood if he had any doubts about Hoyt Kelly killing William Moore.

No, he said.

"God's going to take care of everything he's done," he said. "He's going to have to answer for everything bad that he's done. God's got it. I wouldn't want to be in his shoes or his socks. He should be done to what he's done to others."

Kenneth and Veronica Underwood said they heard their relatives talk about the murder of William Moore.

"My grandmother told me about it," Veronica said. "She said she fed him and gave him dinner."

Like her husband, Veronica was sure that Kelly had killed Moore.

"The cops had to be on his [Kelly's] side," she said. "We don't know where he got his power, but he done it. He did whatever he wanted to do."

I told the Underwoods that I believed the murder of William Moore had been the start of that acquisition of power. I informed them of what Kenneth Hammond and Herman Kerley had told me: People in influential positions wanted someone to kill Moore and that the killer, realizing there was power to be gained, decided to grant their wishes after the businessman in Collinsville, the original choice, had turned down Gaddis Killian and Floyd Simpson.

"Well," Kenneth Underwood said, "he [Kelly] jumped on it."

Kenneth believed that Hoyt Kelly used that power for himself and for his most trusted Klan associates, especially those in the southern part of DeKalb County.

"He had them stationed everywhere down there and in Collinsville," Kenneth Underwood said.

"They [African Americans in Fort Payne] would go through Lebanon to go to Collinsville instead of Collbran because you never knew what they had waiting on you there," Veronica said. "They say there were rallies at the store."

Going through Lebanon added another four miles to the drive to Collinsville, but at least Black people lived there.

Kenneth and Veronica Underwood were not afraid, but they told me that the fear remained in Douglas and other parts of Fort Payne when Hoyt Kelly's name was mentioned.

"People still fear that name," Kenneth said.

"If you hear it, they get nervous and scared," Veronica said.

The fear was still in the home of Floyd Jackson, the handyman who drove Minnie Reeves's Cadillac. Kenneth Underwood suggested I go to his house on a hill near the former site of Douglas High School. Jackson was about to eat a late lunch when I knocked on his front door. His wife, Elizabeth, opened the door and invited me to sit in a chair in the living room. A black-and-white rerun of *The Fugitive*, the popular television show that debuted on ABC the year William Moore was killed, played on the Jacksons' big-screen television. I told them that I wanted to talk to them about an incident that happened about the time *The Fugitive* was on television.

At first, Floyd Jackson was proud about his role in local civil rights, almost bold.

"You're talking to the man," he said.

He and Elizabeth told me that he was among the first African American students to integrate the Fort Payne schools in 1964. Floyd attended Williams Avenue Elementary School, and Roscoe Underwood, Kenneth's older brother, went to Fort Payne High School.

Then I informed Floyd of the purpose of my visit. I told him I was interested in the murder of William Moore, the Freedom Walker.

"I know who [the killer] was, but I'm not telling," he said.

I told him that I had heard Hoyt Kelly was the killer. Floyd Jackson's eyes widened and his mouth dropped, as if he was pretending to be astonished.

"Bingo," he said.

He asked me what I planned to do with the information. I told him that I intended to tell the story of the murder, and the fear returned. He said he wasn't the type to hold a grudge, but he admitted that he had been a target of the Klan because he had driven Minnie Reeves's Cadillac.

"I probably dodged getting killed two or three times," he said.

Nevertheless, he was surprised when he learned that William Moore had been killed, as he recalled. But he was now through sharing his memories of the case.

"Everything's going good now," he said. "I'd rather not disturb it."

His wife, though, was more talkative.

"Why would any man think he's better than any other man?" she asked. "That's what I don't understand. My husband looks like a white man. There's no difference."

She told me that she and Floyd had seen Hoyt Kelly and his wife earlier that week. She told me that she liked the Kellys and that Hoyt Kelly "loves on me and kisses on me," like those dark days had never happened.

But those days, as powerful as they were, still seemed to be with Floyd and Elizabeth Jackson, just as they were with almost everyone in Fort Payne who lived through them.

"I'm just proud it's all over with," Floyd Jackson said.

My long hours with my grandfather at those service stations on Sand Mountain taught me that grandfathers held few secrets from their grandsons, so I called Phillip Kimbrell after speaking with Kenneth and Veronica Underwood. I asked him to confirm that his grandfather had told him that Hoyt Kelly was the killer.

"Seems like he did," he said. "I don't know about the other person [in the car]."

He asked me if I planned to identify the killer. I told him that I intended to tell what happened.

"It's going to get some people mad around here," he said.

I asked him why.

"Mr. Kelly's got a lot of family still alive," he said.

"Isn't the truth an open secret?" I asked him.

"Oh, yeah, I think so," he said. "The people who did it wanted it known without being prosecuted."

I figured the most logical way for my search to end was to start at the beginning for Don Whisenant, the closest thing to an eyewitness. About two weeks after I met him at his daughter's home, I drove to a grocery store parking lot at the intersection of U.S. Highway 11 and Alabama 77 in Attalla, near the site where he once pumped Gulf gasoline and changed oil at Cleo's Gulf.

He climbed out of his truck, eased into the passenger's seat of my car, and we headed up Highway 11.

"That's where I used to change the oil," he said, motioning toward a spot near the end of the self-service station that stood where Cleo's Gulf had been on the night of April 23, 1963. "I used to have a lift outside, over there at the end of the building."

We rode through downtown Attalla on a mild, sunny afternoon in early April—nothing like the warm, windy night that he and Paulette encountered when Don drove his 1956 Ford toward their home near Collinsville. On the night of the murder, Don drove past motels and a pipe foundry that had recently reopened before moving into Little Wills Valley. D & J Truck Stop Cabins, the roadhouse that Charlie Hicks and Roy McDowell had suggested to Moore, was tucked in a curve between Reese City and Keener.

Heading out of Reese City and approaching the long straightaway into Keener, Don Whisenant pointed out the former site of D & J Truck Stop Cabins. It was now a clump of underbrush and trees that needed pruning.

As we neared the murder site, he said, "I told you there was a little rise here. That's where he [the killer] was sitting. There was a tree here when I topped the hill, and I saw the taillight."

I pulled past Harry Sizemore's dairy farm and into the former roadside park, in front of the William Moore historical marker. The black Buick, Don said, was parked under the black walnut tree, behind the historical marker.

"There was a tree right here by the marker," he said. "They were at least fifteen or twenty feet off the road. It was dark here, dark everywhere."

The road had almost no traffic. He didn't recall seeing the Greyhound bus at the top of the hill, rushing toward Attalla, as Paulette had.

"People weren't out late, certainly not eating at no picnic table," he said. "I feel like he was shot from inside the car. I wonder where he fell."

I told Don about the crime scene photo. Moore was slumped forward, lying on the right side of his face, his feet tangled in his cart. His body appeared to be almost twisted, straddling the warning stripe of the highway, a pool of blood forming on the dirt at the edge of the roadside park.

"He must have been moved over after the first shot," Don said.

I asked him if perhaps Moore was moved so the murderer could climb out of the car and fire the second shot—the shot that entered Moore's neck and exited the back of his head. Maybe so, Whisenant said. He believed Moore was also moved so the murderer could turn left and make his getaway down Stephens Gap Road, past Harry Sizemore's farm.

"He could have dodged everything," Don said, "and he'd be out of here in a heartbeat."

I pulled onto Highway 11, and I asked him if he'd mind going to Collbran.

"No," he said, "go on."

We drove past Hilltop Grocery and through the woods at the border of Etowah and DeKalb Counties. He showed me where he and Paulette lived on the night of the murder and the old roadhouse clip joint known as Ab's.

It was nineteen miles from the murder scene to Floyd Simpson's store. Heading out of Collinsville and toward Portersville, I sensed some of Don's old anxieties were returning.

"We're getting close to the store, aren't we?" Whisenant said.

It won't be long, I told him, just up the straightaway and around the curve, past the Killian Cemetery. Entering Collbran, I drove by Gravel Hill Baptist Church, and we saw the store. Don Whisenant seemed almost excited.

"There's the store," he said. "The car was parked right over there, to the left of the store."

Sitting in the store parking lot on the day after the murder, the tensions high in Collbran, he believed the murderer was somewhere near him, either in the store or lurking close to the highway.

"I was just scared," he said. "That's all I remember with the police and proving somebody killed somebody. They just said, 'You think that's the car at the picnic table?' I said, 'One brake light is off and a hubcap is off. Looks like it to me.'"

It had taken me twenty-four years to find a white man in northeast Alabama who wanted justice. Even Bozo Hammond, as outspoken as he had been in our discussions at the Valley Head town hall, was not interested in prosecuting Hoyt Kelly. Don Whisenant, though, wanted someone in power to solve the case.

"Well, I would have thought somebody would have tried to find the murderer before now," he said. "My biggest thought is if it happened today, it wouldn't have been covered up like it was then."

Did he have any doubt about who killed William Moore?

"No, no doubt who murdered him," he said. "The people who did it wanted everybody to know they did it, but they didn't want the consequences. They felt like they were heroes."

"You think he has any remorse?" I asked as we pulled out of the parking lot and headed toward Hoyt Kelly's house.

"No, I don't think so," he said. "If he had any remorse, he would have admitted it."

We talked about the influence of the Klan in Fort Payne and Gadsden and the power of Hoyt Kelly's family.

"The Klan had to be controlling a little piece of everything," Whisenant said. "I think the Klan was even bigger than I suspected. If the Klan threatened the judge, they're not going to find somebody guilty."

We passed Hoyt Kelly's house on the way back to Keener. An appliance repairman from Fort Payne was parked in the driveway. I asked Whisenant what he would tell Hoyt Kelly if he had a chance to speak to him.

"I'd tell him the whole bunch got away with murder," he said. "I think that's what happened. All the Kellys knew about it. They got all the attention they wanted and served no time. They were glad everybody knew about it. I believe before I passed, I would admit to it."

But Don Whisenant knew there would be no public confession after more than sixty years. Hoyt Kelly had said all he was going to say about the murder. His interview for the documentary and his call to me months later were apparently the end.

"Life is hell," William Moore wrote months before his death. "It is a terrible lottery, an awful game whereby no one really wins and none ever survives. As a reward for having to struggle through life on earth, heaven is but a fitting payment."

Heading out of Collbran, I believed I had found my fitting payment, at last. Life had once been hell for Don Whisenant and the residents of Douglas who had lived in fear and ducked into their homes when the hooded man rode through the streets, shining his lights on them. Now, though, they shone the light on him.

I thought of Hoyt Kelly again six months later. I knew that he was about to celebrate his eighty-ninth birthday, and I wondered if perhaps he had returned to Facebook and made a reference to the occasion on social media. I imagined him reveling in his strength and vibrancy, proud that he had carried on his family's history of longevity. I never considered the possibility of death. But there it was on the website of one of the funeral homes in Fort Payne. Hoyt Kelly's obituary had been posted almost two weeks earlier. Todd Simpson was among the many who gave online tributes. I was surprised that no one from my family or any of my acquaintances in Fort Payne had called to tell me that he had died, but the people of the valley always protected their own, especially in death.

On a crisp, sunny morning in late fall, I returned to the mountain and the valley again to see Hoyt Kelly's widow, Jean.* A relative told me that Jean had encountered some recent health issues, but she assured me that Jean would be glad to see me. As I headed down Sand Mountain, past the road to my maternal grandparents' former home, I saw the traffic slow near the cutoff to Z. Z. Richey's old store. A convoy of trucks with Donald Trump for President flags and stickers moved toward Fort Payne less than two weeks before the election. They passed down the right side of the four-lane highway, but they caused such congestion that I nearly rear-ended the car in front of me when it stopped suddenly in front of Walmart.

I had not seen Jean Kelly in ten years, and I wondered if she would remember me. I knocked on her door only once. I could see her through the storm door as she approached because the front door had been open since her youngest son's visit earlier that morning. She smiled as she saw me. She

* Pseudonym. To be known from hereon as Jean Kelly.

remembered me, but she had forgotten my name. She had gray sprinkled through her black hair, and she was thin and fitter than my relative had thought she was. Her broken wrist was still in an air cast, but she did not need a walker.

She led me toward the back of the house, to the den where Hoyt and I had talked about his years in the Klan. I recognized many of the photos from those visits, including one of her and Hoyt when he came home on leave from the navy after he graduated from high school. The television in front of us flashed footage of Trump, and we discussed the election.

"I do so hope he wins," she said.

I mentioned her husband's death.

"He died where you're sitting," she said, motioning toward the edge of the couch. "He laid down and never woke up."

Some recent heart issues had caused his doctors to insert five stents, she said, but the problems worsened. He never made it to an appointment that was scheduled only days after his death.

Even one month after the funeral, she was amazed by the outpouring of support.

"I've never seen so many people," she said. "There were people everywhere."

I told her that I thought he was one of the most memorable people I had ever met.

"Yes," she said, "I remember you saying that."

Then I told her something I had never told her.

"You know that incident down at Keener, the man who was killed?" I said. "I've always had an interest in that. People say that Hoyt killed him. Are they telling me wrong?"

Her eyes appeared to glisten, and she paused before answering.

"He was on a trip that night," she said. "He was down there at Keener, but he went on that trip."

Hoyt had refused to tell me which direction he had gone on U.S. 11 on the night of the murder. But his wife was telling me that he had gone south, toward Keener.

"Is that what they're saying?" she said. "That he did it? He couldn't have done it. There is no way he could have done it."

I didn't ask her to elaborate. I couldn't bring myself to ask the question. To my surprise, she didn't drop the subject.

"We stopped and looked at that sign in Keener when we went to Gadsden about two years ago," she said. "We didn't usually stop, but we did that day."

He read the marker in silence, she recalled. His only reaction, she said, came when they resumed their drive to Gadsden.

"He said, 'There's no way Floyd Simpson could have done it,'" she said. "I guess we'll never know."

We talked about how she and Hoyt had raised a family in Collbran. They had moved here in 1962, when Hoyt became the exalted cyclops of the Fort Payne Klan. He had also been a Klansman when they lived in the Birmingham suburb of Tarrant, their home before returning to northeast Alabama.

"Yes," she said. "I didn't like that."

She rose to check on a chicken casserole in the kitchen that she was making for an ill friend. She asked me to help her remove it from the stove because of her broken wrist, and I obliged. She wanted to show me the rest of her home. We walked to the porch at the side of the house, and she pointed out the grocery store and gas station that she and Hoyt once owned. She had operated the store while Hoyt hauled shipments in his eighteen-wheeler.

We walked to the dining room, and I remarked about the craftsmanship of the table and the benches. My favorite uncle, her older brother, had made the table and benches for her almost fifty years earlier, when he churned out one piece of furniture after another for his relatives at his woodworking shop in northwest Georgia.

"He was so talented," she said.

She walked me to the front door, and I told her that I might come back to talk some more. She leaned over to hug me and said, "Come back anytime."

And then she shut the door.

NOTES ON SOURCES

This book is based extensively on hundreds of interviews with northeast Alabama residents, especially Kenneth Hammond, Herman Kerley, Jim McGee, Mickey Strickland, Don and Paulette Whisenant, and Hoyt Kelly. Their help was crucial in giving me the understanding of how Moore was murdered and why the murder was never solved. I also benefited from hundreds of pages of FBI files, grand jury notes that Strickland gave me, and testimony from congressional hearings on the demonstrations in Gadsden in 1963. Some records were obtained from the Freedom of Information Act. Most information, though, came from years of interviews with residents of northeast Alabama, northwest Georgia, and southern Tennessee. Travis Nail, Louise Robinson, Jarvis Adams, and Rick Correll provided great insight into what life was like in Keener in the early 1960s. I am also indebted to Herman Kerley, Kenneth and Veronica Underwood, and Robert Avery for their memories of Ku Klux Klan terrorism on African Americans during the civil rights era and beyond. J. P. Nation, a resident of Lookout Mountain and a longtime certified public accountant in Gadsden, told me in an October 2010 interview that the Gadsden police had been active in the Ku Klux Klan. He confirmed what the *Gadsden Times* hinted in its reporting after the infamous photograph of the lead Klan car through downtown on the night of March 5, 1949: Fay Boman, the longtime police chief, was believed to be the Klansman in the front passenger seat. Nation referred to Boman as "the [Klan] ringleader." A *Birmingham Post-Herald* story on April 2, 1979, quoting Gadsden Police Chief Charles Cary's remarks in the *Wall Street Journal* two months earlier, verified how influential the Klan had been. Twelve members of the Gadsden Police Department were members of the Klan, Cary said, and others were sympathizers.

A profile of George Wallace in the *Chicago Tribune* ("George Wallace Tosses an Old Hat into Familiar Ring," published on May 26, 1982) chronicled the origins of Wallace's longtime friendship with Bill Beck, including the details of how Beck arranged for Wallace's struggling family to move out of a filthy apartment in downtown Montgomery in the late 1940s. I interviewed Virgil Pittman in 2006, but a *Mobile Press-Register* profile of Pittman ("The Judge Who Changed Mobile," published on May 7, 2006) provided additional context of how the Ku Klux Klan harassed Pittman before the Floyd Simpson grand jury trial. A 2017 blog post by Karen Spears Zacharias, *Raised Up White in Alabama*, gave a more complete account of Ace Williams's visit to Frank Helderman's office in 1959, after Frank Helderman Jr., then a journalism student at the University of Alabama, drove his car past a Klan sign in Tuscaloosa, trying to help a student photographer get a photograph. "The two ended up being chased by Klan members but they were never caught. The next day, the Grand Dragon of the Klan paid Frank's father a visit, warned him that if Frank didn't back off, somebody was going to get hurt. Frank didn't drive his car for a week after that," wrote Zacharias, sharing the memories of Jennie Miller Helderman, Frank Helderman Jr.'s wife.

I relied on several books about the civil rights movement. They included *Freedom Ride* by James Peck; *This Is What We Found* by Ralph and Carl Creger; *My Undercover Years in the Ku Klux Klan* by Gary Thomas Rowe; *The Martyrs* by Jack Mendelsohn; *We Shall Overcome* by Michael Dorman; *Fighting the Devil in Dixie* and *Watch Out for George Wallace* by Wayne Greenhaw; and *A Fire You Can't Put Out* by Andrew M. Manis. *General Walker and the Murder of President Kennedy* by Jeffrey H. Caufield provided information on the alliances among some of the most notorious racists in northeast Alabama and southern Tennessee, including Kenneth Adams's connections to the Ku Klux Klan in Collbran. His visit to Collbran on May 2, 1963, nine days after the murder of William Moore, was among the earliest indications of a longtime relationship between Hoyt Kelly and Adams. *Freedom Walk*, Mary Stanton's 2003 account of the murder, was also helpful. William Moore's autobiography, *The Mind in Chains: The Autobiography of a Schizophrenic*, was essential to understanding Moore's childhood and his complicated relationship with his father, Robert. *Lewis Brandon and His Descendants* by Douglass R. Brandon, the genealogy of the Simpson and Brandon families, provided the best details of Floyd Simpson's life.

For information about Joe Louis's and Sugar Ray Robinson's difficulties with the segregation laws at Camp Sibert during World War II, I relied mostly on *Sweet Thunder: The Life and Times of Sugar Ray Robinson* by Wil Haygood. I found rich details about Gadsden's labor troubles in the 1930s in "Gadsden Is Tough" by Maxwell Stewart, published in the *Nation* on July 17, 1937, and in the *Akron Beacon-Journal*'s reporting.

Several newspapers helped me piece together the narratives of Moore's walk, the murder investigation, the demonstrations in Gadsden, and the institutional racism in northeast Alabama. I relied mostly on the *Gadsden Times*, *Etowah News-Journal*, *Birmingham News*, *Birmingham Post-Herald*, *Huntsville Times*, *Montgomery Advertiser*, *Alabama Journal*, *Chattanooga Times*, *Baltimore Sun* and *Baltimore Evening Sun*, *Baltimore Afro-American*, *Pittsburgh Courier*, *Fort Payne Times-Journal*, *Collinsville Courier*, *New York Times*, *Los Angeles Times*, *Brooklyn Eagle*, *New York Age*, *Rochester (N.Y.) Democrat and Chronicle*, *Binghamton Evening Press* and *Sun-Bulletin*, *Washington Afro-American*, *Washington Evening Star*, *Dade County Times* of Trenton, Georgia, and *Atlanta Journal-Constitution*. Moore's diary, of course, was the best account of his walk. The *Gadsden Free-Press*, a newspaper founded in 1961 by Gadsden businessman R. H. Hardin, provided significant details about the economic distress in Gadsden in the early 1960s. The *Petal Paper*, P. D. East's iconoclastic newspaper in Petal, Mississippi, published several articles by Moore after he and East met in Binghamton in 1961. Among them was "Blessed Are the Damned," an October 19, 1961, editorial that contained Moore's faith in Jesus Christ and heaven, an important perspective because it opposed the widespread belief that he was an atheist.

Harold Morrison, the *Canadian Press*'s Washington correspondent, produced an outstanding series on the racial troubles in Alabama, Mississippi, and Georgia in 1963. He traveled approximately 2,100 miles through the Deep South during the late spring and summer, and he provided detailed reporting on the racial attitudes in Gadsden in the aftermath of the William Moore murder and during the Reverend Martin Luther King Jr.'s visit in

June 1963. His stories include Circuit Judge A. B. Cunnington's view of the electric cattle prods that were used on demonstrators ("only gave them a little bit of a shock"), an African American's belief that Gadsden is "a living hell," and a Gadsden resident's view that *Brooklyn Eagle* columnist Robert Ferrell's stories about Gadsden "are not lies." Madeleine Sherwood's first-person account of her role in the William Moore Memorial Walk, *My Crime Was to Take Five Steps on a Freedom Walk*, was another insightful piece that appeared in a Canadian newspaper. It appeared in the *Vancouver Sun* on May 9, 1964, and told revealing stories of the harassment that activists faced in Gadsden after Moore's death.

The best reporting on the murder investigation was done by Bill Kovach and Murray Kempton, two of the nation's legendary journalists. Kempton, then at the peak of his newspaper and magazine career, wrote *Pilgrimage to Jackson* for the May 10, 1963, edition of the *New Republic*. Kovach was in his early years at *The Tennessean* of Nashville when he came to Gadsden to write about the murder investigation. He later became a distinguished journalist at the *New York Times* and the *Atlanta Journal-Constitution*.

Kovach's reporting helped show how the Southern media was also involved in the cover-up. He was the only journalist who reported that Ace Williams, the one-time head of the Gadsden Ku Klux Klan, huddled with Etowah County District Attorney William Rayburn and Alabama state trooper officials before Roy McDowell, the chief investigator, took Floyd Simpson's rifle to the FBI Laboratory in Washington, D.C. His reporting was crucial in reinforcing my belief that several entities, including the media, were responsible for Moore's murder going unsolved for more than sixty years.

The *Baltimore City Paper*, an alternative weekly newspaper that folded in 2017, published *Kill the Messenger: The Last March of Bill Moore* in May 1993, the thirtieth anniversary of the murder. The author, Jim Duffy, gave me insight into Moore's childhood and his life after he married Mary. *Time*, *Jet*, and the *Saturday Evening Post* were among the leading magazines of the civil rights era, and their reporting of the murder and the racial climate in Alabama was valuable. I am especially indebted to *Time* for "In Bill Moore's Footsteps," its article on the murder in its May 10, 1963, issue. It was the inspiration for this book.

Perhaps most of all, I am grateful for the help of Kenneth Hammond, Herman Kerley, Jim McGee, Mickey Strickland, and Don and Paulette Whisenant. They were always willing to talk whenever I had a question. I am also indebted to Glenn T. Eskew, my former Auburn classmate, and Jerry Batts for their support in the final years of the project. They are the reason this book is possible.